The Intelligent REIT Investor

HOW TO BUILD WEALTH WITH REAL ESTATE INVESTMENT TRUSTS

Stephanie Krewson-Kelly
R. Brad Thomas

WILEY

Published by John Wiley & Sons, Inc., Hoboken, New Jersey.
Published simultaneously in Canada.

For general information on our other products and services or for technical support, please contact our Customer Care Department within the United States at (800) 762-2974, outside the United States at (317) 572-3993 or fax (317) 572-4002.

Wiley publishes in a variety of print and electronic formats and by print-on-demand. Some material included with standard print versions of this book may not be included in e-books or in print-on-demand. If this book refers to media such as a CD or DVD that is not included in the version you purchased, you may download this material at http://booksupport.wiley.com. For more information about Wiley products, visit www.wiley.com.

Library of Congress Cataloging-in-Publication Data is available:

ISBN 9781119252719 (Hardcover)
ISBN 9781119252740 (ePDF)
ISBN 9781119252764 (ePub)

Cover Design: Wiley
Cover Image: © Leonardo Patrizi/iStockphoto

Printed in the United States of America

10 9 8 7 6 5 4

To William,
so that someday you understand
why Mommy
turned the dining room
into "an office" for a year

Contents

Part II Investing in REITs   85

Foreword

The ability to understand the characteristics and value of an asset when others do not is often the key to investment success. For my entire professional life, REITs have been one of the most misunderstood investments. Early on, real estate experts called them stock, and stock market investors called them real estate. As a result, they found no natural home in diversified portfolios. Although that has changed dramatically over the years, there are still many poorly understood aspects of this asset class. That is why this book is such an important resource.

For much of the post-1974 period, the term *REITs* was associated with the mortgage REIT debacle that preceded it. Financial institutions had offloaded mortgage businesses onto this new vehicle and the combination of an economic recession and soaring interest rates precipitated bankruptcies and substantial investor losses. Somehow, the public had a lot of trouble getting over this—it's as if there was no statute of limitations on the damage done in this period. Periodically, investor appetite for current yield irrespective of risk allowed the mortgage REIT to resurface in subsequent cycles, often with similarly disappointing results. Throughout, as Stephanie Krewson-Kelly demonstrates, equity REITs—that is, property owners as opposed to lenders—have delivered consistent and superior investment performance.

The modern publicly traded equity REIT is, quite simply, the purest form of corporate and property ownership. Professional management is employed by shareholders and subject to performance-based compensation. There is strong corporate governance. Portfolio decisions are made with a long-term perspective and not with an arbitrary internal rate of return objective that is used to determine a promoter's compensation. The company has the ability to employ nearly every type of equity and debt financing. And the company pays no taxes; pretax profits of the enterprise are entirely distributed to its shareholders in direct proportion to their ownership stakes.

The importance of this book is that it gives the reader the tools required to properly analyze and evaluate property companies. I often advise investors that they should look at the numbers before they look at the pictures. This book tells you how.

The industry was not always as resilient as it is today. Over the years there were issues with respect to conflicts of interest, high expenses, poor balance sheet management, and lack of clarity of company strategy. (I should add that this, sadly, is still the case with many private or nontraded REITs.) But the natural selection process has been in full force in the industry. Evolution has favored companies that adhered to best practices and became industry leaders, producing excellent returns to investors and earning a place as components of all major indexes. This was also the result of an army of dedicated and professional investors and analysts following these enterprises. So-called corporate activism, whereby a small group of investors challenge management and directors or attempt to affect the liquidation or sale of a company, is not new to the REIT industry. As far back at the late 1970s astute investors seeing share prices that did not reflect underlying values were very effective at producing change.

Despite such progress, there remain a great number of misconceptions about the nature and behavior of equity REITs. For example, many believe that share price performance is directly related to the level and direction of interest rates. Empirical evidence of this is lacking. In fact, it is the economy that most strongly influences property and REIT fundamentals and, when rising interest rates accompany a robust economy, REITs perform exceptionally well. Many direct real estate investors complain that the volatility of this publicly traded asset class makes it an inferior investment to that which doesn't trade at all. Being long-term investors, they are happy to sit on their asset until there is a final outcome—that is, sale. It could be argued that if one is truly a long-term investor, day-to-day volatility should be ignored, unless it presents an occasional compelling trading opportunity.

The Intelligent REIT Investor will help you understand and appreciate the newest innovations and developments in the REIT industry. The most important is the rise in popularity of exchange-traded vehicles that provide broad diversification and liquidity. Although many active managers are capable of outperforming popular indexes, the low expense ratios and tax efficiency of ETFs make them a compelling choice—so much so that they are experiencing greater capital inflows than actively managed real estate mutual funds. Also new are REITs that own formerly uninvestable assets such as single-family homes, an outgrowth of the housing crisis. Here, as it has in the past, the public market has filled a capital void, providing an opportunity to investors.

There are more positive developments in the REIT industry on the horizon. Rules governing the taxation of foreign owners of U.S. assets have been relaxed. Already, REITs are extremely popular among Japanese investors and this interest is quickly spreading to other parts of Asia. In 2016 real estate has been given its own sector in the Global Industry Classification Standard (GICS). Formerly part of the *Financial* sector, this separation significantly raises the profile of the asset class.

Publicly traded real estate companies have become a cornerstone of investment portfolios. I trust that this new edition will provide the reader the tools required to find appreciation of, and profit from, this asset class.

Martin Cohen
April 2016

Preface

Over the 15-year period that ended on December 31, 2015, Real Estate Investment Trusts (REITs) were the best performing investments, delivering annualized total returns of 11.1 percent. By contrast, the S&P 500 and NASDAQ Indexes achieved annualized total returns of only 5.0 percent and 4.8 percent, respectively, over that same time period. Yet many investors are unfamiliar with equity REITs—companies that own commercial property, such as office buildings or apartments—or with mortgage REITs, which invest in real estate–based loans.

In 2016, the REIT industry will experience a watershed event that will likely increase demand for REIT shares dramatically: Standard & Poor's Dow Jones Indices (S&P) and MSCI Inc. (MSCI) will create a new Global Industry Classification Standard (GICS) sector called *Real Estate*. S&P is a leading provider of financial market indexes and, historically, has classified REITs as part of the *Financials* sector. MSCI is a leading provider of investment-decision-support tools. Together, the organizations determined that investors' view of real estate has evolved such that it is regarded as a distinct asset class—one that is different from banks and financial institutions. Accordingly, after the market's close on August 31, 2016, publicly traded equity REITs and other listed real estate companies will be removed from Financials and be promoted into their own GICS code. (Note that mortgage REITs will remain in S&P's Financials sector.) The creation of the Real Estate GICS sector should elevate investor awareness of REITs and broaden the industry's appeal to individuals and institutions alike.

The Intelligent REIT Investor conveys essential information about REITs in a concise, easy-to-understand format. Even novice investors can gain a thorough understanding of the REIT market by reading the relevant industry background and simple examples presented in these pages. Part I, An Introduction to REITs, presents basic information that will help investors quickly gain an understanding of what

REITs are in order to have more informed conversations with their financial advisors. Part II, Investing in REITs, is more technical in nature, with content geared for individuals who want to analyze and evaluate specific REITs before investing in them. *The Intelligent REIT Investor* is a steppingstone that provides critical information about the REIT industry and individual companies and, in sharp contrast to other REIT books, can be read cover-to-cover in less than a day.

Here are a few industry background facts to get started:

- The REIT industry's aggregate equity market capitalization has increased exponentially from a mere $8.7 billion at the beginning of 1990 to its December 31, 2015, level of $939 billion, for a compounded annual growth rate of 34 percent (see Table 1.1).
- Innovations to the REIT structure that eliminated conflicts of interest between management and shareholders helped fuel the industry's explosive growth. Perhaps the most significant event in modern REIT history occurred in October 2001, when the first equity REIT was added to the S&P 500 Index. Since then, REIT shares have attracted an increasingly broader array of investors, including general money managers, pension funds, hedge funds, and individual investors. As a result, the average daily trading volume for REITs increased from approximately 16 million shares in 2000 to 175 million shares a day in 2015, according to S&P Global Market Intelligence.
- Despite the industry's outperformance and the upcoming creation of the Real Estate GICS sector, most investor portfolios are under-allocated to real estate securities. The 2015 *Institutional Real Estate Allocations Monitor*, published by Cornell University's Baker Program in Real Estate and Hodes Weill & Associates LP, found the average institutional portfolio contains an 8.5 percent investment in real estate versus their targeted investment level of 9.56 percent. REITs are viewed as an established investment class, and demand for REIT shares has increased by multiples since 2000—but they are not yet mainstream.
- Just as the demand for REITs has increased, the marketplace for REIT shares has also evolved dramatically. As previously mentioned, the average daily trading volume for component companies in the FTSE NAREIT All REITs Index, which at

December 31, 2015, tracked 223 publicly traded REITs, has increased exponentially. By dollar volume, the average daily trading volume of companies in the FTSE NAREIT All REITs Index increased from $400 million in 2000 to $6.2 billion in 2015 (source: NAREIT).

- In addition to higher trading volume, REIT volatility also has increased dramatically. The MSCI® US REIT Index (ticker symbol: RMZ) is an index that tracks approximately 150 publicly traded equity REITs. According to S&P Global Market Intelligence, during the 1,508 trading days in the 2000–2005 period, the RMZ rose or fell by more than 3 percent only 13 times; in the 1,508 trading sessions of 2010–2015, the RMZ saw 51 such daily swings. With greater volatility comes greater risk, but also greater potential returns.

As a final observation, given the industry's rapid growth in the last 15 years, it is surprising that basic information about REITs is not easy to find. Even something as simple as a complete listing of publicly traded companies in the REIT industry is difficult or expensive to obtain, as each brokerage firm typically has access only to information about the REITs actively covered by their research department's analysts (the individuals who analyze and rate stocks as *buy, hold,* or *sell*). To remedy this information gap, the appendices of this book list the 223 REITs that comprised the FTSE NAREIT All REITs Index at the end of 2015, as well as some basic information about each company. The following chapters present information in a progressive manner. Read as much or as little as you require, and welcome to the world of REITs.

Note: Unless noted otherwise, all prices, total returns, and data used in this book are as of December 31, 2015.

Acknowledgments

Sincere thanks to the following individuals and organizations for their permission to reproduce select material and for the time they invested in editing this book's more technical content:

- Paul Reeder at S&P Global Market Intelligence (formerly SNL Financial)
- Matthew Bechard, John Barwick, John D. Worth, Ph.D., Christopher T. Drula, and Kurt Walten at the National Association of Real Estate Investment Trusts (NAREIT)
- Cohen & Steers, Inc. (NYSE: CNS)
- Green Street Advisors

At the risk of omitting someone, I would also like to thank numerous colleagues at Corporate Office Properties Trust (NYSE: OFC), the executives at Pebblebrook Hotel Trust (NYSE: PEB), and Andrew T. DiZio at Sterling Capital Management for their technical readings of select chapters.

Sincere thanks to R. Brad Thomas for discovering my prior book and realizing its potential.

A very special thanks to Ralph L. Block, author of *Investing in REITs*. His work and writings have inspired and influenced countless investors and REIT industry veterans, including myself and Brad Thomas. We both thank him for his love of real estate and generosity of spirit to educate a still young industry.

Last but never least, I want to thank my family and friends for their support and patience during the many months it took to compose this work.

About the Author

Stephanie Krewson-Kelly is head of investor relations at Corporate Office Properties Trust (NYSE: OFC), a publicly traded office REIT. Her experience in the REIT industry dates back to 1994 and includes work as a senior associate in investment banking (1994–1997) and as a research analyst (1997–2009) in New York City at Salomon Smith Barney (which today is part of Citi Global Markets) and J.P. Morgan, followed by five years as the head of REIT research at BB&T Capital Markets in Richmond, Virginia. In between retiring from Wall Street and joining her current firm, Ms. Krewson-Kelly authored *REIT Roadmap: An Insiders Guide to Successful Investing in Real Estate Investment Trusts* (second edition published in 2012 under her maiden name, Krewson; now out of print).

Prior to her career in REITs, Ms. Krewson-Kelly worked as an internal auditor for a global corporation headquartered in Paris, France. In 1992, Ms. Krewson-Kelly graduated from the University of Pennsylvania's College of Arts & Sciences and Wharton School of Business, where she earned her respective BA in English and BS in Economics.

Ms. Krewson-Kelly also authored *4-Leaf Clovers* (Cedar Tree Books, 2015), a new and original children's book that explains why the finder of a four-leaf clover gets one wish.

Brad Thomas has over 25 years of experience in commercial real estate. He is currently the senior analyst for iREIT Forbes and the editor of the Forbes Real Estate Investor (monthly subscription-based newsletter).

He is an active real estate analyst and business journalist for both Seeking Alpha and Forbes.com where he has a combined following of over 27,000. He has consistently been ranked as the number-one REIT and finance analyst on Seeking Alpha and in 2014 he was ranked by TipRanks as the number-one analyst on Seeking Alpha.

Thomas has also written articles or has been featured in *Forbes* magazine, *Kiplinger's*, *US News & World Report*, *Money*, NPR, *Institutional Investor*, GlobeStreet, The Motley Fool, The Street, Investopedia, and Fox, CNN, and Fox Business.

Over the last five years Thomas has written over 1,500 articles that have generated over 7.5 million annual page views. In 2015 his articles generated 3 million annual page views and on Seeking Alpha he authored over 280 articles, of which 75 percent were Editor's Picks.

Thomas considers himself a value investor and much like Warren Buffett, his investment strategies are rooted in the same margin-of-safety principles taught by the legendary investor, Benjamin Graham.

Thomas considers fundamental research to be the key to intelligent investing, and in the words of Ben Graham, "You are neither right nor wrong because the crowd disagrees. You are right because the data and reasoning are right."

Thomas received a bachelor of science degree in business from Presbyterian College and he resides in South Carolina with his wife and children.

Part I

An Introduction to REITs

Part I of this book begins with very basic information that will be helpful to individuals with little or no prior knowledge of REITs. Chapter 1 addresses industry size, the different ways REITs are classified, and on-line resources for learning more about the industry and individual companies. Chapter 2 provides an overview of the benefits of investing in REITs. Chapter 3 discusses REIT dividends in great detail, in terms of yield, ways to quickly assess if a dividend is safe, and how dividends generally are taxed at the investor level. Chapter 4 provides an overview of different lease structures used by the REITs that own various property types, followed by a discussion of the REIT property sectors and subsectors tracked by NAREIT in Chapter 5. This includes the "major food groups" of office, industrial, retail, residential, and hotel properties, as well as specialized assets, such as data centers and timber.

What Is a REIT?

A real estate investment trust (REIT, pronounced "reet") is an entity that receives revenue through owning or financing income-producing property. Similar to other industries, REITs can be private organizations or they can be publicly traded on a stock exchange. (Chapter 6 discusses the benefits of publicly traded REITs versus private or nontraded REITs.) By being public, REITs are accessible to investors of all types, who can benefit from receiving real estate income without purchasing, managing, or financing property directly.

Publicly traded REITs can be bought or sold like the stock of any other public company. Unique to REITs, however, is their tax status. The *Real Estate Investment Trust Act of 1960* legislation that created the REIT structure exempts companies that qualify as REITs from paying corporate income tax, provided they distribute their taxable income as dividends. To qualify as a REIT in the eyes of the Internal Revenue Service (IRS), a company must meet many specific criteria. The most widely known provision is that a REIT must pay shareholders a dividend equal to at least 90 percent of its otherwise taxable income. (Chapter 6 lists the primary fundamental technical hurdles companies must clear to qualify for REIT tax status.)

The National Association of Real Estate Investment Trusts (NAREIT) is the worldwide representative voice for REITs and publicly traded real estate companies with an interest in U.S. real estate and capital markets. NAREIT's website, www.reit.com, provides investors with educational resources, research, and data and index information, as well as news and information about the industry.

Size of the REIT Industry

According to the All REITs Index produced by FTSE NAREIT, there were 223 publicly traded REITs with a combined public equity market capitalization (or size) of $939 billion on December 31, 2015. Table 1.1 presents year-end data on the REIT industry's capitalization going back to 1971. The market capitalization shown excludes operating partnership (OP) units, which are similar to shares of stock in the REIT, but which are not publicly traded. (OP units are discussed in detail in Chapter 6.) Among the 223 publicly traded REITs in the FTSE NAREIT All REITs Index, 198 were listed on the New York Stock Exchange (NYSE) and the remaining 25 were listed on either the National Association of Securities Dealers Automated Quotation System (NASDAQ) or the American Stock Exchange (AMEX).

Before delving into the benefits of investing in REITs, investors will find it instructive to understand how different types of REITs operate.

Categories of REITs

The two broadest categories for REITs—equity and mortgage—are based on the types of investments they make and the nature of their revenues. Equity REITs will be included in S&P's Real Estate GICS sector effective September 1, 2016; mortgage REITs will remain in Financials. REITs are also classified by the type of property they own, such as office or apartment buildings, and by other means discussed in the following pages. Before buying or selling any stock, investors should know whether the REIT is an equity REIT or a mortgage REIT, and what type(s) of property it owns. NAREIT tracks equity REITs according to property type and mortgage REITs according to whether their investments are backed by residential or commercial real estate. Chapter 5 provides additional information to help investors identify REITs that fit their portfolio objectives.

Equity REITs

Equity REITs derive the majority of their revenue from rents paid by tenants according to the terms of leases that exist between the REIT (the landlord or lessor) and its tenants (the lessees). These REITs usually have *fee simple interest* in their properties and use debt to finance a percentage of the purchase price. This investment

Table 1.1   Historical REIT Industry Market Capitalization and Total Returns

Year Ended	FN All REITs			FN All Equity REITs			FN Mortgage REITs			Hybrid REITs		
	# of REITs	EMC[a] ($MMs)	Total Return	# of REITs	EMC[a] ($MMs)	Total Return	# of REITs	EMC[a] ($MMs)	Total Return	# of REITs	EMC[a] ($MMs)	Total Return
1971	34	$1,494	–	12	$332	–	12	$571	–	10	$592	--
1972	46	$1,881	11.2%	17	$377	8.0%	18	$775	12.2%	11	$729	11.4%
1973	53	$1,394	-27.2%	20	$336	-15.5%	22	$517	-36.3%	11	$540	-23.4%
1974	53	$712	-42.2%	19	$242	-21.4%	22	$239	-45.3%	12	$232	-52.2%
1975	46	$900	36.3%	12	$276	19.3%	22	$312	40.8%	12	$312	49.9%
1976	62	$1,308	49.0%	27	$410	47.6%	22	$416	51.7%	13	$483	48.2%
1977	69	$1,528	19.1%	32	$538	22.4%	19	$398	17.8%	18	$592	17.4%
1978	71	$1,412	-1.6%	33	$576	10.3%	19	$340	-10.0%	19	$496	-7.3%
1979	71	$1,754	30.5%	32	$744	35.9%	19	$377	16.6%	20	$633	33.8%
1980	75	$2,299	28.0%	35	$942	24.4%	21	$510	16.8%	19	$847	42.5%
1981	76	$2,439	8.6%	36	$978	6.0%	21	$541	7.1%	19	$920	12.2%
1982	66	$3,299	31.6%	30	$1,071	21.6%	20	$1,133	48.6%	16	$1,094	29.6%
1983	59	$4,257	25.5%	26	$1,469	30.6%	19	$1,460	16.9%	14	$1,329	29.9%
1984	59	$5,085	14.8%	25	$1,795	20.9%	20	$1,801	7.3%	14	$1,489	17.3%
1985	82	$7,674	5.9%	37	$3,270	19.1%	32	$3,162	-5.2%	13	$1,241	4.3%
1986	96	$9,924	19.2%	45	$4,336	19.2%	35	$3,626	19.2%	16	$1,962	18.8%
1987	110	$9,702	-10.7%	53	$4,759	-3.6%	38	$3,161	-15.7%	19	$1,782	-17.6%
1988	117	$11,435	11.4%	56	$6,142	13.5%	40	$3,621	7.3%	21	$1,673	6.6%
1989	120	$11,662	-1.8%	56	$6,770	8.8%	43	$3,536	-15.9%	21	$1,356	-12.1%
1990	119	$8,737	-17.4%	58	$5,552	-15.4%	43	$2,549	-18.4%	18	$636	-28.2%
1991	138	$12,968	35.7%	86	$8,786	35.7%	28	$2,586	31.8%	24	$1,596	39.2%
1992	142	$15,912	12.2%	89	$11,171	14.6%	30	$2,773	1.9%	23	$1,968	16.6%
1993	189	$32,159	18.6%	135	$26,082	19.7%	32	$3,399	14.6%	22	$2,678	21.2%
1994	226	$44,306	0.8%	175	$38,812	3.2%	29	$2,503	-24.3%	22	$2,991	4.0%
1995	219	$57,541	18.3%	178	$49,913	15.3%	24	$3,395	63.4%	17	$4,233	23.0%
1996	199	$88,776	35.8%	166	$78,302	35.3%	20	$4,779	50.9%	13	$5,696	29.4%
1997	211	$140,534	18.9%	176	$127,825	20.3%	26	$7,370	3.8%	9	$5,338	10.8%
1998	210	$138,301	-18.8%	173	$126,905	-17.5%	28	$6,481	-29.2%	9	$4,916	-34.0%
1999	203	$124,262	-6.5%	167	$118,233	-4.6%	26	$4,442	-33.2%	10	$1,588	-35.9%
2000	189	$138,715	25.9%	158	$134,431	26.4%	22	$1,632	16.0%	9	$2,652	11.6%
2001	182	$154,899	15.5%	151	$147,092	13.9%	22	$3,991	77.3%	9	$3,816	50.8%
2002	176	$161,937	5.2%	149	$151,272	3.8%	20	$7,146	31.1%	7	$3,519	23.3%
2003	171	$224,212	38.5%	144	$204,800	37.1%	20	$14,187	57.4%	7	$5,225	56.2%
2004	193	$307,895	30.4%	153	$275,291	31.6%	33	$25,964	18.4%	7	$6,639	23.9%
2005	197	$330,691	8.3%	152	$301,491	12.2%	37	$23,394	-23.2%	8	$5,807	-10.8%
2006	183	$438,071	34.4%	138	$400,741	35.1%	38	$29,195	19.3%	7	$8,134	40.9%
2007	152	$312,009	-17.8%	118	$288,695	-15.7%	29	$19,054	-42.3%	5	$4,260	-34.8%
2008	136	$191,651	-37.3%	113	$176,238	-37.7%	20	$14,281	-31.3%	3	$1,133	-75.5%
2009	142	$271,199	27.5%	115	$248,355	28.0%	23	$22,103	24.6%	4	$741	41.3%
2010	153	$389,295	27.6%	126	$358,908	28.0%	27	$30,387	22.6%	§	—	—
2011	160	$450,501	7.3%	130	$407,529	8.3%	30	$42,972	-2.4%	§	—	—
2012	172	$603,415	20.1%	139	$544,415	19.7%	33	$59,000	19.9%	§	—	—
2013	202	$670,334	3.2%	161	$608,277	2.9%	41	$62,057	-2.0%	§	—	—
2014	216	$970,428	27.2%	177	$846,410	28.0%	39	$61,017	17.9%	§	—	—
2015	223	$938,852	2.3%	182	$886,488	2.8%	41	$52,365	-8.9%	§	—	—

*Information prior to 1971 is not available.
§NAREIT discontinued its FTSE NAREIT Hybrid REIT Index in 2010.
aNAREIT calculates equity market capitalization (EMC) as the year-end share price times the number of common shares outstanding. The number does not include operating partnership units (OP units), which are not publicly traded and which are discussed in Chapter 6.
Source: Reproduced by permission of the National Association of Real Estate Investment Trusts® ("NAREIT") and is used subject to the Terms and Conditions of Use set forth on the NAREIT website, including, but not limited to, Section 9 thereof.

approach is similar to how individuals purchase homes in that the REIT generally uses some amount of debt and pays the remainder in cash. Fee simple interest in real estate means the buyer receives title to the land and improvements, improvements being the building and any structures that exist on the land. The debt an equity REIT uses to finance a portion of a property can either be a mortgage (which is also called *property-level* debt) or corporate-level bonds (also called *senior* or *unsecured* debt).

Sometimes, equity REITs own properties according to a leasehold interest, which is also called a *ground lease*. In this case, the REIT does not own the land on which the building(s) sit(s). The REIT pays the landowner (or *lessor*) a monthly fee for an agreed-upon time period—usually several decades—in exchange for the right to use the land as needed to support the building's operations.

Particularly since the *REIT Modernization Act of 1999* (RMA), equity REITs increasingly operate as fully integrated real estate companies that also derive income from a range of real estate–related business activities. As of December 31, 2015, 182 of the 223 publicly traded REITs in the FTSE NAREIT All REITs Index were equity REITs. These companies had an aggregate equity market capitalization of $886.5 billion (excluding OP units), constituting the largest category of REITs in the United States. Chapter 5 provides more detail on equity REITs according to the different types of commercial properties they own.

Mortgage REITs

Mortgage REITs lend money to real estate owners directly, by issuing mortgages, or indirectly, by acquiring existing loans or mortgage-backed securities. Mortgage REITs, which are also referred to as *mREITs*, derive the majority of their revenues from interest received on commercial mortgage loans or from investments in residential- or commercial-based real estate instruments.

Mortgage REITs are analogous to banks that lend almost exclusively to commercial real estate developers and landlords, except mREITs do not have customer deposits from which to lend. Instead, they raise capital by issuing debt and equity in private or public capital markets. Their revenue comprises the principal and interest payments received from their investments.

As of December 31, 2015, FTSE NAREIT All REITs Index listed 41 mortgage REITs with a combined equity market capitalization of

$52.4 billion (excluding OP units). Since the *Dodd–Frank Wall Street Reform and Consumer Protection Act* (the Dodd-Frank Act) was signed into law in July 2010, the number of publicly traded mREITs tracked by NAREIT has increased 52 percent, from 27 companies at the end of June 2010 to 41 at the end of 2015. This is because the Dodd-Frank Act tightened regulation on traditional banks and lenders. Mortgage REITs essentially stepped in to fill the credit void created by this and other legislation.

Hybrid REITs

Prior to 2011, there was a third category of REITs, then called *hybrid REITs*. These companies combined the ownership strategies of equity and mortgage REITs, depending on the investment opportunities available. Historically, hybrid REITs represented the smallest class of REITs industry and, in December 2010, NAREIT reclassified the four remaining hybrid REITs as mortgage REITs.

Classification by Property Type

Most often, investors refer to REITs by the type of commercial property in which they invest, such as offices, apartments, or warehouse buildings. In the past few years, the IRS ruled that rental income from less traditional property types can also qualify as *good income* for REITs. (The concept of good or bad REIT income is addressed in Chapter 6.) As a result, the industry now includes REITs that own billboards, cell phone towers—even gas and electric transmission lines—and other highly specialized real estate. NAREIT classifies these new comers to the industry as *specialty* REITs. Chapter 5 discusses the industry's different property types in greater detail, and Appendix C provides summary information on the 223 REITs that were publicly traded at the end of 2015.

Size and Index Inclusion

In describing each classification of REIT, size is one important investment criterion, because companies that are large (as measured by their equity market capitalization) trade differently than small companies. Chapter 8 details how to calculate a REIT's equity market capitalization (also referred to as simply *market cap* or *EMC*) and other important metrics.

An important detail to keep in mind when looking at REIT data is that, in addition to the shares held by public shareholders, most REITs also have private, nontraded ownership units called *operating partnership (OP) units* outstanding. Specific to REITs, OP units are similar to shares of common stock in that they represent a percent ownership in a REIT (see Chapter 6). Generally, OP units can be exchanged on a one-for-one basis into common stock of the REIT and receive the same level of common dividend as stock. The main difference between OP units and stock is that OP units are not publicly traded (also referred to as not being *liquid*). Unless expressly noted otherwise, market capitalizations for REITs that are available on financial service outlets, such as Yahoo! Finance, exclude OP units.

One of the reasons why large and small cap REITs trade differently is that larger REITs simply have a greater supply of common shares available to buy or sell on stock exchanges; the number of common shares outstanding is also referred to as a company's *float*. Larger-cap REITs with greater float tend to have higher average daily trading volumes.

Approximately 100 REITs, or less than 50 percent of the industry, have market capitalizations and daily average trading volume levels that have qualified them for inclusion in major stock indexes. Index inclusion is a significant factor in long-term REIT performance. This is because money managers typically have to allocate money to invest in stocks that are part of the broader indexes against which they *benchmark*. Benchmarking is simply measuring the performance of an investment strategy against a standard, such as an index. Money managers may aim to match the performance of their targeted benchmark(s); others may aim to exceed their benchmarks.

REITs that are included in the S&P 500, 400, or 600 Indexes are more visible to investors and money managers, and tend to outperform nonindex REITs when REITs are in favor as an investment class. In contrast, when investors do not want to own REITs, the index companies often experience disproportionate declines (albeit, temporary) compared to nonindex REITs. (Chapter 7 discusses factors that affect REIT performance in more detail.)

The 24 large-cap REITs that were included in the S&P 500 Index at the end of 2015 are listed in Table 1.2. With REITs outperforming most other asset classes in the last few years, there have been a number of initial public offerings, or *IPOs*, by small and mid-cap REITs.

Table 1.2   REIT Constituents of the S&P 500 Index[a]

Company Name (Ticker)	Ticker	Property Focus	EMC[b]
Simon Property Group	SPG	Retail—Malls	$60.4
Public Storage	PSA	Self-Storage	42.8
American Tower Corporation	AMT	Infrastructure—Wireless	41.0
Equity Residential	EQR	Residential—Apartments	29.7
Crown Castle International	CCI	Infrastructure—Wireless	28.9
AvalonBay Communities	AVB	Residential—Apartments	25.2
General Growth Properties	GGP	Retail—Malls	24.0
Welltower, Inc.*	HCN	Health Care	23.9
Prologis, Inc.	PLD	Industrial	22.5
Boston Properties	BXP	Office	19.6
Vornado Realty Trust	VNO	Diversified	18.8
Ventas, Inc.	VTR	Health Care	18.7
Equinix Inc	EQIX	Data Centers	18.6
HCP, Inc.	HCP	Health Care	17.8
Essex Property Trust	ESS	Residential—Apartments	15.7
Weyerhaeuser Company[†]	WY	Timber	15.3
Realty Income Corporation	O	Retail—Free Standing	12.9
Macerich Company	MAC	Retail—Malls	12.7
Host Hotels & Resorts	HST	Lodging/Resorts	11.6
SL Green Realty Corp	SLG	Office	11.3
Kimco Realty Corporation	KIM	Retail—Shopping Centers	10.9
Plum Creek Timber Company[†]	PCL	Timber	8.3
Apartment Investment and Management	AIV	Residential—Apartments	6.3
Iron Mountain, Inc.	IRM	Specialty	5.7
Total for all 24 REITs			$502.4

[a]In 2016, Extra Space Storage (NYSE: EXR) and UDR, Inc. (NYSE: UDR) will be added to the S&P 500, becoming the 25th and 26th REITs in this index.
[b]Equity market caps are in billions of dollars.
*Formerly known as Health Care REIT, Inc.
[†]These two timber REITs are merging; the transaction is expected to be complete in the first half of 2016.
Source: Reproduced by permission of the National Association of Real Estate Investment Trusts® and is used subject to the Terms and Conditions of Use set forth on the NAREIT website, but not limited to, Section 9 thereof.

Although these smaller companies are not as liquid as larger-cap stocks, they nonetheless can offer strong value for longer-term investors. The 35 and 32 REITs that, respectively, were included in the S&P 400 Mid Cap and 600 Small Cap Indexes at the end of 2015 are listed in Tables 1.3 and 1.4.

Geographic Focus

REITs typically own and operate regional or national portfolios of properties. Investors interested in investing in "the U.S. office

Table 1.3   REIT Constituents of the S&P 400 Mid Cap Index

Company Name (Ticker)	Ticker	Property Focus	EMC[a]
Extra Space Storage Inc.[†]	EXR	Self Storage	$10.9
Federal Realty Investment Trust	FRT	Retail—Shopping Centers	10.1
UDR, Inc. [†]	UDR	Residential—Apartments	9.8
Duke Realty Corporation	DRE	Industrial	7.3
Mid-America Apartment Communities, Inc.	MAA	Residential—Apartments	6.8
Camden Property Trust	CPT	Residential—Apartments	6.6
Omega Healthcare Investors, Inc.	OHI	Health Care	6.5
Alexandria Real Estate Equities, Inc.	ARE	Office	6.5
Regency Centers Corporation	REG	Retail—Shopping Centers	6.4
Kilroy Realty Corporation	KRC	Office	5.8
National Retail Properties, Inc.	NNN	Retail—Free Standing	5.5
Lamar Advertising	LAMR	Specialty—Billboards	4.9
BioMed Realty Trust, Inc.[‡]	BMR	Office	4.8
American Campus Communities, Inc.	ACC	Residential—Apartments	4.6
Taubman Centers, Inc.	TCO	Retail—Malls	4.6
Liberty Property Trust	LPT	Industrial	4.6
Douglas Emmett, Inc.	DEI	Office	4.5
Weingarten Realty Investors	WRI	Retail—Shopping Centers	4.3
Highwoods Properties	HIW	Office	4.2
Hospitality Properties Trust	HPT	Health Care	4.0
Sovran Self Storage, Inc.	SSS	Self Storage	3.8
Senior Housing Properties Trust	SNH	Health Care	3.5
Equity One, Inc.	EQY	Retail—Shopping Centers	3.5
Post Properties, Inc.	PPS	Residential—Apartments	3.2
Tanger Factory Outlet Centers, Inc.	SKT	Retail—Shopping Centers	3.1
Corrections Corporation of America	CXW	Specialty—Prisons	3.1
LaSalle Hotel Properties	LHO	Lodging/Resorts	2.8
Communications Sales & Leasing	CSAL	Infrastructure	2.8
Rayonier Inc.	RYN	Timber	2.7
Care Capital Properties, Inc.	CCP	Health Care	2.6
Urban Edge Properties	UE	Retail—Shopping Centers	2.3
Mack-Cali Realty Corporation	CLI	Office	2.1
Corporate Office Properties Trust	OFC	Office	2.1
WP Glimcher Inc.	WPG	Retail - Malls	2.0
Potlatch Corporation	PCH	Timber	1.2
Total for all 35 REITs			$163.8

[a]Equity market caps are in billions of dollars.
[†]In 2016, Extra Space Storage and UDR, Inc. will be added to the S&P 500 Index.
[‡]In January 2016, BioMed Realty Trust (former NYSE: BMR) was taken private.
Source: Reproduced by permission of the National Association of Real Estate Investment Trusts® and is used subject to the Terms and Conditions of Use set forth on the NAREIT website, including, but not limited to, Section 9 thereof.

Table 1.4   REIT Constituents of the S&P 600 Small Cap Index

Company Name (Ticker)	Ticker	Property Focus	EMC[a]
EPR Properties	EPR	Specialty—Cineplex	$3,493
Healthcare Realty Trust Incorporated	HR	Health Care	2,843
Medical Properties Trust	MPW	Health Care	2,738
PS Business Parks	PSB	Industrial	2,354
Acadia Realty Trust	AKR	Retail—Shopping Centers	2,282
Kite Realty Group Trust	KRG	Retail—Shopping Centers	2,151
GEO Group	GEO	Specialty—Prisons	2,144
Education Realty Trust	EDR	Residential—Apartments	2,099
Cousins Properties Inc.	CUZ	Office	2,042
DiamondRock Hospitality Company	DRH	Lodging/Resorts	1,937
Lexington Realty Trust	LXP	Diversified	1,888
EastGroup Properties, Inc.	EGP	Industrial	1,796
Retail Opportunities Investments Corp.	ROIC	Retail—Shopping Centers	1,768
CoreSite Realty Corporation	COR	Data Centers	1,738
Parkway Properties, Inc.	PKY	Office	1,737
American Assets Trust, Inc.	AAT	Diversified	1,722
LTC Properties, Inc.	LTC	Health Care	1,533
Pennsylvania REIT	PEI	Retail—Malls	1,512
Chesapeake Lodging Trust	CHSP	Lodging/Resorts	1,501
Sabra Health Care REIT, Inc.	SBRA	Health Care	1,318
Government Properties Income Trust	GOV	Office	1,128
Saul Centers, Inc.	BFS	Retail—Shopping Centers	1,082
Inland Real Estate Corporation[†]	IRC	Retail—Shopping Centers	1,068
Franklin Street Properties Corp.	FSP	Office	1,037
Summit Hotel Properties, Inc.	INN	Lodging/Resorts	1,035
Capstead Mortgage Corporation	CMO	Mortgage—Residential	835
Universal Health Realty Income Trust	UHT	Health Care	665
Agree Realty Corporation	ADC	Retail—Free Standing	642
Cedar Realty Trust, Inc.	CDR	Retail—Shopping Centers	596
Getty Realty Corp.	GTY	Retail—Free Standing	573
Care Trust REIT Inc	CTRE	Health Care	527
Urstadt Biddle Properties	UBA	Retail—Shopping Centers	511
Total for all 32 REITs			$50,291

[a]Equity market caps are in millions of dollars.
[†]This REIT is in the process of being acquired and will no longer be publicly traded.
Source: Reproduced by permission of the National Association of Real Estate Investment Trusts® and is used subject to the Terms and Conditions of Use set forth on the NAREIT website, including, but not limited to, Section 9 thereof.

market" could invest in a REIT, such as Boston Properties, Inc. (NYSE: BXP), that owns office buildings in major U.S. cities. By contrast, an investor who wants to capitalize on a rise in demand for office space in, say, Philadelphia, Pennsylvania, could focus on stocks such as Brandywine Realty Trust (NYSE: BDN).

Certain larger-cap U.S. REITs have expanded their real estate holdings outside the United States. Stocks like Prologis (NYSE: PLD) provide a way for investors to participate in the economics of owning warehouse/distribution space in the global marketplace. Similarly, Simon Property Group, Inc. (NYSE: SPG) affords individuals the opportunity to invest in the company's globally diversified portfolio of high-end shopping malls.

Risks and Rewards of Geographic Concentration

There are risks and rewards associated with each REIT's degree of geographic concentration and the supply-and-demand character-istics associated with their property markets. Landlords that own apartment buildings in New York City's Manhattan market will likely generate different levels of rent growth, occupancy, and shareholder returns than apartment landlords in Dallas, Texas. In all cases, the competency and discipline of a company's senior management and property management teams are key determinants of a REIT's ability to increase shareholder value, regardless of geography or property focus. That said, investors who strongly believe one region or market in the country will experience disproportionately better—or worse—economic times than the rest of the country can capitalize on their conviction by investing in (or selling out of) REITs based on the geographic concentrations of their portfolios.

Growth Strategy

A less common but nonetheless important way of classifying REITs (at least for investment purposes) is according to the tactics they use to grow earnings and cash flow. Every REIT can be broken down into three activities that support their financial results:

1. Internal growth generated by managing assets the REIT already owns; also sometimes called "organic" growth
2. External growth generated by acquiring or developing properties
3. Financing that growth through issuing new debt or equity, and/or by selling properties

There is no one "right way" for REITs to grow earnings, though each company's cost of capital affects the opportunities on which a management team can capitalize. Chapter 7 discusses cost of capital in more detail, but for purposes of this chapter, the following rule is sufficient:

> Companies with lower costs of capital are able to grow faster and with higher quality investments than companies with higher, less competitive costs of capital.

Each REIT's management team pursues the strategy they deemed to be optimal for that company's chosen real estate markets, opportunities, and cost of capital. The following truisms should assist investors in evaluating individual companies before making an investment.

Risk Axioms for Growth Strategies:

Developing = More Risk Than Acquiring Properties

Acquiring = More Risk Than Actively Managing Existing Properties

More Debt = More Risk

- **Development**—Growing earnings by developing properties is riskier than acquiring assets that already exist, especially in property types that take a year or more to construct. The added risk associated with development is why companies expect to earn a higher yield, or return, on monies they invest in development. The higher returns compensate the higher risk of potential failure. Many REITs have been able to execute successful development strategies, however, by being extremely careful in their selection of location, by achieving some level of pre-leasing prior to commencing construction, and/or by operating their business with lower levels of debt. Examples of such REITs include: Armada Hoffler Properties (NYSE: AHH),

Corporate Office Properties Trust (NYSE: OFC), and the various data center–focused REITs such as Digital Realty Trust (NYSE: DLR).

- **Acquisitions**—Acquiring assets bears more risk than managing properties a REIT already owns. Managing existing assets can include redeveloping them to reposition them in their markets, which generally is less risky than new acquisitions. When a REIT buys a property, management underwrites the local trade area surrounding that asset. If management overestimates the demand for space in the new market, the acquired property will underperform expectations. By the same token, if management underestimates the supply outlook for a new market, and other landlords develop too many competing buildings, then the acquired property will likely underperform expectations due to the REIT's difficulty in raising rents to keep pace with inflation.

- **Financing**—Regarding how a REIT pays for existing operations and any level of external growth, it is hard to find a REIT—or any company—that went bankrupt because it had *too little* debt. REITs are like any company in that more debt, which also is referred to as *leverage*, equates to higher risk and lower certainty of future earnings and cash flow.

> No REIT ever went bankrupt from having *too little* debt.

At a minimum, the amount of debt a REIT carries can affect its ability to take advantage of market opportunities. For example, a REIT that has a debt-to-gross book value ratio of 40 percent has greater financial flexibility than a REIT with a 60 percent ratio. (Please refer to Chapter 8 for a definition of gross book value.) The REIT with lower leverage should be able to successfully navigate adverse economic times without lowering its common dividend or selling assets at fire-sale prices. Low-levered companies should also be able to purchase strategic, premium-quality assets that distressed sellers may bring to market during times of economic adversity, such as during the Great Recession of 2008–2009. Last but definitely not least, companies with low levels of debt typically can raise debt and equity capital at lower prices than more highly leveraged companies.

Where to Find Information on REITs

In addition to NAREIT, there are several resources to consult for additional information on the industry and individual REITs. The resources detailed below should provide sufficient information for analyzing the majority of REITs that were publicly traded at the end of 2015.

FTSE NAREIT All REITs Index

The FTSE Group is a joint venture between the Financial Times of London and the London Stock Exchange and is the largest provider of financial indexes in the United Kingdom. The acronym *FTSE* is pronounced "footsie" and stands for Financial Times Stock Exchange.

Appendix A and B provide listings of the 223 REITs that comprised the FTSE NAREIT All REITs Index at December 31, 2015. Companies are listed alphabetically by their name in Appendix A and by their stock exchange (or *ticker*) symbol in Appendix B. Chapter 5 and Appendix C of this book also list each REIT according to property focus and present summary information on each company, including website addresses.

Company-Specific Websites

Once an investor knows which REIT(s) suits his or her investment criteria, each REIT's website will provide the most complete and timely information, including press releases, annual reports, and quarterly statements filed with the Securities and Exchange Commission (SEC), as well as other useful information.

In December 2015, the Internet Corporation for Assigned Names and Numbers (or ICANN) designated NAREIT to operate a dot-REIT top-level domain registry. As more REITs adopt the .REIT identifier for their websites, searching for companies that are REITs by using the Internet will become faster and easier. See Appendix C for the website addresses of the 223 REITs in the FTSE NAREIT All REITs Index.

Indexes for Tracking REIT Performance

In 1985, Cohen & Steers, Inc. (NYSE: CNS) created the first real estate mutual fund and, today, is a global investment manager specializing in liquid real assets, including real estate securities, listed infrastructure, commodities and natural resource equities, as well as preferred securities and other income solutions. They offer two real estate indexes:

- Cohen & Steers Realty Majors Portfolio Index (RMP), which tracks the largest, most liquid U.S. REITs.
- Cohen & Steers Global Realty Majors index (GRM), which tracks global real estate securities that stand to lead or benefit most from the securitization of commercial real estate worldwide.

NAREIT and MSCI, a leading provider of investment-decision-support tools, provide indices that track REIT performance:

- MSCI US REIT Index, ticker symbol RMZ on the American Stock Exchange, is a real-time, price-only index that tracks approximately 99 percent of the publicly traded equity REITs in the United States. At the end of 2015, 150 equity REITs composed the RMZ. Mortgage and certain equity REITs are not included in this index. Investors can obtain real-time quotes for the RMZ on financial websites, such as Google Finance and Yahoo Finance, and can learn more about the index by going to www.msci.com.
- MSCI also publishes the RMS, a daily total return version of the RMZ, which encompasses the companies' dividend yields. The RMS is not a real-time index; the total return of the REITs that compose the index is published at the end of the day.
- NAREIT indexes. In conjunction with FTSE, NAREIT publishes several indexes to track U.S. REIT performance; the three most popular indexes, and the number of companies that comprised each one at December 31, 2015, are as follows:
  1. FTSE NAREIT All REITs Index—tracks publicly traded equity and mortgage REITs (223 companies)
  2. FTSE NAREIT Equity REITs Index—tracks publicly traded equity REITs (160 companies)
  3. FTSE NAREIT Mortgage REITs Index—tracks publicly traded mortgage REITs (37 companies)

S&P Dow Jones Indices LLC (www.spdji.com), a part of McGraw Hill Financial, is the world's largest, global resource for index-based concepts, data, and research. Home to iconic financial market indicators, such as the S&P 500® and the Dow Jones Industrial Average®, S&P Dow Jones Indices LLC has over 115 years of experience constructing innovative and transparent solutions that fulfill the needs of investors. S&P Dow Jones Indices publishes many stock market indices, including the Dow Jones Equity All REIT Index (REI):

- The REI contains all the publicly traded U.S. equity REITs in the Dow Jones U.S. stock universe, which totaled 177 companies at December 31, 2015.
- The REI is calculated and disseminated every 15 seconds during the trading day. More information about the Dow Jones REIT indexes can be found at www.djindexes.com.

Exchange-Traded Funds for Investing in REITs

The indexes in the preceding paragraphs only track and report REIT performance. Several exchange-traded funds (ETFs) exist that enable investors to purchase an index (or bundle) of REITs—similar to buying a mutual fund that approximates the returns of the S&P 500 Index or other broad-based stock market index. There are even ETFs that will allow investors to *short* (that is, *bet against*) a rise in REIT share prices. Three of the largest REIT ETFs are listed below:

1. **VNQ**—The Vanguard Group's REIT exchange-traded fund that trades under the ticker symbol VNQ is the largest REIT ETF available and is designed to track the performance of the MSCI US REIT Index (see RMZ discussion earlier in this chapter).
2. **IYR**—iShares U.S. Real Estate ETF investment seeks to approximate the price and yield performance of an index of U.S. equities in the real estate sector.
3. **ICF**—iShares Cohen & Steers REIT ETF seeks to track the investment results of the largest, most liquid REITs.

For a more complete listing and discussion of real estate ETFs, Investors should consult with their financial advisors and also review the ETF Lab provided by Forbes and www.IntelligentREITInvestor.com.

CHAPTER 2

Why Invest in REITs?

Many investors buy REITs solely for the attractive dividend yields they offer relative to government bonds and other investments. However, there are many more, equally compelling reasons to include REITs as part of a well-balanced portfolio. Two such reasons are that REITs typically have delivered total returns that exceed those of the S&P 500 Index and that their dividends generally increase faster than inflation (as measured by increases in the Consumer Price Index [CPI]), making REITs an effective hedge against inflation. A third and equally important reason is that REITs are a diversification tool; a wealth of research has proven that investing in REITs helps lower risk and increase returns on a portfolio of stocks and bonds.

Double-Digit Total Returns

Investor total returns on any stock investment are calculated as the sum of dividends received plus any appreciation (or less any declined) in stock price during the time the stock is owned. Due in part to their attractive current yields, REITs have tended to deliver annualized total returns to investors of 10 to 12 percent over time. As shown in Table 2.1, equity REITs delivered average total annual returns of 12.0 percent from 1972 to 2015—or 170 basis points more than the 10.3 percent total return achieved by stocks in the S&P 500 Index over the same period. (A basis point [bps] is equal to 1/100 of a percentage point; for example, 1 percent equals 100 bps.)

Table 2.1   Comparative Compounded Total Annual Returns

Timeframe*	All REITs	All Equity REITs	S&P 500	NASDAQ†	DJIA
2015	2.3%	2.8%	1.4%	7.0%	0.2%
3-Year	10.3%	10.6%	15.1%	19.8%	12.7%
5-Year	11.6%	11.9%	12.6%	14.9%	11.3%
10-Year	6.9%	7.4%	7.3%	9.7%	7.8%
15-Year	10.8%	11.1%	5.0%	4.8%	5.8%
20-Year	10.3%	10.9%	8.2%	8.1%	8.8%
30-Year	9.4%	10.7%	10.4%	9.6%	8.4%
40-Year	12.0%	13.7%	11.4%	11.0%	7.8%
1972 – 2015	9.8%	12.0%	10.3%	8.9%	7.0%

*Compounded annual total returns for the number of years ended December 31, 2015. Shaded areas represent time periods when equity REITs outperformed the S&P 500 Index.
†Price appreciation only. Compounded annual returns from 1972 to 2015 are calculated from the NASDAQ Composite's inception date of December 31, 1973.
Source: Reproduced by permission of the National Association of Real Estate Investment Trusts® and is used subject to the Terms and Conditions of Use set forth on the NAREIT website, including, but not limited to, Section 9 thereof.

Dividends

Dividend income is one of the primary reasons to invest in REITs, in large part because their yields represent an attractive premium to yields offered by other investments. As of December 31, 2015, the average dividend yield from REITs in the FTSE NAREIT All REITs Index was 4.3 percent, or approximately 200 basis points higher than the 2.3 percent yield on 10-year U.S. Treasuries and the 2.2 percent yield from the S&P 500 Index.

REITs are an attractive investment for people seeking current income, provided that the REIT has a conservatively leveraged balance sheet and well-located assets that are competitively managed. When a REIT possesses these qualities, it generally can sustain—and preferably grow—the dividend it pays to shareholders. Chapter 3 discusses the characteristics of REIT dividends and dividend yield, as well as quick calculations investors can perform to assess the sustainability of a REIT's dividend.

Liquidity

Publicly traded REITs offer investors the ability to add real estate returns to their portfolios without incurring the liquidity risk that accompanies direct real estate investment. This is because REITs that are publicly traded on stock exchanges can be bought or sold in an instant, like other stocks, through a financial advisor or online trading services. (Nontraded and private REITs do not offer similar liquidity; these structures are discussed in Chapter 6.) In contrast, direct investments in real estate can take several months or even years to sell. Publicly traded REITs, therefore, enable investors to participate in real estate–based investments in a liquid manner.

Portfolio Diversification

REITs are a proven diversification tool for portfolio management, a fact that has been demonstrated in multiple studies by various prominent investment advisory firms using different techniques, data sources, and time periods. In simplistic terms, diversification means that adding a particular investment to a portfolio increases the overall expected returns of that pool of investments while also reducing risk. Note that risk is also referred to as *volatility*.

The reason for this diversification benefit is because real estate and, by extension, REITs represent one of the three fundamental investment asset classes, the other two being stocks (also called *equities*) and bonds. As Figure 2.1 shows, U.S. investment real estate (which excludes single-family homes) is estimated to represent $17 trillion, or 21 percent of the $79 trillion investable assets in the United States. Because real estate has its own unique drivers and cycle that are separate from that of other equities and bonds, real estate investments promote portfolio diversification. (Chapter 7, REIT Performance, discusses the real estate cycle in detail.)

In the past decade, six major studies have been performed to determine what allocation to REITs will maximize their diversification benefits. (*Allocation* speaks to what percent of the total portfolio amount is invested in an asset class. For example, an individual may invest 20 percent of his or her portfolio in REITs, 40 percent in equities, and 40 percent in bonds.) Figure 2.2 summarizes their findings.

Fact

A $1,000 portfolio invested in a combination of equities, bonds, and equity REIT shares will produce greater returns and exhibit less risk than a $1,000 portfolio that does not include an allocation to equity REITs.

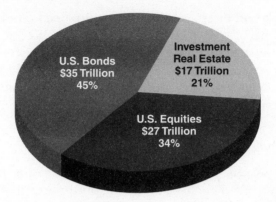

Figure 2.1   Investment Real Estate Is the Third Largest Asset Class in the United States.

Source: Reproduced from NAREIT materials by permission of the National Association of Real Estate Investment Trusts® and is used subject to the Terms and Conditions of Use set forth on the NAREIT website, including, but not limited to, Section 9 thereof.

Although many investors believe investing (or allocating) between 5 and 10 percent of their portfolio in REITs is "about right," these six studies have shown that the optimal allocation to REITs is as high as 20 percent—which is proportionate with the size of the investment real estate market shown in Figure 2.1.

For example, the 2016 Wilshire Associates study commissioned by NAREIT, *The Role of REITs and Listed Real Estate Equities in Target Date Fund Asset Allocations* (the "2016 Wilshire Report," reference in Figure 2.2), found that the optimal portfolio allocates up to 17 percent of assets to REITs. The study showed that a diversified portfolio that included REITs had nine less basis points of risk (and generated 33 basis points of additional return) than a similar portfolio that did not include REITs. Although 0.33 percent may not seem meaningful on the surface, over time the additional return adds up.

A portion of this outperformance can be attributed to the robust dividend yields and above-average returns REITs offer, but an equally important factor is the low correlation with which REITs trade relative to bonds and other stocks. A correlation of +1 between two investments means that they trade in complete lockstep with one another; conversely, a correlation of −1 means they trade proportionally in opposite directions. The 2016 Wilshire Report showed that from 1975 through 2015, REIT share prices moved with a 0.58 correlation with the Wilshire U.S. Large Cap Index and a 0.65 correlation with the Wilshire U.S. Small Cap Index.

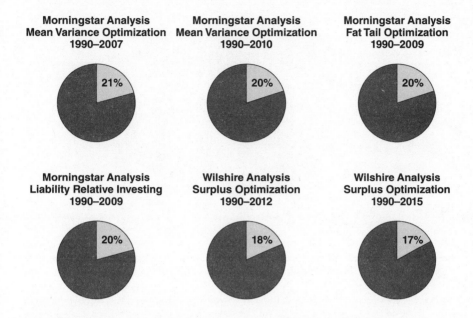

Figure 2.2   Portfolio Allocations to Global Real Estate (different researchers, methodologies, and time periods)

Source: Reproduced from NAREIT materials by permission of the National Association of Real Estate Investment Trusts® and is used subject to the Terms and Conditions of Use set forth on the NAREIT website, including, but not limited to, Section 9 thereof.

As a final note, a groundbreaking study completed recently by CEM highlighted the advantages of owning publicly traded REITs rather than private real estate. According to a summary of the CEM study provided by NAREIT, the study tracked returns from over 200 public and private pension plans with combined assets of over $2.5 trillion. The results, which are summarized in Figure 2.3, clearly demonstrated that publicly traded REITs had the highest return (net of expenses), with an annualized total return of 11.31 percent. Private real estate returned just 7.61 percent.

Hedge Against Inflation

Equity REITs rent their properties to tenants according to leases, the terms of which tend to protect the REITs' margins from the effects of inflation. As discussed in Chapter 4, most leases provide

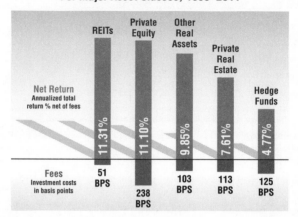

Figure 2.3 CEM Benchmarking Study: U.S. Defined Benefit Pension Plan Performance

Source: Reproduced from NAREIT materials by permission of the National Association of Real Estate Investment Trusts® and is used subject to the Terms and Conditions of Use set forth on the NAREIT website, including, but not limited to, Section 9 thereof.

that landlords will bill tenants for various costs (utilities, taxes, insurance, landscaping, etc.) after they have been incurred. In the case of triple-net leases, the landlord does not pay any of these operational costs; instead, tenants pay the costs directly. Apartment landlords typically have one-year leases, and generally can increase their rents (also called *marking-to-market*) to keep pace with inflating costs. The ability to pass along increases in operating costs enables REIT revenues to keep pace—albeit with some lag—with rising prices in times of inflation. The result is that REITs generate inflation-adjusted earnings, which makes their stocks attractive investments during times of inflation.

Table 2.2 is excerpted from the 2016 Wilshire Report referenced earlier in this chapter, and shows how often different investments—namely REITs, commodities (as represented by the S&P GSCI Total Index), the S&P 500 Index, and Treasury Inflation Protected Securities (TIPS)—generated total returns that exceeded inflation. The higher the percentage shown, the more effective the investment was at protecting (or *hedging*) against inflation. From 1975 through 2015, REIT total returns exceeded inflation 74 percent of the time on a rolling 6-month basis, and 75 percent of the time on

Table 2.2   Percent of Rolling Periods in Which Total Return Met or Exceeded
Inflation: 1975–2015

	FTSE All Equity REITs Index	S&P GSCI Total Index	S&P 500 Index	Barclays Capital U.S. TIPS Index*
6-month rolling returns	74%	56%	69%	69%
12-month rolling returns	75%	57%	72%	74%

*Barclays Capital U.S. TIPS Index inception was October 1, 1997.
Sources: Wilshire Compass; U.S. Department of Labor, Bureau of Labor Statistics. Reproduced from the 2016 Wilshire Report and by permission of the National Association of Real Estate Investment Trusts® ("NAREIT") and is used subject to the Terms and Conditions of Use set forth on the NAREIT website, including but not limited to, Section 9 thereof.

a rolling 12-month basis. REITs' ability to produce total returns that were greater than inflation was comparable to owning TIPS, which exceeded inflation 69 percent of the time over a 6-month period and 74 percent of the time over a 12-month period. Although it is not surprising that REITs' inflation protection exceeded that of stocks in the S&P 500 Index (69 percent and 72 percent on 6- and 12-month rolling returns, respectively), it may surprise investors to learn that REITs also were a much more effective hedge against inflation than commodities, where returns exceeded inflation only 56 percent of the time on a rolling 6-month basis and 57 percent of the time on a 12-month basis.

Transparent Corporate Structures

The REIT industry is highly transparent in part because, as publicly traded firms, each company faces a high degree of scrutiny every quarter. There are over 30 firms in the United States. that provide equity research on REITs. Additionally, based on data provided by S&P Global Market Intelligence, 80 of the 223 REITs in the FTSE NAREIT All REITs Index at the end of 2015 were investment-grade rated and another 24 were rated but below investment grade, for a total of 104 rated REITs. (Please see Appendix D, *REITs with Credit Ratings.*) These 104 companies represent approximately 80 percent of the industry's equity market capitalization and have at least one fixed-income analyst also scrutinizing their quarterly results. If a management team pursues a questionable business practice, such as using short-term variable rate debt to finance growth, one of these analysts is bound to report on it, alerting investors and likely causing that REIT's valuation to suffer. Against the backdrop of accounting scandals like the Enron Corporation (former NYSE: ENE) in 2001 and Ponzi schemes like that of Bernie Madoff, which was revealed in 2008, investors increasingly take comfort in REITs because of the daily scrutiny they endure from the analyst communities.

Secondly, REITs are compelled to pay out at least 90 percent of their otherwise taxable income, and many pay out 100 percent or more. REITs also pay their dividends in cash (though the IRS has, in the past, allowed REITs to issue new stock to pay their dividends) and, therefore, operate with limited retained earnings. As a result, they generally issue new public equity every other year in order to finance growth. Whichever Wall Street firm a management team selects to underwrite a stock issuance will subject the REIT to yet another level of scrutiny as part of the investment bank's due diligence. As the accounting irregularities discovered at American Realty Capital Properties' (formerly NYSE: ARCP) in 2014 proved, the REIT industry is not immune to scandal. However, incidents of fraud are few and far between in the REIT world. The difficulty REIT management teams would have in hiding accounting irregularities for any extended period of time, without disrupting their ability to pay dividends or without being found out by the analyst community or underwriters, minimizes the risk of fraud. The heavy scrutiny under which REITs operate, as well as the discipline the dividend payout requirement imposes on management, combine to make REITs a highly transparent investment class that investors increasingly turn to for steady appreciation and attractive yield.

3

REIT Dividends

As Chapter 2 highlighted, many investors are drawn to REITs first and foremost because of the attractive yield they offer relative to bonds or other stocks. A REIT's dividend yield is only attractive, however, if it is sustainable and, preferably, able to be increased over time. This chapter discusses how to calculate a REIT's yield, as well as how to assess the safety and sustainability of a REIT's common dividend. Additionally, because investors pay the taxes on the dividend income they receive, this chapter addresses REIT dividend taxation. Last, this chapter highlights the risks and rewards associated with investing in preferred stock of REITs. Preferred dividends provide a premium yield to common dividends of the same REIT, but there are several potential risks investors need to understand before investing in the preferred stock of any REIT.

Rockland REIT

Rockland REIT (ticker symbol: ROCK) is a fictional company used to illustrate concepts discussed in this and the remaining chapters.

REIT Yields

A REIT's distribution requirement is based on taxable income for IRS purposes, rather than income as calculated in accordance with Generally Accepted Accounting Principles (GAAP) for financial reporting purposes. Because REITs must pay out at least 90 percent

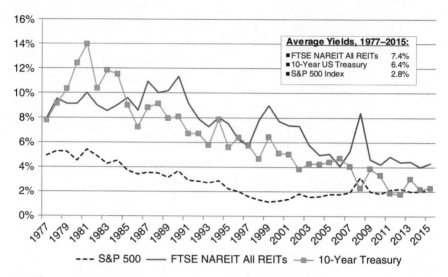

Figure 3.1   REIT Yields versus Yields on Other Investments

Sources: NAREIT; Yahoo! Finance.

of their taxable income each year to shareholders in the form of dividends, their yields tend to be higher than the yields on other income investments, such as U.S. Treasuries and corporate bonds. Figure 3.1 illustrates the average yield REITs have offered investors over time, versus the yield on the S&P 500 Index and on 10-year U.S. Treasuries. At the end of 2015, the FTSE NAREIT All REITs Index offered a 4.3 percent yield, or approximately 200 basis points higher than the 2.3 percent yield on 10-year U.S. Treasuries and the 2.2 percent dividend yield from companies in the S&P 500 Index. Additionally and according to statistics provided by NAREIT, from 1990 through 2015, the 6.4 percent average yield offered by REITs averaged 180 basis points higher than the average yield on 10-year Treasuries during the same period.

As with any stock, a REIT's current yield equals the current stock price divided into the most recently paid dividend, annualized (multiplied by four, in most cases). Because many investors hold investments for several years, it is also important to understand the concept of yield on cost, which is calculated by dividing the current dividend annualized by the investor's cost basis in the REIT's common or preferred stock:

$$\text{Yield on Cost} = \frac{\text{Current quarterly dividend} \times 4}{\text{Shareholder's per share cost basis}}$$

For example, assume an investor paid $10 per share two years ago for common stock of Rockland REIT. Today, Rockland REIT's stock price is $15 per share and it pays a quarterly dividend of $0.25, which annualizes to one dollar. The REIT's current yield is 6.7% (or $1 ÷ $15), but the investor's yield on cost is 10%, calculated as the $1.00 annualized dividend divided by their $10 cost basis. When evaluating whether to sell these REIT shares in order to invest in a different stock or bond, the investor will need to compare the 10% yield on cost to the current yields of competing investments.

A few REITs pay dividends on a monthly, instead of quarterly basis. In such cases, their current dividend needs to be multiplied by 12, rather than 4, to calculate their annualized yield. Note also that REITs sometimes pay special dividends, usually in association with realizing large gains on properties sold. It is important to exclude special dividends from the above yield calculations, as these cash payouts are nonrecurring. Table 3.1 lists those REITs that were paying monthly dividends at the end of 2015.

Table 3.1   U.S. REITs That Pay Monthly Dividends

	Ticker	Type
American Capital Agency	AGNC	Mortgage REIT
Apple Hospitality	APLE	Equity REIT
Armour Residential	ARR	Mortgage REIT
Chatham Lodging Trust	CLDT	Equity REIT
EPR Properties	EPR	Equity REIT
Five Oaks Investment	OAKS	Mortgage REIT
Gladstone Commercial Corporation	GOOD	Equity REIT
Gladstone Land Corporation	LAND	Equity REIT
Global Net Lease	GNL	Equity REIT
Inland Real Estate Corporation	IRC	Equity REIT
Independence Realty Trust	IRT	Equity REIT
Javelin Mortgage	JMI	Mortgage REIT
LTC Properties	LTC	Equity REIT
New York REIT	NYRT	Equity REIT
Orchid Island Capital	ORC	Mortgage REIT
Realty Income	O	Equity REIT
STAG Industrial	STAG	Equity REIT
United Development Funding	UDF	Mortgage REIT
Wheeler Real Estate Investment	WHLR	Equity REIT
Whitestone REIT	WSR	Equity REIT

Source: S&P Global Market Intelligence.

Are REIT Yields Safe?

REIT yields may be attractive, but they are meaningless if the dividend behind them is not sustainable. Brad Thomas, who writes for Forbes on his online platform, www.TheIntelligentREITInvestor .com, often warns readers to avoid REITs that pay a "sucker yield." Investopedia.com defines "sucker yield" as the allure that high-yielding investments have with many investors; hypnotized by the attractively high yield, these investors fail to realize the investment's fundamentals are unpredictable and/or unreliable, which ultimately leads to the dividend being partially or completely cut (i.e., the *sucker punch*).

REITs that offer sucker yields tend to be the exception rather than the norm. Historically, the contractual nature of rental revenue from leases has enabled REITs to pay dividends that have proved to be secure, even during most economic recessions. Equity REITs derive the majority of their income from leases that, depending on their duration and the credit of the tenant, provide REITs with recurring, more bond-like cash flows than most non-REIT companies can offer. Provided a REIT management team does not finance their company's growth with excessive levels of leverage, the preferred and common dividends of that company should be reasonably safe.

That said, the 2007–2008 global financial crisis that precipitated the Great Recession of 2008–2009 served as a grim reminder about economic and market forces that can jeopardize REIT dividends. According to S&P Global Market Intelligence, in 2008–2009 over two-thirds of all REITs cut or suspended their common dividends in order to conserve cash. Equity REIT returns were a dismal negative 37.7 percent in 2008, before rebounding to a positive 28.0 percent in 2009. (Please refer to Table 1.1 in Chapter 1 for annual REIT returns.) Despite widespread dividend cuts, in 2008 REITs underperformed the S&P 500 Index by only 73 basis points and then actually outperformed that index by 153 basis points in 2009.

The rash of dividend cuts by REITs during the Great Recession was similar to the percent of REITs that slashed their dividends in the wake of the savings-and-loan crisis of the late 1980s. In both instances, a broad liquidity crisis translated into dividend cuts for the majority of REITs. Unsurprisingly, the REITs that did not cut or suspend their dividends were ones with lower levels of debt, and also ones with little debt maturing during the crisis years.

Rule of Thumb

In a credit crisis, like the United States endured in 2007–2009 and in the savings-and-loan crisis of the late 1980s, many REIT boards of directors will elect to cut or even temporarily suspend dividend payments to preserve capital. To mitigate the risk of a dividend cut, invest in REITs with lower leverage levels than their peers.

Quantifying Dividend Safety

Investors can use two approaches to quantify dividend safety, the first of which focuses on near-term expected earnings growth and the second of which measures a REIT's balance sheet leverage. Chapter 8 provides the calculations for other metrics that assess the relative health of individual companies.

Dividend/FFO Payout Ratio

A REIT's expected dividend payout ratio is calculated as its current annualized dividend, divided by an estimate of next year's expected funds from operation (FFO) per share. REITs use FFO to measure profitability instead of earnings per share (EPS). Estimates of FFO per share may be obtained from individual company reports generated by investment banks' research departments and from data service providers, such as S&P Global Market Intelligence and Thomson's First Call. The resulting dividend/FFO payout ratio (which is also referred to as an *FFO payout ratio*) gives a quick thumbnail sketch about a REIT's ability to pay its current dividend. An FFO payout ratio below 1.0 indicates that Wall Street expects that REIT to generate FFO sufficient to cover its current annualized dividend. By contrast, an FFO payout ratio above 1.0 should generate immediate concern and cause potential investors to dig deeper into a REIT's expected earnings ability.

Investor Tip

If the Dividend/FFO ratio for a REIT is greater than 1.0, the dividend may be at risk.

Debt Ultimately Determines Dividend Safety

REITs can enhance the safety of their dividend by managing their operations with lower amounts of debt. Common dividends represent the most junior claim on a company's cash flow, meaning that a company is obligated to pay interest and principal due to lenders and dividends associated with any preferred stock before paying the dividend due to common shareholders. Accordingly, the less debt a company has, the more likely it will be able to pay its common dividend. Investors can calculate two leverage metrics—debt-to–total market capitalization and debt-to–gross book value—to determine if a REIT potentially has too much debt. Chapter 8 walks through the calculation of both metrics, so this chapter simply cites some historical data.

Debt-to–Total Market Capitalization Ratio

As of December 31, 2015 and according to NAREIT, equity REITs average debt-to–total market capitalization ratio was 36.0 percent. Including mortgage REITs, this ratio was 46.4 percent. Because the debt-to–total capitalization ratio changes depending on a REIT's current stock price, this ratio can over- or understate a company's leverage, depending on market conditions. For example, if Rockland REIT has $100 million of debt and 10 million common shares that trade at $15 a share, then it has a debt-to–total market capitalization ratio of 40 percent:

$100 of debt ÷ ($100 of debt + [$15 × 10 shares of ROCK]) = 40%

If Rockland REIT's stock dips to $10 per share, however, its debt-to–total market capitalization ratio increases to 50 percent:

$100 of debt ÷ ($100 of debt + [$10 × 10 shares of ROCK]) = 50%

Because a variety of events influence a company's stock price, not all of which are within a management team's control, a more certain way of gauging a REIT's leverage is to use a REIT's debt-to–gross book value ratio.

Debt-to–Gross Book Value Ratio

Gross book value can be calculated by taking total assets listed on the balance sheet of the financial statements, less any goodwill or

> ## Less Is More
>
> To minimize the risk of investing in REITs that offer sucker yields, investors should focus on REITs whose debt-to–gross book value is 50 percent (or less).

intangibles, plus any accumulated depreciation and amortization (generally listed in the footnotes to the financial statements). As of December 31, 2015, the average debt-to–gross book ratio of equity REITs was 36 percent (including mREITs, this ratio was 46 percent). Putting this industry statistic into context, private landlords, including private equity firms that have taken publicly traded REITs private in 2005–2007, had employed as much as 90 percent leverage to finance their real estate purchases. At the end of 2006, which was the last year before the 2007–2008 global financial crisis, equity REITs had an average debt-to–gross book value of 57 percent. Although some REITs exceeded what, in hindsight, were prudent levels of leverage, REITs nonetheless were more conservative in their use of leverage than the average private real estate investor.

In fact, out of the 130 REITs that composed the FTSE NAREIT All REITs Index at the end of 2006 and before the global financial crisis, only one REIT, General Growth Properties (NYSE: GGP), filed for protection from its creditors under Chapter 11 bankruptcy. Before the crisis, General Growth Properties' debt-to–gross book value ratio was 74 percent, or 17 percentage points higher than the industry average. The company restructured its debt in the bankruptcy courts and, in November 2010, emerged from bankruptcy. At the end of 2015, General Growth Properties' debt-to–gross book value ratio was 54 percent, which is still higher than the industry average ratio, but much more conservative than the company's historical levels. (Note that most of the debt-to–gross book value ratios cited in the section were provided by S&P Global Market Intelligence.)

Legal Standing of Leases Supports Dividend Safety

As is discussed in Chapter 4, Leases, bankruptcy courts view leases as operating expenses, which are legally senior to non-operating expenses—meaning the tenant is obligated to pay their rent before paying any interest or principal on outstanding debt, or any dividends on preferred or common stock. Therefore, even if a REIT's tenant goes bankrupt, the tenant must continue paying the REIT its contractual rent until the bankruptcy court judge allows the tenant to reject the lease. As a result, REITs generally do not go bankrupt, even when some of their tenants do. The relative stability and visibility of these underlying cash flows are a primary reason that investors view real estate and REITs as defensive investments that pay reasonably safe dividends.

REIT Dividends and Taxation

The two most widely known features of REITs are that they pay relatively high dividends and that they generally do not pay corporate income taxes. To qualify each year as a REIT for IRS purposes, REITs must pay their common and preferred shareholders dividends that equal at least 90 percent of what would otherwise be taxable income. If a REIT pays out only 90 percent of its taxable income, it will owe corporate taxes on the 10 percent it retains. By distributing 100 percent of taxable income (including capital gains) and satisfying other REIT requirements, REITs can avoid paying corporate income taxes. The REIT shareholders then pay their appropriate taxes on the dividend income received. As the example in Table 3.2 illustrates, the REIT structure provides higher after-tax income to shareholders, based on the following assumptions:

- C-Corp and REIT both have 35 percent marginal tax rates.
- C-Corp and REIT both have 90 percent payout ratios.
- The personal marginal tax rate for investors is 25 percent.

The 90 percent minimum distribution requirement governing REITs helps shareholders in two ways. First, it translates into above-average dividend income (almost always in cash). In the simple example in Table 3.2 the investor pockets an extra $23.62 (or $67.50 minus $43.88) in after-tax dividend income from the REIT investment versus the regular C-corporation investment. Second, REIT management teams must manage their portfolios and balance sheets conservatively enough to be able to maintain the dividend. REITs can elect to reduce or cut their common dividends, but not without severely damaging short-term stock price performance in the process. This chapter addresses basic facts investors should know before buying REITs for dividend income.

Table 3.2   Example of After-Tax Income for C-Corporations versus REITs

	C-Corp		REIT
Earnings before taxes	$100.00	Earnings before taxes	$100.00
– Taxes (35%)	–35.00	– Dividends (90%)	–90.00
Net income	65.00	Taxable income	10.00
– Dividends (90%)	–58.50	– Taxes (35%)	–3.50
Retained earnings	$6.50	Retained earnings	$6.50
	Investor		Investor
Dividend income	$58.50	Dividend income	$90.00
– Personal tax (25%)	–14.63	– Personal tax (25%)	–22.50
After-tax income	$43.87	After-tax income	$67.50

REITs Do Not Pay Out All of Their Cash in Dividends

Investors often make the mistake of thinking REITs pay out all of their free cash flow in the form of dividends. In fact, the cash REITs generate from their properties typically is greater than the dividends they pay to shareholders. From an accounting perspective, taxable income for IRS purposes is often less than the dividend paid to shareholders, resulting in no tax obligation to the REIT. Taxable income is calculated according to rules set by the IRS, whereas net income for public reporting purposes to the SEC is determined by GAAP. In calculating both types of income, REITs are permitted to deduct many noncash expenses, such as the annual depreciation of their buildings. Note that only the buildings themselves, and not the land on which buildings are constructed, are depreciable.

For example, if Rockland REIT buys a building for $11 million, and the land under it is worth $1 million, then Rockland REIT will depreciate the $10 million building over a 40-year period. This annual $250,000 expense (equal to $10 million divided by 40 years) reduces Rockland REIT's income for IRS and GAAP purposes; because the $250,000 represents an expense only for GAAP purposes, the company does not use cash to pay it. Instead, Rockland REIT reduces its basis in that building by $250,000 each year. Continuing the example, after four years, the Rockland REIT's basis in the property will be $9 million, calculated as the building's initial

$10 million cost, less four years of $250,000 depreciation expense (i.e., $10 million less [4 years × $250,000 annual depreciation expense]).

The Components of a REIT's Common Dividend

The example in Table 3.2 was an oversimplified illustration of how REITs' common dividends are taxed at the individual investor level. Rarely is a REIT's dividend taxed entirely as ordinary income. Instead, a REIT dividend generally consists of a combination of three types of income, which are taxed at different levels. These three income classifications are:

1. Ordinary dividends (individual shareholders' tax rates apply)
2. Capital gains (generally 15% at December 31, 2015), and
3. Returns of capital (nontaxable)

REITs typically disclose the tax treatment of each year's dividends in a press release issued in late January or early February. (Refer to each REIT's website for current and past press releases. Website addresses for the 223 REITs in the FTSE All REITs Index at the end of 2015 are provided in Appendix C.) The "dividend treatment" press release typically contains a table that clearly states how much of the common dividend should be taxed as ordinary dividend income, how much is a classified as capital gains, and how much, if any, is a non-taxable return of capital.

Ordinary Dividend Income

Generally, the majority of REIT common dividends are characterized and taxed as ordinary income, meaning that the business activities that generated the cash flow being paid out as dividends to share-holders were "ordinary," such as from collecting rents. So if investors receive $1.00 per share in dividends and are in the 25 percent ordinary income tax bracket, they will owe $0.25 of federal taxes on every dollar of REIT dividends they receive. However, if a REIT engages in transactions during its fiscal year that are not ordinary, such as selling a building at a gain or loss relative to its investment basis, the REIT may recognize long-term capital gains and/or returns of capital, both of which are discussed next.

Capital Gains

If a REIT sells an asset for more money than its depreciated basis (also referred to as its *net book value* in the property), the REIT will recognize a capital gain on the sale. The REIT can then pass the capital gains through to shareholders by classifying part of the common dividend as capital gains. Capital losses are not passed through to investors, however, because REITs are not limited partnerships. (See Chapter 6 for a comparison between REITs and limited partnerships.) Shareholders pay taxes on this portion of the dividend, but at the then-current capital gains rate, which for individuals in the 25 percent federal income tax bracket at December 31, 2015, generally was 15 percent.

Returns of Capital

If a REIT distributes more than its taxable income for IRS purposes, the additional amount paid to shareholders that exceeds 100 percent of taxable income is classified as a return of capital. Returns of capital are not taxed. Rather, they lower an investor's basis in a common stock (see examples in Tables 3.3 and 3.4) and eventually may be taxed in the form of capital gains when the investor sells his or her shares. Returns of capital, therefore, increase both an investor's tax-adjusted current yield, as well as the after-tax total return he or she realizes upon sale of the shares. Table 3.3 provides a simple practical example of how a portion of a REIT's dividend may be classified as a return of capital.

In summary, a REIT's common dividend generally consists of one or more types of income for taxation purposes: ordinary

Table 3.3   Return of Capital Calculation

Assumptions
Rockland REIT has taxable income of $1.25 per share in Year 1. Also in Year 1, Rockland REIT pays an annual dividend of $1.50 per share.
Conclusions
The amount of the dividend that exceeds 100% of Rockland REIT's taxable income—$0.25 per share in this case—is classified as a return of capital. Assuming Rockland REIT engaged only in ordinary business in Year 1, the remaining $1.25 per share of the dividend will be classified as ordinary income to be taxed at the investor level.

Table 3.4   Sample Calculations of Taxes on Rockland REIT's Dividend

Assumptions

- Rockland REIT pays a dividend of $1.00 per share
- The shareholder paid $20.00 for each share of ROCK (so original basis equals $20.00)
- The individual ordinary income tax rate is 25%
- The individual long-term capital gains tax rate is 15%
- **Example A**—Rockland REIT classifies 100% of its dividend as ordinary income
- **Example B**—Rockland REIT classifies 60% of its dividend as ordinary income, 25% as a long-term capital gain, and 15% as a return of capital

	Example A	Example B
Shareholder's dividend received from Rockland REIT	$1.00	$1.00
× Percent of dividend classified as ordinary income	× 100%	× 60%
Income taxable at ordinary rate	$1.00	$0.60
× Federal tax rate on ordinary income	× 25%	× 25%
(A) Income tax due on ordinary income	$0.25	$0.15
Shareholder's dividend received from Rockland REIT	—	$1.00
× Percent of dividend classified as long-term capital gains	—	× 25%
Income taxable at capital gains rate	—	$0.25
× Federal tax rate on long-term capital gains	—	× 15%
(B) Income tax due on long-term capital gains	—	$0.04
Shareholder's dividend received from Rockland REIT	—	$1.00
× Percent of dividend classified as return of capital	—	× 15%
Income taxable as return of capital	—	$0.15
× Federal tax rate on capital gains	—	—
(C) Income tax due on returns of capital	—	$0.00
(D) Shareholder's total tax liability (A + B + C)	$0.25	$0.19
Effective tax rate for shareholder	25%	19%
Shareholder's original basis in Rockland REIT shares	$20.00	$20.00
− Return of capital received	—	($0.15)
(E) New basis in Rockland REIT	$20.00	$19.85
After-tax yield on Rockland REIT shares [($1.00 − D)/E]	3.8%	4.1%

income, which is taxed at the highest individual or "ordinary" rate; capital gains, which are taxed at the long-term capital gains tax rate; and returns of capital, which are not taxed and which lower a shareholder's cost basis in each share. When a REIT classifies portions of its dividend as long-term capital gains or returns of capital, the shareholder's effective tax rate is lower than if the dividend were classified entirely as ordinary income.

Examples A and B in Table 3.4 illustrate how an individual investor in the 25 percent income tax bracket would calculate his tax liability on Rockland REIT's common dividend using 2015 tax rates.

Example A in Table 3.4 illustrates the investor's tax liability assuming the entire dividend is ordinary income. Example B in Table 3.4 illustrates how having some of the dividend classified as long-term capital gains or returns of capital lowers an investor's effective tax rate on dividends.

REIT Dividends and the Bush Tax Cuts

The *Jobs and Growth Tax Relief Reconciliation Act of 2003* (also known as the *Bush Tax Cuts*) lowered the individual's tax rate on previously taxed earnings of C-corporations paid out to shareholders as dividends to a maximum of 15 percent. The distinguishing characteristic of REITs continues to be that their dividends are exempt from the "double taxation" to which other C-corporation dividends are subject. As the example in Table 3.2 at the beginning of this chapter illustrated, dividends paid by C-corporations are taxed at both the corporate and investor levels. REIT dividends are not taxed at the corporate level, so the portion of a REIT's dividend that is characterized as ordinary taxable income does not qualify for the lower tax rate; that is, REIT dividends are not *qualified dividends* under this law. The Bush Tax Cuts did not affect the taxation rate shareholders pay on the ordinary income components of REIT dividends. In 2008, when they were originally designed to sunset, Congress extended the Bush Tax Cuts to 2012, at which time they again were extended and, as of now, have no expiration date. Should Congress ever decide to end the Bush Tax Cuts, the effective after-tax yield of other C-corporations will decline, whereas the current taxation of REIT dividends and the expected after-tax yield will not change.

Preferred Stock Dividends

As mentioned earlier, REITs can satisfy their 90 percent payout requirement by paying dividends to both its common *and* preferred shareholders. At the end of 2015 and according to S&P Global Market Intelligence, the liquidation value of REIT preferred shares outstanding totaled $29.8 billion, or only 3 percent of public REIT common equity. Though the market for REIT preferred stock is small, it nonetheless is worth knowing a few basic facts—and potential pitfalls—associated with its attractive yield.

Preferred Stock Basics

Preferred stock is often viewed as a hybrid security in that it shares characteristics with debt and common stock investments. Like a bond, preferred shares are sold according to a face (or *par*) value, which, in the case of preferreds, is usually $25 per share. Unlike bonds, perpetual preferred stock has no maturity date. Typically, a REIT that issues preferred shares has the right to redeem (or *call*) those shares at par after five years; if the REIT can issue new preferred shares or debt that has a lower recurring payment than the old preferred shares, then management will likely call those preferred shares and issue lower-cost capital to pay for the redemption. Similar to common stock, preferred shares pay investors a quarterly dividend. Like a bond, the preferred dividend is often a fixed amount based on par value, though sometimes the preferred shares contain a ratchet feature so that the preferred dividend increases by the same percentage as the common dividend in subsequent years.

Risks to Owning Preferred Shares

There are three risks investors need to keep in mind when investing in preferred shares for dividend income, each of which involves liquidity or lack thereof. First, the secondary market for REIT preferred stock is not as liquid as the market for common stock in the same company. This means that investors may have some difficulty selling (or even pricing) their preferred shares when they want or need their principal back.

> ### Unintentional Mezzanine Lenders
> During a change in control, investors of many REIT preferred stock issuances bear the risk of becoming unwilling mezzanine lenders, as the acquiring entity often is not required to "cash-out" holders of the target REIT's preferred stock.

Second, it is important to read and understand the term sheet in the prospectus of each preferred stock issuance before investing. Although the preceding paragraph detailed general terms that are typical for preferred stock issuances, there is no consistent underwriting standard to which issuers of preferred stock must conform. The difference that may exist between what preferred stock investors *assume* they are buying and the *reality* of what they actually bought can lead to unpleasant and costly surprises. For example, a REIT that pays a $0.75 per share annualized common dividend may issue a preferred stock that pays $1.00 per share each year. If that preferred stock does not contain a ratchet feature or some other covenant to protect the preferred yield relative to that of the common shares, the management team legally could increase the annual common dividend to be greater than $1.00 per share. If that happens, the preferred issuance will become illiquid, making it extremely difficult (or impossible) to sell the securities anywhere close to par. The investors in the preferred stock in this example will likely have to sell their shares at a steep discount if they want to exit this investment.

The third level of liquidity risk relates to when there is a change in control at a REIT, such as when a private equity firm or competing REIT buys a REIT that has preferred shares outstanding. In all too many instances, the preferred equity investors of the acquired (or *target*) REIT discover that the terms of their preferred stock allow an acquiring company to suspend their preferred dividend and/or that the acquiring entity has no obligation to "cash out" the target REIT's preferred shareholders. As a result, acquiring companies often treat existing preferred stock as a form of mezzanine financing to increase their returns on the deal. The preferred stock investors become financially marginalized in the new entity, and have no recourse. In contrast, the target REIT's common stockholders will receive cash, stock in the acquiring entity, or both as compensation for their investment.

Conclusion

The income that investors can access by investing in REITs is a powerful wealth-building tool, but only if the REITs can sustain and preferably grow their dividends over time. The wealth destruction and underperformance associated with REITs that have cut their common dividends in the past is examined more thoroughly in Chapter 7, REIT Performance.

CHAPTER 4

Leases

Prior to exploring the different types of commercial properties that REITs own, it is instructive to understand the different types of leases that REITs, as landlords, use. A lease is a legal agreement between a landlord (the *lessor*, which is the REIT) and a tenant (the *lessee*) whereby the tenant agrees to pay rent for a defined period of time in exchange for the right to occupy the landlord's space. Most leases require monthly payments of rent, but other intervals—for example, as annual payments—can also exist. It depends on the terms agreed to between the landlord and tenant. The terms of the lease discussed in this chapter are negotiated between the landlord and tenant and spelled out in the lease agreement.

Along with the length of each lease, which is usually expressed in months or years, different lease structures translate into different cash flow streams to a landlord. Tenants and landlords negotiate all aspects of a lease, including the length of time a property will be leased (lease *length, term,* or *duration*), who will pay for which operating expenses, and who will pay for improvements to the tenant's space. Each type of lease allocates different costs to the landlord or tenant and determines which person bears the risk of paying higher costs if utility or other expenses increase. Lease length and structure, therefore, are fundamental predictors of REIT stock price performance, which is discussed at length in Chapter 7. The content of this chapter provides an overview of the four major types of leases, including which structures are most commonly used among different property types.

43

Lease Terminology

Most people are familiar with the concept of paying rent, but many are not aware of the different types of rent they will pay under different scenarios. An asking rent of $15 per square foot listed on a building's "for rent" sign means something very different under a gross lease than under a full-service lease, both of which are addressed on the following pages. Before discussing the four basic types of leases, it is helpful to become familiar with some basic terminology:

- **Base year** is the 12 months of a lease or the period that ends with the first full calendar year of a lease. In the latter instance, the base year will be more than 12 months. It is often used to set the expense stop (defined below) in a full-service or modified gross lease.
- **Common area maintenance (CAM)** are charges the landlord incurs to maintain areas of a multi-tenanted property (which simply is a building that has more than one tenant) that are accessible to all tenants, such as the landlord's property management fee, labor costs associated with the building's engineering team, lobbies, shared restrooms, and a parking area. In a multi-building office park or campus, CAM fees can also include costs associated with a fitness center or foodservice area that are accessible by tenants throughout the campus. CAM fees are in addition to a tenant's base rent, and the landlord typically bills tenants according to the percentage of the building they rent. For example, if a tenant's space represents one-third of the building's rentable square footage, then that tenant would be billed for one-third of the CAM associated with the building's upkeep.
- **Escalation clauses**, or escalators, are set future increases in rent that the tenant agrees to pay during the course of a lease. Escalations can be expressed in dollar amounts or as a percent and typically occur on an annual basis. Rent escalations tend to be tied to increases in the Consumer Price Index (CPI) or expressed as fixed periodic increases. As an example, a tenant may agree to pay a monthly base rent of $1,000 in year 1, and then an additional $100 per month each subsequent year for the duration of the lease. In year 5, therefore, the tenant's

monthly rent would have escalated to $1,400 (Year 1 = $1,000; Year 2 = $1,100; Year 3 = $1,200; Year 4 = $1,300; Year 5 = $1,400).

- **Expense stops** are most common in full-service and modified gross leases. The landlord will bear the operating expenses and CAM associated with the tenant's space up to the expense stop amount; the tenant will bear any expense overage. For example, operating expenses and CAM on Tenant A's space in Year 1 are $4.50 per square foot, so the expense stop is set for the duration of the lease at that level. For the remainder of the lease, the landlord will use $4.50 of the base rent received to pay the tenant's operating expenses, and will bill the tenant for any amounts that exceed this expense stop.
  - ○ **Capped expenses** are similar to expense stops and, in some areas of the country, are referred to as expense stops. However, instead of being a fixed dollar amount, expense stops are a maximum percentage increase in expenses.
- **Leasing commissions (LCs)** are paid to real estate brokers who represent the tenant and/or landlord. (Tenants' brokers are often referred to as *tenant reps*.) Typically the brokers are paid 50 percent of their LC upon lease execution and 50 percent upon lease commencement. The LC generally is calculated as 2 to 8 percent of the total rent payable for the initial term of the lease. So if a tenant will pay a landlord total annual rent of $10,000 for three years, and the leasing commission rate in that market is 4 percent, then the landlord will need to pay the leasing agent $1,200 ($10,000 × 3 years × 4 percent). If there is a broker representing the landlord, then an additional LC would be owed following a similar schedule.
- **Operating expenses** are costs associated with operating and maintaining the rented area of a building. Such costs include real estate taxes, property insurance, utilities, and janitorial services for tenant-specific areas (as opposed to common areas shared with other tenants). Operating expenses do not include capital expenditures for structural maintenance of the building, and they do not include interest payments on any mortgage associated with the property being leased. Each lease specifically identifies what can and cannot be included as part of the operating expenses.

- **Rent**—There are different types of rental revenue a landlord can receive. Table 4.1 summarizes the different types of rent, including escalations (as described in the preceding text):
  - ○ **Total, base, gross, or contract rent** are all ways of describing the amount of money a tenant will have to pay the landlord each period, as defined in the lease. It includes agreed-upon expense stops and reflects any rent escalations that have become effective.

Table 4.1 Comparison of Different Types of Rent

Assumptions

- 15,000-square-foot rentable area
- 5-year lease term
- $25.00 base rent per square foot
- $4.50 expense stop & CAM

- 3% annual escalations on base rent
- 4% leasing commission
- 4 months of rent (after concessions)
- TI allowance of $15 per square foot

	Year 1	Year 2	Year 3	Year 4	Year 5
Total rent per square foot	$25.00	$25.00	$25.75	$26.52	$27.32
+ Escalation	—	$0.75	$0.77	$0.80	$0.82
New total rent per square foot	$25.00	$25.75	$26.52	$27.32	$28.14
× Rentable square feet	15,000	15,000	15,000	15,000	15,000
Total rent	$375,000	$386,250	$397,838	$409,773	$422,066
− Expense stop[a]	−67,500	−67,500	−67,500	−67,500	−67,500
Net rent before concessions	307,500	318,750	330,338	342,273	354,566
− 4 months of free base rent	−125,000				
Effective rent landlord realizes	182,500	318,750	330,338	342,273	354,566
Less:					
Tenant improvement allowance[b]	−225,000				
Leasing commission[c]	−61,137				
Net effective rent received by landlord	−$103,637	$318,750	$330,338	$342,273	$354,566
Aggregate net effective rent received	$1,242,289				
Net effective rent per square foot[d]	$16.56				

[a]Expense stop and CAM is calculated as $4.50 × 15,000 rentable square feet.
[b]TI is calculated by multiplying the $15 TI allowance times the rentable square feet, or $15 × 15,000.
[c]LC is calculated by adding the "Effective rent landlord realizes" in all five years, times 4%.
[d]The net effective rent per square foot equals the "Aggregate net effective rent received," divided by the rentable square feet, divided by the lease term ($1,242,289 ÷ 15,000 SF ÷ 5 years).

- ○ **Net rent** is the amount of rent a landlord retains each period, after paying (or *net of*) expenses associated with property operations and maintenance.
- ○ **Effective rent** is net rent, adjusted to reflect the cost of any concessions and leasing commissions the landlord has agreed to as part of the lease agreement. The most common concessions are tenant improvements and free rent, both of which are discussed later in this chapter.
- ○ **Free rent** is a period of time (usually a few months but sometimes up to one year) during which time a landlord grants the tenant occupancy rights to the rental space without requiring contract rent be paid. Free rent is a concession a landlord is willing to pay to entice a tenant to lease a space.
- ○ **Market rent** is the rental rate associated with comparable spaces in similar buildings and locations.
- **Square feet**—There also are different ways of measuring the same building, depending on the information needed:
  - ○ **Gross square feet (or gross building area)** measures a building's total constructed area to the outside of its walls. Gross square feet generally is not used for leasing purposes unless the tenant leases the entire building, in which case the gross square feet equals the rentable square feet.
  - ○ **Rentable square feet** is the sum measurement of a tenant's useable area, plus that tenant's pro rata share of the building's common areas.
  - ○ **Useable square feet (or useable area)** measures the amount of space that can be used by tenants within the walls defining the space they have rented. Note that if a building is leased entirely to a single tenant, then rentable square feet equals useable square feet.
- **Tenant improvement (TI) allowance** is an amount of money the landlord is willing to spend on a space to retain an existing

To summarize square footage measurements:
- Multi-tenanted building: Gross > Rentable > Useable
- Single-tenant building: Gross = Rentable = Useable

tenant or entice a new tenant to lease a space. Note that TIs paid by a landlord that improve the future leaseability of a space—such as lobby and bathroom improvements—are depreciated on a different schedule than the building itself. Tenant improvements typically are depreciated over a 7-year life, versus a 15-year life for leasehold improvements, and 40 years for the base building.

o **TIs for first-generation space**—When space is newly constructed, the landlord typically budgets for a higher TI allowance because the tenant will need to build out space from a shell (also referred to as *unimproved*) condition. Because of the greater expense associated with building out new space, tenants that lease first-generation space typically sign longer-term leases of five or more years. Tenants often exceed the landlord's TI allowance and invest additional money into their space. The more a tenant invests its own money into rental space, the more likely that tenant is to renew the lease at the end of the lease term.

o **TIs for second-generation space**—When a space has been occupied previously, it is called second-generation space. The TI dollars a landlord pays to retain the existing tenant tend to be for cosmetic improvements, such as new carpet and painting walls. If the lease length being negotiated is long enough or if the landlord is trying to re-tenant the space with a new tenant (perhaps one with better credit), then TIs are likely to be higher and include some modest structural improvements, such as updating the tenant's bathroom(s).

The Four Major Types of Leases

There are four broadly defined types of lease agreements: gross, net, modified gross, and full service. The name of each lease structure is *not* universal in nature; each region of the country tends to have its own nomenclature and lease standards. Putting precise terminology aside, any lease that results from landlord–tenant negotiations reflects risks and rewards that both parties agree upon and are willing to bear. Table 4.2 summarizes the major types of leases, including a simplified example of the different payments made by a tenant to

Table 4.2   Comparison of Major Lease Types

	Gross	Net*	Modified Gross	Full Service
Contractual rent per square foot paid to landlord	$15.00	$15.00	$19.00	$23.00
– Base year expense stop and CAM[†]	n/a	n/a	−4.00	−8.00
Net rent to landlord	15.00	15.00	15.00	15.00
+ Reimbursement for expense overage[‡]	n/a	n/a	2.00	2.00
Total rent per square foot paid to landlord	$15.00	$15.00	$17.00	$17.00
Risk of cost increase borne by:	Landlord	Tenant	Tenant [†]	Tenant[†]
Who pays what:				
• Nonstructural repair and maintenance	Landlord	Tenant	**	Tenant
• Operating expenses (utilities, janitorial, etc.)	Landlord	Tenant	**	Tenant
• Property taxes	Landlord	Tenant	**	Tenant
• Insurance	Landlord	Tenant	**	Tenant
• CAM	Landlord	Tenant	**	Tenant
Property type(s) most associated with this lease structure:	Lower-priced, lower-quality properties	Retail Industrial Single-tenant	Industrial Office	Office

*Example illustrates a triple-net lease.
[†]With a base-year expense stop, the tenant reimburses the landlord for any cost overruns. The only risk the landlord bears is during the first (or base) year of the lease: if actual expenses per square foot end up being higher than the amount forecasted in lease negotiations, then the landlord will have to absorb the cost difference. Also, if the lease is a full-service lease without a base-year expense stop, the landlord would have to absorb any increases in cost.
[‡]To the extent operating and CAM costs exceed established expense stops, the tenant will need to reimburse the landlord.
**Depends on the terms of the lease. Generally in a modified gross lease, the tenant pays taxes and insurance.

the landlord according to the general terms associated with each type of lease, which are described as follows:

1. **Gross lease**—a lease in which the tenant pays the landlord a fixed monthly rent and the landlord assumes responsibility for paying all operating expenses, taxes, and insurance

associated with the property. If costs rise, the landlord absorbs them, which is another way of saying a gross lease shifts all the risks onto the landlord during the term of the lease. The tenant's rent does not change. Unsurprisingly, the gross lease is rarely (if ever) used, and often only for short periods of time and at lower-quality properties.

2. **Net lease**—a lease in which the tenant pays the landlord a fixed monthly rent and is also responsible for paying all or some of the expenses associated with operating, maintaining, and using the property. There are three levels of "net" that express which expenses the tenant pays in addition to rent:
   - Maintenance, which includes items like utilities, water, janitorial, trash collection, and landscaping
   - Taxes
   - Insurance

   A net lease generally implies the tenant pays rent and property taxes. In a double-net lease the tenant pays rent, property taxes, and insurance; the landlord bears the other costs (though often with an expense stop). A double-net lease more often is referred to as a "modified gross" or "gross industrial" lease, which is described in the following paragraph. In a triple-net lease, in addition to the monthly rent, the tenant pays all costs associated with property operations, maintenance, insurance, and taxes. The landlord essentially collects monthly "coupon" payments from the tenant, similar to receiving monthly interest income from having invested in a bond.

   Triple-net leases are used most often by landlords leasing a freestanding building to a single tenant, where that tenant wants the operating flexibility associated with the triple-net structure. Examples of the types of buildings REITs own that generally are leased using the triple-net structure include fast-food restaurants, industrial warehouses, healthcare facilities, or office buildings that serve as corporate headquarters.

3. **Modified gross lease**—a lease that is similar to the double-net lease described in the preceding discussion on net leases. Often called a gross industrial lease, the modified gross lease is one in which the tenant pays the rent plus the property taxes and insurance, and any increases in these items over

the base year. The landlord pays the operating expenses and sometimes the maintenance associated with the property. In the case in which a landlord uses modified gross leases and has multiple tenants in one building, the landlord will charge the tenants a CAM fee. As described at the beginning of this chapter, CAM charges are additional rent charged for maintenance that benefits all tenants, such as snow removal and outdoor lighting. Tenants generally will be charged a dollar amount representing their proportionate share of expenses, based on the square feet they lease. Modified gross leases most often are used with multi-tenant office buildings, industrial properties, and retail properties.

4. **Full-service lease**—a lease in which the tenant pays the landlord a fixed monthly rent that includes an expense stop calculated off the base year. The landlord pays all the monthly expenses associated with operating the property, including utilities, water, taxes, janitorial, trash collection and landscaping and charges the tenant in subsequent years to the extent operating expenses exceed the expense stop. The tenant gets full service in exchange for the monthly rent and does not have to contract with service providers directly. Full-service leases most often are associated with office buildings.

Leases and Tenant Bankruptcy

In the event that a REIT's tenant goes into bankruptcy, that tenant still has to pay the rent due under its lease(s) with the REIT. This is because the leases are viewed by bankruptcy courts as operating expenses, which have a senior claim over that of creditors or investors on the cash flows of the company reorganizing under bankruptcy laws.

> Fact: Leases between a REIT and a tenant are viewed by bankruptcy courts as operating expenses, which are senior to the bankrupt tenant's debt obligations to lenders. Accordingly, a tenant must continue to pay rent to their landlord (the REIT), even while going through bankruptcy.

The tenant must continue to pay the REIT its contractual rent until the bankruptcy court judge allows the tenant to "reject" the lease. The fact that leases are legal, senior claims on the cash flows of tenants is a major reason that REITs do not necessarily go bankrupt, even when some of their tenants do. Please see Chapter 3, REIT Dividends, for further discussion of this concept.

FASB and the New Standard for Accounting for Leases

In February 2016, the Financial Accounting Standards Board (FASB) issued significant and final changes to the accounting treatment of operating leases (described earlier in this chapter). FASB is the organization that establishes standards of financial accounting for U.S. companies, and the SEC recognizes those standards as being appropriate. Historically, tenants did not capitalize operating leases on their balance sheets and, instead, treated rent payments as expenses that were accounted for in their income statements. The biggest change introduced by FASB's new standard, which goes into effect for REITs on January 1, 2019, will cause tenants to create an asset, which is their right of use on leased space, and a matching liability on their balance sheets equal to the present value of lease payments agreed to in their leases. The anticipated change to the REIT industry is that tenants may prefer to use shorter duration, triple-net leases in order to minimize the liability they will begin showing on their balance sheets. Although the bottom-line economics to REITs should not change, companies will need to adjust their reporting outputs and leasing processes, accordingly.

Lease Duration and REIT Stock Price Performance

On a fundamental level, a REIT's cash flow is the sum of all cash received from tenant leases less any overhead costs for paying management and employees, and the financing costs of any debt the REIT may have outstanding. Property fundamentals, meaning the supply of and demand for real estate, differ widely among the various types of commercial properties and ultimately are the largest governors of REIT returns. However, the length and structure of a lease also dictate how stable (or volatile) a landlord's cash flows are over time. Understanding the type of lease a REIT uses with tenants will help predict how its common shares will trade during different economic scenarios.

Knowing the average lease length and the type of lease structure a REIT uses helps predict how its shares may trade during times of economic expansion and contraction.

Chapter 7 discusses the relationship between lease length and stock price performance in more detail, but it is worth highlighting here, as well. Shorter leases translate into more volatile future earnings and, by extension, wider daily swings in price for those REITs' shares. In contrast, longer leases generate steady income that is similar to receiving interest payment from a bond. This consistent income stream tends to translate into stock-price movements that reflect the underlying stability in rents. Both extremes—short-term and long-term lease durations—have their respective opportunities and risks.

CHAPTER 5

REITs by Property Type

As discussed in the first chapter, one of the primary ways to classify REITs is by the type of property in which they invest. This chapter provides a basic overview of the major property types owned by equity REITs, as well as detail on mortgage REITs. This chapter also provides sublists of the 181 equity REITs and 42 mortgage REITs that compose the FTSE NAREIT All REITs Index, sorted according to NAREIT's property sector and subsector classifications. (Appendix C presents additional information on each company, including website addresses.)

Each type of real estate is associated with distinct supply-and-demand fundamentals that in turn assign certain risks and rewards to the landlords' expected income. Although these risks and rewards become most apparent during times of economic boom or bust, they constantly govern the profitability of different property types and by extension affect stock-price performance. This chapter also highlights economic factors that influence demand for each property type; Chapter 7 provides a more in-depth discussion of the links between current economic news such as changes in interest rates or employment trends, and their effects on the stock prices of different types of REITs.

Diversified and Specialized REITs

Diversified REITs are equity REITs that invest in two or more types of commercial property (see Table 5.1). On the opposite end of the property spectrum are specialty REITs (Table 5.2), which own

Table 5.1   Diversified REITs

Company Name	Ticker Symbol	Total Assets*	Website Address
Vornado Realty Trust	VNO	$21,143	www.vno.com
VEREIT, Inc.[a][b]	VER	17,406	www.vereit.com
NorthStar Realty Finance Corp.	NRF	15,403	www.nrfc.com
W. P. Carey Inc.[a]	WPC	8,755	www.wpcarey.com
Lexington Realty Trust[a]	LXP	3,830	www.lxp.com
Global Net Lease[a]	GNL	2,548	www.globalnetlease.com
Washington Real Estate Investment Trust[†]	WRE	2,191	www.washreit.com
Investors Real Estate Trust	IRET	1,998	www.iret.com
American Assets Trust, Inc.	AAT	1,978	www.americanassetstrust.com
Alexander's, Inc.	ALX	1,448	www.alx-inc.com
BRT Realty Trust	BRT	836	www.brtrealty.com
Gladstone Commercial Corporation	GOOD	833	www.GladstoneCommercial.com
Whitestone REIT	WSR	784	www.whitestonereit.com
Winthrop Realty Trust	FUR	746	www.winthropreit.com
Armada Hoffler Properties, Inc.	AHH	690	www.armadahoffler.com
One Liberty Properties, Inc.	OLP	650	www.onelibertyproperties.com
HMG/Courtland Properties, Inc.	HMG	32	www.hmgcourtland.com
Total for 17 REITs:		$81,271	

*As of December 31, 2015, in millions of dollars.
[a]Indicates that the associated REIT generally uses long-term triple-net leases.
[b]Former name: American Realty Capital Properties (formerly NYSE: ARCP).
[†]This REIT is in the process of being acquired and will not remain publicly traded.
Source: NAREIT, S&P Global Market Intelligence.

only one type of highly specialized real estate, such as billboards, correctional facilities, or farmland. Many of the specialty REITs are new to the industry, though other specialized property types are more established and now have their own NAREIT classification. Data center REITs (Table 5.3) own, develop, and manage wholesale data center properties and data center shells. Infrastructure REITs (Table 5.4) invest in communications, energy and transportation projects. Timber REITs (Table 5.5) own acres of forest, the trees on which are harvested for paper and wood products production. In 2015, there were 44 REITs in these combined categories with total assets of $214.1 billion.

REITs that use Triple-Net-Leases

Recall from Chapter 4 that a triple-net lease is one in which the landlord collects a base rent that excludes—meaning it is net of—taxes, insurance, and maintenance expenses associated with

Table 5.2   Specialty REITs

Company Name	Ticker Symbol	Total Assets*	NAREIT Sub-Property Type	Website Address
Iron Mountain Incorporated	IRM	$6,351	Data Center	www.ironmountain.com
EPR Properties	EPR	4,217	Cineplex Theater	www.eprkc.com
Outfront Media	OUT	3,845	Billboards	www.outfrontmedia .com
GEO Group, Inc.	GEO	3,503	Prison	www.geogroup.com
Lamar Advertising	LAMR	3,392	Billboards	www.lamar.com
Corrections Corporation of America	CXW	3,356	Prison	www.cca.com
Gaming and Leisure Properties, Inc.	GLPI	2,448	Casino	www.glpropinc.com
Farmland Partners Inc.	FPI	345	Land	www.farmlandpartners .com
Gladstone Land Corporation	LAND	230	Land	www.gladstoneland .com
American Farmland Company	AFCO	190	Land	www.americanfarmland company.com
Total for 10 REITs:		$27,877		

*As of December 31, 2015, in millions of dollars.
These REITs generally use long-term triple-net leases and/or ground leases.
Source: NAREIT, S&P Global Market Intelligence.

Table 5.3   Data Center REITs

Company Name	Ticker Symbol	Total Assets*	Website Address
Digital Realty Trust, Inc.	DLR	$11,451	www.digitalrealty.com
Equinix	EQIX	10,357	www.equinix.com
DuPont Fabros Technology, Inc.	DFT	2,815	www.dft.com
CyrusOne Inc.	CONE	2,196	www.cyrusone.com
QTS Realty Trust, Inc.	QTS	1,758	www.qtsdatacenters.com
CoreSite Realty Corporation	COR	1,163	www.CoreSite.com
Total for 6 REITs:		$29,739	

*As of December 31, 2015, in millions of dollars.
These REITs may use long-term triple-net leases at some or all of their properties.
Source: NAREIT, S&P Global Market Intelligence.

Table 5.4   Infrastructure REITs

Company Name	Ticker Symbol	Total Assets*	Website Address
American Tower Corp	AMT	$26,904	www.americantower.com
Crown Castle International Corp	CCI	22,036	www.crowncastle.com
Communications Sales & Leasing	CSAL	2,543	www.cslreit.com
InfraREIT, Inc.	HIFR	1,664	www.infrareitinc.com
CorEnergy Infrastructure Trust	CORR	678	www.corenergy.corridortrust.com
Power REIT	PW	22	www.pwreit.com
Total for 6 REITs:		$53,847	

*As of December 31, 2015, in millions of dollars.
These REITs generally use long-term triple-net leases and/or ground leases.
Source: NAREIT, S&P Global Market Intelligence.

Table 5.5   Timber REITs

Company Name	Ticker Symbol	Total Assets*	Website Address
Weyerhaeuser Company[†]	WY	$12,486	www.weyerhaeuser.com
Plum Creek Timber Company, Inc.[†]	PCL	4,990	www.plumcreek.com
Rayonier Inc.	RYN	2,319	www.rayonier.com
Potlatch Corporation	PCH	1,017	www.potlatchcorp.com
CatchMark Timber Trust, Inc.	CTT	599	www.catchmark.com
Total for 5 REITs:		$21,411	

*As of December 31, 2015, in millions of dollars.
These REITs generally use long-term triple-net leases and/or ground leases.
[†]These two timber REITs are merging; the transaction is expected to be complete in the first half of 2016.
Source: NAREIT, S&P Global Market Intelligence.

occupying the property. These and other operating expenses are paid directly by the tenant to the various service providers. REITs that use triple-net leases typically lease their properties to a single tenant for 10 or more years. NAREIT no longer includes a *triple-net* property category. However, companies categorized by NAREIT as specialty, data center, infrastructure, and timber REITs generally use triple-net leases (including ground leases), as do some of the diversified REITs.

Risks and Rewards of REITs That Use Triple-Net Leases

During times of economic expansion, landlords that use long-term, triple-net leases do not profit as much as other landlords that use shorter-term, gross, or full-service leases because they cannot capture rising market rents. However, triple-net landlords do benefit from steady, bond-like cash flows generated by their leases. As a result, triple-net REITs are viewed as the most defensive, least volatile REITs and tend to outperform other REITs during times of economic uncertainty.

One source of risk in the triple-net REIT model relates to how these companies grow. Few if any of the triple-net REITs grow through development, and their internal growth is embedded in the long-term nature of their leases (often indexed to inflation). This leaves acquisitions as the only source of external growth for these REITs. As such, it is imperative that these companies attain and then maintain a low cost of capital. (See Chapters 7 and 8 for a discussion of REITs' cost of capital.) By way of a simple example, if the investment yield on a property leased pursuant to a long-term triple-net lease is 7 percent, then the triple-net REIT needs to have a cost of capital that is less than 7 percent in order for the acquisition to be additive to its future cash flow.

In the last decade, the number of income-oriented investors competing to buy buildings that are triple-net leased to creditworthy tenants has increased dramatically. The near-decade of super-low interest rates in the United States that followed in the wake of the Great Recession of 2008–2009 was a primary cause of the increase in demand for many high-yield investments, including triple-net properties that generate yields of 5 percent or more. Although higher interest rates in the future may cause a marginal decline in property values, implying higher yields from real estate than today, management teams of triple-net REITs—or any REIT that relies on acquisitions to grow—need to remain vigilant about their costs of capital.

Health-Care REITs

NAREIT lists 17 health-care REITs with combined assets of $114.3 billion (Table 5.6). Health-care REITs receive their income primarily from leasing facilities to health-care providers, usually on a triple-net

Table 5.6   Health-Care REITs

Company Name	Ticker Symbol	Total Assets*	Website Address
Welltower Inc.	HCN	$29,024	www.welltower.com
Ventas, Inc.	VTR	22,262	www.ventasreit.com
HCP, Inc.	HCP	21,450	www.hcpi.com
Omega Healthcare Investors, Inc.	OHI	8,019	www.omegahealthcare.com
Senior Housing Properties Trust	SNH	7,184	www.snhreit.com
Medical Properties Trust, Inc.	MPW	5,609	www.medicalpropertiestrust.com
Healthcare Trust of America, Inc.	HTA	3,172	www.htareit.com
New Senior Investment Group	SNR	3,017	www.newseniorinv.com
Care Capital Properties, Inc.	CCP	2,955	www.carecapitalproperties.com
Healthcare Realty Trust	HR	2,817	www.healthcarerealty.com
Sabra Health Care REIT, Inc.	SBRA	2,486	www.sabrahealth.com
National Health Investors, Inc.	NHI	2,146	www.nhireit.com
Physicians Realty Trust	DOC	1,645	www.docreit.com
LTC Properties, Inc.	LTC	1,275	www.ltcreit.com
CareTrust REIT, Inc.	CTRE	673	www.caretrustreit.com
Universal Health Realty Inc Tr	UHT	459	www.uhrit.com
Community Healthcare Trust Incorporated	CHCT	143	www.communityhealthcaretrust.com
Total for 17 REITs:		$114,337	

*As of December 31, 2015, in millions of dollars.
These REITs generally use long-term triple-net leases and/or ground leases.
Source: NAREIT, S&P Global Market Intelligence.

or modified-gross basis. (Please refer to Chapter 4 for detail on lease structures.) Property types include senior and assisted-living/ rehabilitation facilities, medical clinics, medical office buildings (also referred to as *MOBs*), health-care laboratories, and hospitals.

Population growth, aging demographics, and shifts in consumer preference have all fueled the growth in nonhospital health-care locations and in turn health-care REITs. In their January 2013 report, *U.S. Healthcare Industry and Medical Office Market Overview*, the Rosen Consulting Group ("RCG") wrote:

> The healthcare industry has been growing at a strong pace for decades. Looking forward, this trend is expected to accelerate as baby boomers reach retirement age and echo boomers begin to establish their own facilities. As demand for medical services increases, this will further increase the need for physicians, lab technicians, and other medical support staff, driving demand for the high-quality . . . MOBs that house them.

The *Patient Protection and Affordable Care Act*, which is commonly referred to as the *Affordable Care Act* (ACA or "Obama Care") was signed into law in March 2010. By increasing the number of Americans who have access to health insurance, the ACA is viewed as an additional source of demand in the health-care real estate industry, as a greater number of cost-efficient facilities will be required to administer health services.

Growth in MOBs and other specialty health-care real estate has also expanded dramatically in the past few decades. As RCG observes in the same 2013 report previously stated:

> Evolution in the healthcare industry is also contributing to opportunities in the medical office space. Driven by shifting consumer preferences, limited space in hospitals, and lower costs, procedures that have traditionally been performed in hospitals, such as surgery, have been moving to outpatient facilities. Additionally, increased specialization in the medical field has been driving demand for medical office facilities suited to the needs of the particular profession.

Risks and Rewards of Health-care REITs

Health-care REITs should continue to benefit from robust demand for an increased number of health-care facilities required to support the expanding U.S. population, in as cost-efficient a manner possible. Where there is growth in demand, there is also the possibility for too much new supply being built at once. Investors should be aware of this potential risk when evaluating where different health-care REITs are building and buying facilities.

Health-care REITs' tenants are doctors and health-care service providers, who in turn have varying degrees of exposure to government policy vis-à-vis reimbursement levels for Medicare and Medicaid. Most REITs have minimized their exposure to potential changes in Medicare and Medicaid reimbursement levels by leasing to tenants that emphasize private-pay care. Even so, health-care REITs' total returns remain subject to risk associated with potential reductions to government Medicare and Medicaid reimbursement rates. Even if no changes are made, if investors believe reimbursement rate cuts are possible, all health-care REITs are likely to underperform other property types.

The final risk to consider when reviewing health-care REITs is their use of long-term triple-net leases with the tenants who operate (no pun intended) out of their facilities. In a rising interest rate environment, REITs that use triple-net leases tend to be valued like long-term bonds, in that their stock prices typically underperform other types of REITs that use shorter-term leases. (See Chapter 7 for more information about the factors that influence REIT share price performance.)

Industrial REITs

There are 11 industrial property REITs in the FTSE NAREIT All REIT Index, with combined assets of $60.2 billion (Table 5.7). Industrial properties are leased to businesses for a variety of purposes, including distribution warehousing, light manufacturing, and research and development (R&D).

Industrial property is among the most stable, least-volatile asset classes in the United States. National warehouse/industrial occupancy in the United States typically ranges between 88 percent and 92 percent, evidencing the steady supply-and-demand fundamentals associated with warehousing and distribution facilities. The fact that supply of newly constructed industrial property tends to track demand for new facilities is one of the primary reasons behind the sector's stability.

Demand for industrial property is correlated to consumer spending and growth in the country's gross domestic product (GDP).

Table 5.7   Industrial REITs

Company Name	Ticker Symbol	Total Assets*	Website Address
Prologis, Inc.	PLD	$31,395	www.prologis.com
Duke Realty Corporation	DRE	6,917	www.dukerealty.com
Liberty Property Trust	LPT	6,558	www.libertyproperty.com
DCT Industrial Trust Inc.	DCT	3,632	www.dctindustrial.com
First Industrial Realty Trust, Inc.	FR	2,718	www.firstindustrial.com
PS Business Parks, Inc.	PSB	2,187	www.psbusinessparks.com
STAG Industrial, Inc.	STAG	1,906	www.stagindustrial.com
EastGroup Properties, Inc.	EGP	1,666	www.eastgroup.net
Rexford Industrial Realty, Inc.	REXR	1,153	www.rexfordindustrial.com
Terreno Realty Corporation	TRNO	1,152	www.terreno.com
Monmouth Real Estate Investment Corporation	MNR	916	www.mreic.com
Total for 11 REITs:		$60,200	

*As of December 31, 2015, in millions of dollars.
Source: NAREIT, S&P Global Market Intelligence.

The more demand for consumer goods—whether they are purchased at traditional brick-and-mortar locations like malls, or online with the Internet—the greater the need for warehouses to store and distribute goods to consumers. Supply increases through new development. Industrial properties are fairly simple to build, consisting essentially of four walls tilted up on a six-inch slab of concrete, with a roof that holds it all together. As such, it typically takes only six-to-nine months to construct an industrial property after breaking ground. Due to the relatively short development cycle, industrial property markets tend not to get overbuilt.

Risks and Rewards of Industrial REITs

The trade-off for the industrial sector's stability is these REITs do not enjoy the rapid price appreciation associated with other, more volatile property sectors. Because industrial property is so essential to any economy, shares of industrial REITs tend to perform well throughout the economic cycle. Industrial REITs may not dazzle, but they also rarely disappoint.

Lease Terms

Industrial property landlords employ triple-net or modified-gross leases. As explained in Chapter 4, the tenant is responsible for all of a property's maintenance, taxes, and insurance in the former case; in the latter, the landlord/REIT typically pays basic property taxes and insurance. Lease lengths range from one-to-three years for small-space users with local distribution needs, and five, seven, or 10 years+ for larger tenants distributing goods regionally or nationally. At either end of the spectrum, tenant renewal rates tend to be high (roughly 65 percent or more), since distribution space is a critical component of a tenant's supply chain. (Tenants cannot get their goods to end users without some degree of warehousing and distribution.) Industrial leases tend to include rent escalations every one, two, or three years; these contractual rent bumps typically are indexed to increase with inflation.

Lodging/Resort REITs

In 2015 there were 20 lodging/resort (hotel) REITs in the FTSE NAREIT All REITs Index with $61.3 billion of total assets (Table 5.8). The majority of U.S. hotels are affiliated with national or international franchises or brands. REITs generally own hotels branded under the most widely recognized flags, and tend to focus on the urban markets. Popular brands (and their respective *flags*) include Marriott International (Courtyard, Residence Inn), Hilton (Hilton Garden Inn, Hampton Inn), and InterContinental Hotels Group (Intercontinental, Holiday Inn). Hotels are frequently classified by the quality-level of guest services offered, such as luxury, upper-upscale, upscale, midscale, or economy or by their location such as urban, suburban, resort, and airport.

Hotel Revenue

Location and quality levels is a key driver of a hotel's maximum revenue per available room (RevPAR), which is the product of a hotel's average daily room rate (ADR) and its occupancy rate. Close proximity to a desirable attraction, such as a beach, a central business district, a large university, or a convention center can be a competitive advantage, enabling an operator to charge higher room rates and maintain higher occupancies than hotels that operate in secondary locations. The latter tend to be roadside, limited- or economy-service hotels that compete primarily on price.

Hotel Expenses

Labor represents the most significant expense in hotel operations. As a result, hotels will have large fixed costs to operate the hotel since a minimum number of employees are required to open, run, and clean a hotel each day, regardless of occupancy levels. For this reason, hotels often reduce room rates to increase occupancy during off-seasons or in slow to declining economic times.

Technical Aspects Specific to Hotel REITs

Hotel REITs differ structurally from other equity REITs in that, according to REIT rules (see Chapter 6), hotel owners are not permitted to directly operate the properties they own. This is because earning profit from operating hotels is active and differs from the more passive business of collecting rent on hotels leased to third-party operators. As a result, hotel REITs must retain a third-party hotel manager to operate its hotels. The third-party hotel manager is in charge of all operating facets of the hotel, including hiring and managing the employees, revenue management, and maintenance. In exchange, the third-party manager receives a base

Table 5.8 Lodging/Resort REITs

Company Name	Ticker Symbol	Total Assets*	NAREIT Sub-Property Type	Website Address
Host Hotels & Resorts, Inc.	HST	$11,784	Full-service Hotel	www.hosthotels.com
Hospitality Properties Trust	HPT	6,408	Limited-service Hotel	www.hptreit.com
Ashford Hospitality Trust, Inc.	AHT	4,965	Full-service Hotel	www.ahtreit.com
LaSalle Hotel Properties	LHO	4,075	Full-service Hotel	www.lasallehotels.com
RLJ Lodging Trust	RLJ	3,980	Full-service Hotel	www.rljlodgingtrust.com
Sunstone Hotel Investors, Inc.	SHO	3,863	Full-service Hotel	www.sunstonehotels.com
Apple Hospitality REIT, Inc.	APLE	3,723	Hotel	www.applehospitalityreit.com
DiamondRock Hospitality Company	DRH	3,320	Hotel	www.drhc.com
Pebblebrook Hotel Trust	PEB	3,063	Hotel	www.pebblebrookhotels.com
Xenia Hotels & Resorts, Inc.	XHR	3,006	Hotel	www.xeniareit.com
Ryman Hospitality Properties, Inc.	RHP	2,331	Full-service Hotel	www.rymanhp.com
Chesapeake Lodging Trust	CHSP	2,094	Full-service Hotel	www.chesapeakelodgingtrust.com
Hersha Hospitality Trust	HT	1,970	Limited-service Hotel	www.hersha.com
FelCor Lodging Trust Incorporated	FCH	1,884	Full-service Hotel	www.felcor.com
Summit Hotel Properties, Inc.	INN	1,581	Limited-service Hotel	www.shpreit.com
Ashford Hospitality Prime, Inc.	AHP	1,353	Hotel	www.ahpreit.com
Chatham Lodging Trust	CLDT	1,340	Hotel	www.chathamlodgingtrust.com
SoTHERLY Hotels Inc.	SOHO	393	Full-service Hotel	www.sotherlyhotels.com
Condor Hospitality Trust, Inc.	CDOR	144	Limited-service Hotel	www.condorhospitality.com
InnSuites Hospitality Trust	IHT	27	Limited-service Hotel	www.innsuitestrust.com
Total for 20 REITs:		$61,304		

*As of December 31, 2015, in millions of dollars.
Source: NAREIT, S&P Global Market Intelligence.

management fee (typically 2 to 4 percent of hotel revenues) plus potentially an incentive fee if certain profitability thresholds are achieved. Hotel REITs generally will retain asset managers to oversee the third-party hotel manager.

Risks and Rewards of Hotel REITs

Hotels are more like an operating company than a REIT because they have no leases to guarantee future revenues for some duration of time. Instead, hotel REITs have to "lease" their properties from scratch every day. During times of strong economic growth, hotels can increase prices immediately; as a result, during certain points in the economic cycle, hotel REITs can achieve some of the highest annual total returns of any property type (see Chapter 7 for more detail). In addition, since the lease rate for hotel rooms can be reset daily, in a rising inflationary economy, hotel REITs have an advantage as they can reprice their "leases" daily. As a result, hotel REITs tend to be the least interest rate sensitive class of investment real estate. When it looks like the economy is coming out of a recession, hotel REITs tend to outperform other REIT asset classes, as investors anticipate strong revenue growth and profitability. In a declining economy, however, hotel operators often have to cut their daily rates, and a portion of their employees, to maintain profitability. Unsurprisingly, hotel REITs tend to underperform other REIT sectors when the economy is slowing or at risk of slipping into recession.

Mortgage REITs

The FTSE NAREIT All REITs index listed 41 mortgage REITs (mREITs) at the end of 2015. Early in 2016, a 42nd mREIT was added, bringing the subsector to a total of 42 mREITs with combined assets of $457.2 billion (Table 5.9). Similar to banks and other financial institutions, mREITs lend money to real estate owners directly by issuing mortgages, or indirectly by acquiring existing loans or mortgage-backed securities. In contrast with equity REITs that derive the majority of their revenues from leases, mREIT revenue equals the principal and interest payments received from real estate-based loans.

Mortgage REITs originate residential and commercial mortgages, and they also invest in securities backed by residential

Table 5.9   Mortgage REITs

Company Name	Ticker Symbol	Total Assets*	Website Address
Home Financing:			
Annaly Capital Management	NLY	$75,191	www.annaly.com
American Capital Agency Corp	AGNC	57,021	www.agnc.com
Invesco Mortgage Capital	IVR	16,773	www.invescomortgage capital.com
Hatteras Financial	HTS	16,138	www.hatfin.com
Chimera Investment	CIM	15,345	www.chimerareit.com
New Residential Investment Corp	NRZ	15,193	www.newresi.com
Two Harbors Investment	TWO	14,576	www.twoharborsinvestment .com
Capstead Mortgage	CMO	14,446	www.capstead.com
CYS Investments	CYS	14,331	www.cysinv.com
MFA Financial	MFA	13,167	www.mfafinancial.com
ARMOUR Residential REIT	ARR	13,055	www.armourreit.com
New York Mortgage Trust	NYMT	9,060	www.nymtrust.com
Anworth Mortgage Asset	ANH	6,636	www.anworth.com
Redwood Trust	RWT	6,231	www.redwoodtrust.com
PennyMac Mortgage Investment Trust	PMT	5,827	www.pennymac mortgageinvestmenttrust .com
American Capital Mortgage Investment	MTGE	5,482	www.mtge.com
Dynex Capital	DX	3,670	www.dynexcapital.com
Apollo Residential Mortgage[b]	AMTG	3,663	www.apolloresidential mortgage.com
Western Asset Mortgage Capital	WMC	3,415	www.westernassetmcc.com
AG Mortgage Investment Trust	MITT	3,164	www.agmit.com
Five Oaks Investment Corp	OAKS	2,498	www.fiveoaksinvestment.com
Altisource Residential	RESI	2,458	www.altisourceresi.com
Orchid Island Capital	ORC	2,242	www.orchidislandcapital.com
Ellington Residential Mortgage REIT	EARN	1,557	www.earnreit.com
JAVELIN Mortgage Investment[b]	JMI	874	www.javelinreit.com
ZAIS Financial Corp	ZFC	775	www.zaisfinancial.com
Cherry Hill Mortgage Investment	CHMI	$636	www.chmireit.com
Great Ajax	AJX	615	www.great-ajax.com
Subtotal for 28 Residential Mortgage REITs:		$324,039	
Commercial Financing:			
Starwood Property Trust Inc	STWD	$85,738	www.starwoodpropertytrust .com
Colony Capital	CLNY	10,039	www.colonyinc.com
Blackstone Mortgage Trust	BXMT	9,377	www.blackstonemortgage trust.com
Ladder Capital Corp[a]	LADR	5,895	www.laddercapital.com

(continued overleaf)

Table 5.9   (*continued*)

Company Name	Ticker Symbol	Total Assets*	Website Address
iStar Inc	STAR	$5,623	www.istar.com
RAIT Financial Trust	RAS	4,447	www.rait.com
Resource Capital	RSO	2,760	www.resourcecapitalcorp.com
Apollo Commercial Real Estate Finance[b]	ARI	2,720	www.apolloreit.com
Arbor Realty Trust	ABR	1,827	www.arborrealtytrust.com
Hannon Armstrong Sustainable Infrastructure	HASI	1,470	www.hannonarmstrong.com
Newcastle Invt Corp	NCT	1,468	www.newcastleinv.com
Ares Commercial Real Estate	ACRE	1,379	www.arescre.com
Owens Realty Mortgage Inc	ORM	273	www.owensmortgage.com
Jernigan Capital	JCAP	105	www.jernigancapital.com
Subtotal for 14 Commercial Mortgage REITs:		133,122	
Total for 42 Mortgage REITs:[a]		$457,161	

*As of December 31, 2015, in millions of dollars.
[a]LADR was not included in the FTSE NAREIT All REITs Index at 12/31/2015, but was added in 2016. At the end of 2015, there were only 41 mREITs in the FTSE NAREIT All REITs Index.
[b]In February 2016, AMTG agreed to be acquired by ARI.c.
[b]This REIT is in the process of being acquired and will not remain publicly traded.
Source: NAREIT, S&P Global Market Intelligence.

> **Note**
>
> mREITs will not be included in S&P's Real Estate GICS sector; they will remain in Financials.

mortgages (RMBS) and commercial mortgages (CMBS). A mortgage-backed security (MBS) is a bond-like investment, supported by interest income generated by an underlying mortgage or collection of mortgages. The MBS issuer typically is a government agency or investment bank that purchases the loan(s) and then *securitizes* (or *packages*) them into loan-like securities that appeal to different investors. The purpose of creating these "loans from loans" is to diversify the risk of one borrower by pooling loans together or, in the case of an MBS based on one loan, to restructure the interest and principal payments so investors can buy a piece of the loan with a lower (or higher) risk profile to meet their investment objectives.

Mortgage REITs typically focus on either the residential or commercial mortgage markets. According to NAREIT:

- Most residential mREITs invest in agency RMBS, which are issued by Fannie Mae and Freddie Mac, often referred to as U.S. government–sponsored enterprises (GSEs), or Ginnie Mae. Agency RMBS constitute the bulk of assets held by mREITs today. However, residential mREITs also may invest in RMBS issued by other financial institutions (nonagency or private-label RMBS) and residential mortgage loans.
- Commercial mREITs provide financing for commercial real estate. They may invest in commercial mortgages and commercial real estate loans, as well as both rated and unrated CMBS, mezzanine loans, subordinated securities, or construction loans, and may participate in loan securitizations.

Risks and Rewards of Mortgage REITs

Because mREITs lend money at one rate and borrow it at another, their profitability is affected by changes in the interest rate environment. (Note that increases in interest rates do not directly affect equity REIT profitability. See Chapter 7, REIT Performance, for more detail.) Like banks, mREITs generally make higher profits in a higher-interest-rate environment, where the difference (or *spread*) between where they can borrow and where they lend funds may be greater. However, if interest rates rise rapidly and/or unexpectedly, mREIT profitability can get squeezed because the rate at which management now needs to borrow is higher than the rates at which they have already invested. Most mREIT management teams are

Basics of Investing in mREITs
- Rising interest rates = Margin on investments vs. cost of funds declines; profits fall → Avoid!
- Falling interest rates = Higher prepayments; profits likely to fall → Avoid!
- Stable interest rates = Steady profits → Okay to Invest

diligent about matching durations between their loans receivable and those that are payable. Although duration match-funding mitigates exposure to interest rate increases, investors won't truly know how good (or bad) a job management has done until it may be too late to avoid unexpected losses.

Mortgage REIT profitability can also be challenged in a falling interest rate environment. When rates fall, mortgages and businesses refinance debt at lower interest rates. Such prepayment activity will alter the cash flows of the MBS in which mortgage REITs may have invested and dampen the resulting yield. Because mREIT profitability can be challenged by any change in interest rates, investors are better served to invest in these REITs only when they feel confident that the interest rate environment will be stable during their investment period.

Office REITs

In 2015, NAREIT listed 28 companies as office REITs, with total assets of $145.6 billion (Table 5.10). Office REITs own everything from high-rise buildings in major metropolitan areas such as New York City, to low- and mid-rise suburban office space in secondary office markets such as Charlotte, North Carolina. Within each market, location plays a major role in determining current rental rates, future rent increases, and property occupancy. Depending on the market, properties located in a city's central business district (CBD) may garner higher rents than suburban locations due to proximity to public transportation lines, industry resources, and/or the labor force targeted by corporations doing business there. In contrast, suburban office buildings may be attractive to tenants because of their location relative to executive housing, ample parking, and worker preference to drive to work.

Office buildings are also classified based on building quality (construction and materials), conditions of their mechanical and other internal systems, in-building amenities (such a gym or restaurant), and location. Newer buildings typically are deemed to be Class-A properties. Older buildings that have less efficient mechanical and electrical systems, or that are simply less aesthetically pleasing, tend to be classified as Class-B or Class-C. Although these ratings are subjective and vary from market to market, they

Table 5.10   Office REITs

Company Name	Ticker Symbol	Total Assets*	Website Address
Boston Properties, Inc.	BXP	$18,379	www.bostonproperties.com
SL Green Realty Corp.	SLG	19,858	www.slgreen.com
Paramount Group, Inc.	PGRE	8,794	www.paramount-group.com
Alexandria Real Estate Equities	ARE	8,911	www.are.com
BioMed Realty Trust, Inc.[†]	BMR	6,461	www.biomedrealty.com
Hudson Pacific Properties, Inc.	HPP	6,254	www.hudsonpacificproperties.com
Douglas Emmett, Inc.	DEI	6,066	www.douglasemmett.com
Kilroy Realty Corporation	KRC	5,939	www.kilroyrealty.com
Gramercy Property Trust Inc.[a]	GPT	5,841	www.gptreit.com
Equity Commonwealth	EQC	5,244	www.eqcre.com
Select Income REIT	SIR	4,696	www.sirreit.com
Columbia Property Trust, Inc.	CXP	4,678	www.columbiapropertytrust.com
Brandywine Realty Trust	BDN	4,555	www.brandywinerealty.com
Highwoods Properties, Inc.	HIW	4,493	www.highwoods.com
Piedmont Office Realty Trust	PDM	4,435	www.piedmontreit.com
Mack-Cali Realty Corporation	CLI	4,063	www.mack-cali.com
Corporate Office Properties Tr	OFC	3,909	www.copt.com
Parkway Properties, Inc.[b]	PKY	3,619	www.pky.com
Empire State Realty Trust, Inc.	ESRT	3,301	www.empirestaterealtytrust.com
NorthStar Realty Europe	NRE	2,683	www.nrecorp.com
Cousins Properties Incorporated[b]	CUZ	2,598	www.cousinsproperties.com
Government Properties Inc Tr	GOV	2,175	www.govreit.com
New York REIT, Inc.	NYRT	2,072	www.nyrt.com
Franklin Street Properties	FSP	1,921	www.franklinstreetproperties.com
TIER REIT, Inc.	TIER	1,874	www.tierreit.com
First Potomac Realty Trust	FPO	1,450	www.first-potomac.com
Easterly Government Properties, Inc.	DEA	912	www.easterlyreit.com
City Office REIT, Inc.	CIO	444	www.cityofficereit.com
Total for 28 REITs:		$145,626	

*As of December 31, 2015, in millions of dollars.
[†]In January 2016, BioMed Realty Trust (former NYSE: BMR) was taken private.
[a]In December 2015, Gramercy acquired Chambers Street Properties (former NYSE: CSG).
[b]In April 2016, Parkway Properties and Cousins Properties announced they will merge; the transaction is expected to be complete before the end of the year.
Source: NAREIT, S&P Global Market Intelligence.

are useful for benchmarking rents and property values on a local, regional, or national level. It is possible, for example, to have a Class-A building in a B or C market, and, therefore, only achieve rents that are competitive with other Class-B or -C buildings.

Lease Terms

Office leases typically are full-service leases with an initial term of five to seven years, plus one or more multiple-year renewal options. In a full-service lease (see Chapter 4, Leases), the landlord is responsible for all the operating expenses of the property, including landscaping, real estate taxes, and insurance, but generally the landlord is able to pass most expenses back to the tenant in the form of the expense stops associated with the full-service lease, and common-area maintenance, or CAM, charges. Office leases commonly include annual rent escalations (also called *bumps* or *stepups*) that insulate the landlord's profit margin from costs that rise with inflation.

Risks and Rewards of Office REITs

Office REIT returns are more cyclical than the average equity REIT's due to periodic overbuilding. (Also see Chapter 7, REIT Performance.) If demand for new space does not keep pace with the increase in supply, office vacancy in that market will rise and rental rates will decline. The office sector's longer building cycle is a primary contributing factor to historical overbuilding. During the two or more years it generally takes to complete an office tower, local demand for office space, which is a function of job growth and the local economy, can change materially and cause a building to sit vacant or mostly vacant until demand for office space recovers.

The way tenants use their space can also dramatically alter demand for office space, even in a growing economy. The advancement in communications over the past two decades has made working from home a viable alternative for some workers. Although not all office cultures or industries lend themselves to allowing workers to perform their duties offsite, the ability to work remotely has dampened the overall need for office space in most locations. Densification is a second trend that has dramatically reduced the need for office space in the past 15 years. In 2000, employers generally budgeted 250 square feet of space per employee. Today, the range is between 125 and 225 square feet per employee and an average of around 175 square feet per employee, representing an average decrease in demand of 30 percent. Densification, which is simply space planning more employees into the same square feet of office space, has largely run its course, to the relief of office landlords. However, the way people use—or don't use—formal office space to do their jobs is an ongoing challenge the office property sector faces.

Residential REITs

The residential REIT sector encompassed 23 REITs at the end of 2015 with total assets of $123.6 billion. There are three subcategories of residential REITs: apartments (or *multifamily*), manufactured homes, and single-family homes.

Apartment REITs

NAREIT lists 16 apartment REITs with total assets of $93.4 billion (Table 5.11). Historically, apartment REITs included only companies that owned traditional apartment buildings. More recently, however, the group expanded to include REITs that own student housing apartment complexes.

Traditional apartment buildings are classified as either garden-style or high-rise buildings. Garden-style apartments contain multiple buildings that usually are one to four stories in height and are configured around the center of the community, typically a pool or other common area(s). High-rise apartment buildings are just that: high-rise buildings that contain apartments. High-rise apartments typically are built in high-density cities or town centers where the cost of land and the monthly rental rates the landlord can charge support the additional cost per square foot associated with high-rise construction.

In both formats, apartment properties generally contain a mix of studio, one-, and two-bedroom apartment units. Properties also are classified as Class-A, B, or C. Class-A buildings include newer buildings in prime locations. Buildings in Class-B and C categories tend to be older, offer residents fewer amenities, and, perhaps, are located in less desirable locations. Rental agreements for apartment units typically are for 12 months at a time. A tenant generally may cancel a lease, however, by providing one or more months' notice, typically in writing. The landlord is responsible for the cost of

Table 5.11   Apartment REITs

Company Name	Ticker Symbol	Total Assets*	Website Address
Equity Residential	EQR	$23,157	www.equityapartments.com
AvalonBay Communities, Inc.	AVB	16,931	www.avalonbay.com
Essex Property Trust, Inc.	ESS	12,005	www.essex.com
UDR, Inc.[a]	UDR	7,664	www.udr.com
MAA[b]	MAA	6,848	www.maac.com
Apartment Investment and Management Company[c]	AIV	6,144	www.aimco.com
Camden Property Trust	CPT	6,038	www.camdenliving.com
American Campus Communities, Inc.	ACC	6,026	www.americancampus.com
Monogram Residential Trust, Inc.	MORE	3,283	www.MonogramResidentialTrust.com.
Post Properties, Inc.	PPS	2,272	www.postproperties.com
Education Realty Trust, Inc.	EDR	2,002	www.edrtrust.com
Campus Crest Communities[†]	CCG	1,584	www.campuscrest.com
Independence Realty Trust, Inc	IRT	1,392	www.irtreit.com
Preferred Apartment Communities, Inc.	APTS	1,296	www.pacapts.com
NexPoint Residential Trust, Inc.	NXRT	976	www.nexpointliving.com
Bluerock Residential Growth REIT, Inc.	BRG	703	www.bluerockresidential.com
Total for 16 REITs:		$98,321	

*As of December 31, 2015, in millions of dollars.
[a]UDR will be added to the S&P 500 Index in 2016.
[b]Formerly called Mid-America Apartment Communities, Inc.
[c]This REIT most commonly goes by "Aimco" but has not changed its name officially.
[†]This company was taken private in January 2016. Assets shown are as of September 30, 2015.
Source: NAREIT, S&P Global Market Intelligence.

maintaining the property; however, similar to a full-service lease, the tenant's rent essentially covers costs paid by the landlord. Except in properties where it is possible to meter individual utilities, a landlord also factors into the rental rate reasonable costs for water and heating, ventilation, and air conditioning (HVAC) services.

Steady Demand for Apartment Units

Similar to office space, demand for apartments is highly correlated with employment trends. As employment in an area increases, demand for apartments to house new workers who in-migrate to that area also increases. In contrast to the office sector, demand for apartments also increases when employment decreases, as some former homeowners sell their houses and go back to renting. When unemployment rises, apartment landlords tend to decrease monthly rents and/or offer concessions in the form of months of free rent and, depending on local competition, free garage parking and fitness center memberships in order to maintain occupancy levels. When the economy recovers and is expanding, apartment landlords take advantage of their shorter lease lengths to increase rents more aggressively each year and quickly stop offering concessions to attract or retain tenants.

Risks and Rewards of Apartment REITs

Because demand for apartments tends to be fairly steady, the main risk associated with this sector is the risk of oversupply. As rental rates for apartments increase, private developers and public REITs tend to develop more apartment buildings to take advantage of strong demand. As with any property type, too much supply results in lower rental rates and/or occupancy levels in a market. This in turn usually leads to a decline in the stock prices of apartment REITs with meaningful exposure to the market(s) viewed as becoming overbuilt.

Manufactured Housing REITs

There are only three manufactured housing REITs, with combined assets of $8.2 billion (Table 5.12). Commonly known as mobile homes, manufactured housing communities are a lower-cost

Table 5.12   Manufactured Housing REITs

Company Name	Ticker Symbol	Total Assets*	Website Address
Sun Communities, Inc.	SUI	$4,191	www.suncommunities.com
Equity LifeStyle Properties, Inc.	ELS	3,420	www.equitylifestyle.com
UMH Properties, Inc.	UMH	604	www.umh.com
Total for 3 REITs:		$8,215	

*As of December 31, 2015, in millions of dollars.
These REITs generally use ground leases.
Source: NAREIT, S&P Global Market Intelligence.

alternative to homeownership, which makes them popular among retirees and lower-income workers. REITs in this property niche own land that is rented to individuals pursuant to a ground lease. Tenants purchase prefabricated houses that are placed in an approved location within the community. In addition to providing sites for houses, newer manufactured home communities may also include community-focused amenities, such as lighted streets, swimming pools, and a community recreation facility or clubhouse. The landlord (REIT) receives a monthly fee from each tenant for the right to locate his home on the property. Although individuals technically could move out in any given month, the relatively high cost associated with moving the residence to a competing community tends to translate into a very high renewal rate and in turn a fairly stable income stream to the landlord.

Single-Family-Home REITs

At the end of 2015, there were four REITs that own single-family houses for rent, which NAREIT recently carved out of specialty REITs and placed into their own subproperty type called single-family-home REITs (Table 5.13). (Note in Table 5.13 that two of these four companies are merging in 2016.) This subcategory of residential REITs grew out of the business opportunity the Great Recession of 2008–2009 presented to buy houses at deeply discounted prices and lease them back to the former owners or new occupants.

Table 5.13   Single-Family Home REITs

Company Name	Ticker Symbol	Total Assets*	Website Address
Colony Starwood Homes[a]	SFR	$7,700	www.colonystarwood.com
American Homes 4 Rent[†]	AMH	6,808	www.americanhomes4rent.com
American Residential Properties, Inc.[†]	ARPI	1,359	www.amresprop.com/Home
Silver Bay Realty Trust Corp.	SBY	1,224	www.silverbayrealtytrustcorp.com
Total for 4 REITs:		$17,091	

*As of December 31, 2015, in millions of dollars.
These REITs generally use triple-net leases.
[a]In January 2016, Starwood Waypoint Residential Trust (former NYSE: SWAY) merged with Colony American Homes. Assets shown are estimated, based on September 30, 2015 balance sheet data.
[†]In February 2016, these two REITs merged. Assets for ARPI are as of September 30, 2015.
Source: NAREIT, S&P Global Market Intelligence.

Retail REITs

In 2015, the retail REIT sector included 34 REITs with combined assets of $192.3 billion. NAREIT tracks three subcategories of retail REITs: 19 shopping center REITs with $71.7 billion of assets, eight regional mall REITs with $86.8 billion of assets, and seven freestanding retail REITs with total assets of $33.7 billion.

Initial lease terms to anchor tenants—the larger box tenants used to draw traffic to the retail center—generally are negotiated for 15 to 20 years. Inline tenants are the smaller shops in a center and generally lease their space for 5 to 10 years. Retail landlords typically employ net or modified gross leases (please refer to Chapter 4, Leases). Retail landlords also may receive percentage rents in addition to their face rents and CAM fees. Percentage rents are calculated as a portion (typically 1 to 2 percent) of revenue a tenant achieves in any given year above the base (or initial) year revenue. For example, assume Tenant A generates revenue of $100 per square foot (PSF) during the first year of its lease. If Tenant A generates $110 in revenue PSF in the following year and the landlord has negotiated to receive 1 percent of rents above the base-year revenue, then the landlord will receive an additional $0.10 PSF in percentage rents. During times of economic expansion, landlords can enhance the overall yield on their properties from percentage rents. When economic growth slows or contracts, however, the landlord may receive no percentage rents, which would represent downside risk to the retail REIT's earnings.

Shopping Center REITs

The term *shopping center* encompasses a range of formats, from grocery store–anchored neighborhood and community centers to power centers. According to the International Council of Shopping Centers (ICSC), shopping centers range in size from 30,000 to 150,000 square feet and serve the area within a three-mile radius of their locations. Table 5.14 shows the 19 shopping center REITs tracked by NAREIT.

Neighborhood and community centers are among the most defensive property types because, if they are well located, they remain well leased regardless of broader economic trends. Anchor tenants at shopping centers generally are grocery or drugstores,

Table 5.14   Shopping Center REITs

Company Name	Ticker Symbol	Total Assets*	Website Address
Kimco Realty Corporation	KIM	$11,344	www.kimcorealty.com
Brixmor Property Group Inc.	BRX	9,498	www.brixmor.com
DDR Corp.	DDR	9,097	www.ddr.com
Federal Realty Investment Trust	FRT	4,912	www.federalrealty.com
Retail Properties of America, Inc.	RPAI	4,621	www.rpai.com
Regency Centers Corporation	REG	4,191	www.regencycenters.com
Weingarten Realty Investors	WRI	3,902	www.weingarten.com
Kite Realty Group Trust	KRG	3,766	www.kiterealty.com
Equity One, Inc.	EQY	3,376	www.equityone.net
Acadia Realty Trust	AKR	3,032	www.acadiarealty.com
Tanger Factory Outlet Centers, Inc.	SKT	2,327	www.tangeroutlet.com
Retail Opportunity Investments Corp.	ROIC	2,311	www.roireit.net
Ramco-Gershenson Properties Trust	RPT	2,129	www.rgpt.com
Urban Edge Properties	UE	1,919	www.uedge.com
Inland Real Estate Corporation[†]	IRC	1,522	www.inlandrealestate.com
Cedar Realty Trust, Inc.	CDR	1,322	www.cedarrealtytrust.com
Saul Centers, Inc.	BFS	1,304	www.saulcenters.com
Urstadt Biddle Properties Inc.	UBA	861	www.ubproperties.com
Wheeler Real Estate Investment Trust, Inc.	WHLR	314	www.whlr.us
Total for 19 REITs:		$71,747	

*As of December 31, 2015, in millions of dollars.
[†]This REIT was taken private in January 2016 and is no longer public.
Source: NAREIT, S&P Global Market Intelligence.

designed to draw traffic to the center. Shopping center inline tenants tend to sell necessary consumer items and services, such as dry cleaning and shoe repair. As a result, demand for neighborhood and community shopping center space tends to be fairly stable (or *inelastic*), as evidenced by their high historical occupancy rates that typically range between 89 and 94 percent. Similar to industrial properties, new supply of shopping centers tends to track demand due to the short development time.

Power centers consist only of big-box, national retailers such as Bed Bath & Beyond, Petco, Dick's Sporting Goods, and Home Depot. According to ICSC, the average power center is between 250,000 and 600,000 square feet and has a primary trade area of 5 to 10 miles.

Although the goods sold at these stores are everyday in nature, they tend not to be true necessity items. Consumers, therefore, may substitute less-expensive brands during an economic downturn. Part of the major draw to power centers, however, is the convenience of shopping at a center that offers a series of anchor tenants clustered in one location.

Mall REITs

Malls are classified as regional or super-regional, depending on how large they are and what population base they serve. According to ICSC, regional malls are generally between 400,000 and 800,000 square feet in size and have at least two anchor tenants, such as Nordstrom (NYSE: JWN). Super-regional malls are at least 800,000 square feet in size, have at least three anchor tenants, at least one of which offers luxury and/or fashion goods, such as Neiman Marcus; and super-regional malls are the dominant shopping venue within a 25-mile radius. Malls also are classified as being Class-A or Class-B in quality, depending on location, the anchor tenants, average household income in the surrounding trade area, all of which influence a mall's sales per square foot—an essential metric for comparing productivity among different malls. Table 5.15 shows the eight regional mall REITs tracked by NAREIT.

Table 5.15   Mall REITs

Company Name	Ticker Symbol	Total Assets*	Website Address
Simon Property Group, Inc.	SPG	$30,651	www.simon.com
General Growth Properties, Inc.	GGP	24,074	www.ggp.com
Macerich Company	MAC	11,259	www.macerich.com
CBL & Associates Properties, Inc.	CBL	6,480	www.cblproperties.com
WP Glimcher Inc.	WPG	5,479	www.wpglimcher.com
Taubman Centers, Inc.	TCO	3,563	www.taubman.com
Pennsylvania REIT	PEI	2,807	www.preit.com
Rouse Properties, Inc.[†]	RSE	2,529	www.rouseproperties.com
Total for 8 REITs:		$86,841	

*As of December 31, 2015, in millions of dollars.
[†]In January 2016, a private equity firm made an unsolicited offer to take Rouse Properties private; accordingly, this REIT is not likely to remain publicly traded.
Source: NAREIT, S&P Global Market Intelligence.

Anchor tenants may lease their space, though many prefer to own their stores. Since a landlord selects an anchor tenant primarily for that tenant's ability to draw consumers to the mall itself, the choice of anchor tenants is crucial to the overall success of a project. In between anchor tenants are smaller retailers referred to as inline shops. These tenants include national retailers such as The Gap, as well as regional and local retailers. Malls typically are located in close proximity to or within major metropolitan areas and/or areas that have above-average household income levels in order to maximize sales per square foot and profitability.

Freestanding Retail REITs

Freestanding retail properties house a wide array of businesses, including fast-food and sit-down restaurants (such as Burger King and Macaroni Grill, respectively), drugstores, movie theaters, day-care services, automotive care, and gas stations. REITs that own freestanding retail properties typically use triple-net leases with their tenants (see Chapter 4, Leases). By using triple-net leases, the tenants have full control over their property operations, including staying open late or all night for business. Alternatively, if these tenants rented space in a shopping center or mall, they would be subject to that center's operating hours and other criteria. NAREIT tracks seven freestanding retail REITs, as shown in Table 5.16.

Table 5.16   Freestanding Retail REITs

Company Name	Ticker Symbol	Total Assets*	NAREIT Sub-Property Type	Website Address
Realty Income Corporation	O	$11,866	Single-Tenant	www.realtyincome.com
Spirit Realty Capital, Inc.	SRC	7,919	Diversified	www.spiritrealty.com
National Retail Properties	NNN	5,460	Single-Tenant	www.nnnreit.com
STORE Capital Corp	STOR	3,911	Diversified	www.storecapital.com
Seritage Growth Properties	SRG	2,833	Other Retail	www.seritage.com
Getty Realty Corp.	GTY	899	Single-Tenant	www.gettyrealty.com
Agree Realty Corporation	ADC	793	Single-Tenant	www.agreerealty.com
Total for 7 REITs:		$33,681		

*As of December 31, 2015, in millions of dollars.
These REITs generally use long-term triple-net leases and/or ground leases.
Source: NAREIT, S&P Global Market Intelligence.

In the past few years, three of the freestanding retail REITs listed in Table 5.16 (Seritage, Spirit, and STORE) joined the ranks of publicly traded REITs. Growth in this once sleepy subcategory of retail REITs is being fueled by increased comfort tenants have gained to lease rather than own their real estate. In a sale/leaseback transaction, an owner that occupies a property sells the building to a new owner/landlord, then leases back that same space, typically using a long-term triple-net lease. An increasing number of businesses are willing to monetize their real estate holdings through sale/leaseback transactions with REITs. By doing so, the businesses free up precious capital to deploy back into their operations while still maintaining fundamental control over their locations.

Risks and Rewards of Retail REITs

As the 2015 holiday shopping season evidenced, consumers increasingly are shopping for gifts and necessary items online rather than in retail stores. Internet sales, often referred to as e-commerce, are encroaching on the profitability of traditional brick-and-mortar stores. In January 2016, for example, in the wake of weak holiday sales, Walmart Stores (NYSE: WMT) announced it would close 269 stores worldwide in 2016, including 154 in the United States, to focus on its supercenters and e-commerce business. Similarly, Macy's (NYSE: M) announced it would close 36 stores. As e-commerce proliferates, retailers—and the REITs who act as their landlords—will need to innovate to retain market share and profitability. One effective strategy retail REITs use to mitigate the risk of losing tenants and market share to e-commerce retailers, such as Amazon.com, Inc. (NASDAQ: AMZN), is to own the most attractive locations, often measured by the average household and discretionary income levels within a one-, three-, or five-mile radius of retail centers. Such attractive locations tend to support higher sales per square foot leased for their tenants, meaning the space they rent is more productive and profitable than secondary locations. When retailers close stores, they close their least productive ones. A second strategy landlords use to maintain the revenue per square foot at their centers is to lease space to tenants that offer necessary items (such as groceries and dry cleaning) or, at the other end of the consumption spectrum, luxury goods.

Self-Storage REITs

The FTSE NAREIT All REITs Index classifies five companies as self-storage REITs with combined assets of $22.2 billion (Table 5.17). Similar to what drives the apartment sector, demand for self-storage units is driven by population growth, people moving locations for jobs or other reasons, as well as the urge many people have to archive things for future generations or the simple inability to throw anything away. Individuals who rent apartments or who live in condominiums tend to rent self-storage space. Customers select storage facilities based on price, location, security, and suitability of space to their needs. Property owners rarely depend on one customer for large portions of revenue because individual consumers (rather than businesses) represent the majority of self-storage users. The storage units themselves are simple structures located near busy roads in order to ensure visibility. They require little capital expenditures outside of roof or parking lot/pavement repairs.

Risks and Rewards of Self-Storage REITs

Self-storage units are rented on a month-to-month basis, which can create volatility in rental rates during times of weak or robust demand. Historically, oversupply had been the primary risk associated with this sector. Although the facilities take little time to construct, highly fragmented ownership historically led to less

Table 5.17   Self-Storage REITs

Company Name	Ticker Symbol	Total Assets[*]	Website Address
Public Storage	PSA	$9,778	www.publicstorage.com
Extra Space Storage Inc.[†]	EXR	6,071	www.extraspace.com
CubeSmart	CUBE	3,115	www.cubesmart.com
Sovran Self Storage, Inc.	SSS	2,122	www.unclebobs.com
National Storage Affiliates Trust	NSA	1,102	www.nationalstorageaffiliates.com
Total for 5 REITs:		$22,189	

[*]As of December 31, 2015, in millions of dollars.
[†]In 2016, Extra Space Storage will be added to the S&P 500 Index.
Source: NAREIT, S&P Global Market Intelligence.

transparent supply-and-demand information than for other commercial property types. As the REITs in this space have grown by acquiring local operators, the sector's supply issues have waned and the sector has tended to outperform other property types.

Conclusion

REIT performance varies by property sector, as each type of real estate is impacted differently by larger economic trends. Chapter 7 provides a more in-depth analysis of REIT performance, including a comparison by property sector.

Part II
Investing in REITs

Part II of this book builds on the basic information conveyed in Part I. Chapters 6 through 8 are for investors who want to take their academic understanding of REITs accumulated in Chapters 1 through 5 and apply it to actual companies for investment purposes. This includes money managers who are new to REITs, as well as financial advisors who want to better serve their clients by mastering the basics of REIT analysis.

Getting Technical

Before discussing factors that influence REIT performance in Chapter 7 and the various metrics used to analyze REITs in Chapter 8, there are a few technical items specific to REITs that are helpful to understand.

REIT Structures

As discussed at the outset of this book, REITs are companies that own or finance income-producing commercial real estate. The majority of REITs are equity REITs, which generally derive the bulk of their income from rental revenue paid by tenants. Prior to 1992, equity REITs owned their commercial properties directly or through joint ventures. As Figure 6.1 illustrates, the investing public buys shares in the REIT, which invests the monies into rentable properties and in turn pays a dividend back to shareholders from the net income derived from operating the rental properties. As with any other stock, the dividend represents an investor's current return, or yield, on their REIT shares.

So with a traditional REIT structure (Figure 6.1), shareholders essentially owned a portion of the REIT's business enterprise, prorated according to how many shares they owned of the REIT as a percentage of total shares outstanding. If an investor owned 5 percent of a REIT's outstanding shares, they essentially owned 5 percent of that REIT's assets and operations.

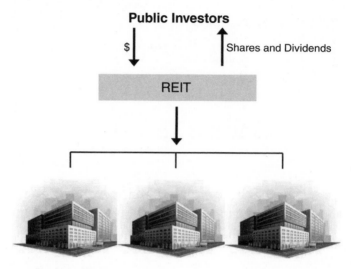

Figure 6.1   REIT Structure

UPREITs

Beginning in 1992, the REIT corporate ownership structure under-went a radical change with the introduction of the Operating Partnership Unit (OP unit) and the Umbrella Partnership REIT (UPREIT) structure. Taubman Centers, Inc. (NYSE: TCO) is credited for innovating the UPREIT structure with its initial public offering (IPO) in 1992.

UPREITs differ from traditional REITs in two ways. First, and as shown in Figure 6.2, in the UPREIT structure, the REIT does not own its properties directly. Instead, the REIT owns (usually a great majority of) units in a limited partnership called an operating part-nership (OP), which in turn owns and operates the properties. As Figure 6.2 illustrates, the UPREIT owns an interest in and is the sole general partner of its OP. When an UPREIT sells common shares or issues debt to the investors, it contributes the proceeds raised to its OP in exchange for additional OP units. The OP technically is the legal entity that buys and/or develops properties and operates them. From the money it earns from operating the properties, it "dividends" money back to the UPREIT, which pays dividends to the investors. The OP, therefore, is a pass-through mechanism that is transparent to public shareholders. Second, UPREITs have an additional currency besides cash and common stock with which its management team can acquire properties: the OP unit.

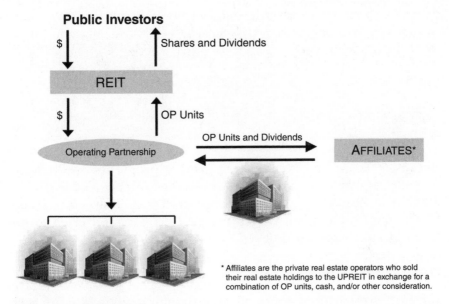

Figure 6.2   UPREIT Structure

OP Units

As is the case for all U.S. partnerships, the operating partnership of an UPREIT can issue OP units to the seller of property as a form of consideration, similar to issuing common shares. OP units are economically the same as shares of common stock in that the OP unit holders receive the same distributions per unit as the UPREIT's stockholders receive on their common shares. Unlike common stock, OP units are not publicly traded and the owner cannot vote regarding UPREIT corporate governance matters. In nearly every instance, OP unit holders can convert each unit on a one-for-one basis into common stock of the UPREIT or for cash (at the UPREIT's option). When unit holders convert to common shares, they become shareholders of the UPREIT. Converting OP units to shares also triggers a taxable event.

It is the nontraded (that is, *illiquid*) characteristic of the OP unit that enables the IRS to view them similarly to like-kind exchanges when a REIT tenders them as consideration for limited partnership (LP) interests in an acquisition property. Said more simply, by accepting OP units rather than cash or stock as payment for a property, the seller of the property may defer the tax liability that otherwise would have been triggered at the time of the asset sale.

Generally, the IRS views the contribution of limited partnership units of real property in exchange for partnership interests, including OP units, as a nontaxable event. As a result, the party that contributed real estate in exchange for OP units may be able to defer the recognition of capital gains (and the associated taxes) until such time as they convert their OP units into shares of the UPREIT or cash.

Because OP units enable REITs to acquire properties on the same basis as regular contributions of properties to partnerships, since 1992 most REITs have opted to adopt the UPREIT structure. Many REITs that were publicly traded before 1992 have converted to the UPREIT structure over time.

OP Units and Estate Planning

Private real estate operators typically own their assets in LPs with each limited partner (investor) having rights to his or her *pro rata* share of the partnership's profits and losses. The Tax Code requires landlords to depreciate the value of a property (excluding land value) over the "useful life" of the building. In the cases where private landlords have owned their properties for a number of years, for income tax purposes, they likely have a very low or even negative basis in each asset. Consequently, the sale of their assets at current market values would trigger a meaningful gain on sale, resulting in a significant tax liability.

Because OP units are similar to any other partnership contribution in the eyes of the IRS, a seller may defer his current tax liability* by accepting a UPREIT's OP units as part of or the entire sales price, instead of cash or common stock. Equally important is the fact that, upon the OP unit holder's death, the basis in his or her OP units is stepped up to the then-current market value of the REIT's common stock. The seller's heirs can then convert the OP units into common shares of the REIT without triggering a capital gain.

---

*Note: Before entering into a transaction, sellers of property should consult with their tax accountant to determine their ability to defer taxes according to then-current U.S. Tax Code.

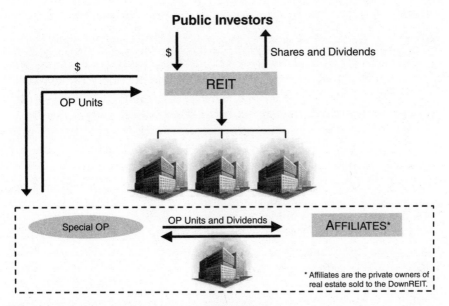

Figure 6.3   Corporate Structure of a DownREIT

DownREITs

In some instances, older REITs found it too costly to convert to an UPREIT structure. For example, the legal process of contributing properties from the REIT to a new OP could trigger potentially massive state-level transfer taxes. To compete with UPREITs in bidding for privately held assets with tax-efficient purchase proposals, some REITs began acquiring assets using DownREIT structures. REITs formed OPs that issued DownREIT OP units to acquire specific portfolios of assets, usually from one seller or partnership. Figure 6.3 shows a REIT that owns assets directly as well as in a DownREIT structure.

Issues emerged with this somewhat restrictive structure, however, such as the REIT's ability to later sell assets owned in a DownREIT. Additionally, DownREIT unitholders often had different voting rights than public shareholders of the REIT, which proved to be an unsustainable conflict. The DownREIT structure has been improved to eliminate prior conflicts and today is a useful tool that many traditional REITs like Kimco Realty (NYSE: KIM) employ when necessary to acquire assets in a tax-efficient manner.

Publicly Traded, Public Nonlisted, and Private REITs

The focus of the chapters leading up to this point has been to provide information and data on publicly traded REITs. In the past two decades, however, private REITs and REITs that are public but nonlisted on any exchange have proliferated. The biggest difference between publicly traded REITs and their public nonlisted REIT (PNLR) cousins is liquidity. However, there are many other differences associated with private and nontraded REITs. Table 6.1 summarizes the major differences between REIT structures.

Volatility versus Liquidity

Investors in PNLRs and private REITs often cite the lack of daily price changes (or *volatility*) among the benefits of investing in these entities. They like the fact that they do not have to worry about the daily price movements in their investments, as do shareholders in publicly traded REITs. However, this semblance of stability comes at the steep price of not having liquidity. Shareholders of publicly traded REITs own liquid investments that can be sold instantly in the stock market. It can take weeks or months to redeem an investment in a private REIT or PNLR; in some instances, redemptions may be forbidden for a specified period of time. If investors need liquidity, they should avoid investing in private REITs and/or PNLRs. Moreover, a FINRA rule going into effect in April 2016 requires customer statements for PNLR investments to show the shareholder's net investment (i.e., subtracting commissions) for the first couple of years and then the shareholder's share of net asset value of the PNLR thereafter. This new rule will make the PNLR shareholder's investment more transparent and therefore possibly more volatile than in the past.

Transparency and Corporate Governance

Publicly traded REITs and PNLRs must file quarterly and annual periodic statements with the SEC. Accordingly, shareholders in these REITs enjoy a high level of transparency and ultimately benefit from a greater alignment of shareholder–advisor interests. In contrast, private REITs do not have to disclose their financial statements.

Table 6.1 Comparison of Public versus Nontraded and Private REIT Structures

	Publicly Traded REITs	Public Nonlisted REITs	Private REITs
Overview	REITs that file with the SEC and whose shares trade on national stock exchanges.	REITs that file with the SEC but whose shares do not trade on national stock exchanges.	REITs that are not registered with the SEC and whose shares do not trade on national stock exchanges.
Liquidity	Shares are listed and traded on major stock exchanges and can be bought and sold instantly during market hours through financial advisors and on-line brokerage houses. Most publicly traded REITs are listed on the NYSE.	Shares are not traded on public stock exchanges. Redemption programs for shares vary by company and are limited. Generally, a minimum holding period for investment exists. Investor exit strategy generally linked to a required liquidation after some period of time (often 10 years) or, instead, the listing of the stock on a national stock exchange or a merger into a traded company at such time.	Shares are not traded on public stock exchanges. Existence of, and terms of, any redemption programs varies by company and are generally limited in nature.
Transaction	Brokerage costs the same as for buying or selling any other publicly traded stock.	Typically, fees of 10–15 percent of the investment are charged for broker-dealer commissions and other up-front costs, although some PNLRs are now spreading out the fees over several years. On-going management fees and expenses also are typical. Back-end fees may be charged.	Varies by company.
Management	Typically self-advised and self-managed.	Typically externally advised and managed, although many may have internal management before a liquidity event.	Typically externally advised and managed.

(continued)

Table 6.1 *(continued)*

	Publicly Traded REITs	Public Nonlisted REITs	Private REITs
Minimum Investment	One share.	Typically $1,000–$2,500	Typically $1,000–$25,000; private REITs that are designed for institutional investors require a much higher minimum.
Independent Directors	Stock exchange rules require a majority of directors to be independent of management. NYSE and NASDAQ rules call for fully independent audit, nominating, and compensation committees.	Subject to North American Securities Administrators Association (NASAA) regulations. NASAA rules require that boards consist of a majority of independent directors. NASAA rules also require that a majority of each board committee consist of independent directors.	Not required.
Investor Control	Investors reelect directors.	Investors reelect directors.	Investors reelect directors.
Corporate Governance	Specific stock exchange rules on corporate governance.	Subject to state and NASAA regulations.	Not required.
Disclosure Obligation	Required to make regular financial disclosures to the investment community, including quarterly and yearly audited financial results with accompanying filings to the SEC.	Required to make regular SEC disclosures, including quarterly and yearly financial reports.	Not required.
Performance Measurement	Numerous independent performance benchmarks available for tracking public REIT industry. Wide range of analyst reports available to the public.	No independent source of performance data available.	No public or independent source of performance data available.

Source: Reproduced by permission of the National Association of Real Estate Investment Trusts® and is used subject to the Terms and Conditions of Use set forth on the NAREIT website, including, but not limited to, Section 9 thereof.

Costs and Fees

Publicly traded REITs list their costs (both property level and corporate general and administrative expenses [G&A]) on their quarterly financial statements, where analysts and investors can scrutinize how efficiently properties and the company in general are managed. In contrast, private REITs are not compelled to disclose any such information. PNLRs historically have been criticized for charging large upfront fees of 12 percent or more, in part to pay financial advisors large commissions for marketing their shares. During the investment period, they also charge fees for buying and managing properties, and then more fees to various advisors, as well.

The real problem with the fees charged by PNLRs is that historically they were not transparent to investors. When an investor would buy a share in a PNLR, typically for $10, the value per share listed on the investor's statement would be the gross $10, not an amount that was net of fees and other costs, which typically consumed $1.20 per share or more. Said another way, the PNLR investor did not realize they were starting out this investment by using at least 12 percent of their initial investment to pay brokers, startup costs, and advisory fees incurred by the PNLR sponsor.

In 2015, the Financial Industry Regulatory Authority (FINRA) addressed these and other disclosure issues associated with PNLRs by modifying NASD Rule 2340 (Customer Account Statements). According to FINRA's January 2015 "Regulatory Notice," effective April 11, 2016, public PNLRs must include per share amounts that reflect current value, "developed in a manner reasonably designed to ensure that per share estimated value is reliable" (FINRA Regulatory Notice, January 2015). As a result, investors in PNLRs now have a better line of sight on how efficiently their investment is being put to use. However, their overall transparency is less than that offered by publicly traded REITs, which trade on stock exchanges.

Externally Advised and Externally Managed REITs

The 223 REITs that composed the FTSE NAREIT All REITs Index at the end of 2015 are publicly traded and, therefore, do not have the features of private REITs and PNLRs discussed earlier. However, there is a small population of publicly traded REITs that are externally advised and externally managed, which is similar to how REITs were structured before the 1986 Tax Act (see section in Chapter 7,

Improvements to the REIT Structure...). The externally advised structure may have conflicts of interest between the REIT advisor and REIT shareholders; these conflicts can lead to suboptimal capital allocation decisions. Furthermore, research published over the years by Green Street Advisors, an independent REIT and real estate research firm, has shown that the average annual total returns of externally managed REITs often lag that of the industry. First, externally advised REITs do not have any employees; instead, they pay a fee to an external, third-party advisor, whose employees oversee the REIT's daily operations. The advisor also earns a fee on any assets the REIT acquires. An incentive for the advisor may be to maximize the amount of properties the REIT owns, not to maximize the performance or profitability of those assets. The conflict between the advisor and shareholders may not be apparent immediately, but over time, externally advised and managed REITs tend to underperform other REITs in the same property sector. To learn if a REIT is an externally advised or managed REIT, be sure to read the "Company Description" located in the first few pages of any recent form 10-Q or 10-K that the REIT has filed with the SEC. If the company states that it is "a self-advised, self-managed real estate investment trust," then it does not have the fee-oriented conflicts of interest just described.

Qualifying as a REIT

Just as The Walt Disney Company (NYSE: DIS) and Apple, Inc. (NASDAQ: AAPL) must comply with aspects of Internal Revenue Code (the Code) that govern C-corporations, a REIT must adhere to certain provisions in order to qualify for and maintain its tax status. A summary of the principal provisions of the Code for REITs follows:

Distribution requirements—a REIT must:
- Pay dividends equal to at least 90 percent of its taxable income. (From 1980 until January 1, 2001, the minimum distribution requirement was 95 percent of taxable income.)

Qualification requirements—a REIT must:
- Be a corporation formed in one of the 50 United States or the District of Columbia.
- Be governed by a board of directors or trustees.
- Have shares that are fully transferable.

- By its second taxable year, have a minimum of 100 shareholders.
- Have no more than 50 percent of its shares held by five or fewer individuals during the last half of each taxable year; this is known as the "5 or fewer rule," or the "5/50 test."

Annual income requirements—annually, a REIT must:
- Derive at least 75 percent of gross income from rents from real property or, as with mortgage REITs, interest on mortgages on real property and gains from the sale of real property; this is known as the 75 percent Income Test.
- Derive at least 95 percent of its gross income from items qualifying under the previously defined 75 percent Income Test, plus dividends and interest income, and gains from the sale of stock or other non–real estate investments (the 95 percent Income Test).
- Derive 5 percent or less of its income from nonqualifying sources, such as third-party management or leasing fees provided to properties the REIT does not own. As a result, REITs often use a structure known as a taxable REIT subsidiary (TRS) to pursue real estate–related business opportunities that enhance management's ability to deliver higher levels of tenant services. Because the TRS is taxed like a regular operating company, the REIT is allowed to own up to 100 percent of each TRS's stock.

Quarterly investment requirements—at the end of each quarter, a REIT must:
- Invest at least 75 percent of its total assets in real estate assets, mortgage loans, cash, and government securities.
- Not own more than 10 percent of another company, other than another REIT, a qualified REIT subsidiary (QRS), or a taxable REIT subsidiary. In the case of TRSs, no more than 25 percent (20 percent after 2017) of a REIT's total asset value may reside in one or more TRS.
- A REIT cannot own stock in any corporation other than a TRS whose value exceeds 5 percent of the REIT's total asset value.

Note that a REIT's board of directors votes on which methodology it will use to measure *total asset value*. Methodologies include using gross asset value (also known as *undepreciated book value*), or methods prescribed by lenders.

REITs Are Not Limited Partnerships

Even though the IRS can treat OP units similar to other contributions to partnerships, REITs are *not* partnerships and have no relation to the real estate limited partnerships (RELPs) of the 1980s. REITs are C-corporations that are allowed a dividends-paid deduction when calculating corporate income taxes. Many REITs are publicly traded, whereas most partnerships are not. Table 6.2 summarizes the many differences between REITs and partnerships.

Table 6.2   Comparison of REITs and LPs

	REITs	Limited Partnerships
Liquidity	Yes. The shares of most REITs are listed and traded on stock exchanges	No. When liquidity exists, generally much less than REITs
Minimum Investment Amount	None	Typically $2,000–$5,000
Reinvestment Plans	Yes, including some at discounts.	No
Ability to Leverage Property Investments without Incurring UBIT* for Tax-Exempt Accounts	Yes; this makes REITs suitable for individual IRAs, 401(k), and other pension plans.	No
Investor Control	Yes, investors reelect directors	No, controlled by general partner who cannot be easily removed by limited partners
Independent Directors	Yes, stock exchange rules or state law typically require majority to be independent of management	No
Beneficial Ownership	At least 100 shareholders required; most REITs have thousands	Shared between any number of limited and general partners
Ability to Grow by Additional Public Offerings of Stock or Debt	Yes	Rarely
Ability to Pass Losses on to Investors	No	Yes
Information to Investors	Form 1099	Form K-1
Subject Investors to State Taxes	Only in state where investor resides	Yes, for all states in which it owns properties

*UBIT stands for Unrelated Business Income Tax.
Source: Reproduced by permission of the National Association of Real Estate Investment Trusts® and is used subject to the Terms and Conditions of Use set forth on the NAREIT website, including, but not limited to, Section 9 thereof.

CHAPTER 7

REIT Performance

Historical Total Returns

This chapter examines the market forces that influence demand for REIT shares and, ultimately, REIT performance relative to other investments. Understanding the various factors that influence REIT stock price performance will enable investors to make better buy, hold, or sell decisions among the various REITs that are publicly traded. With an aggregate equity market capitalization of $939 billion, REITs are an established asset class, but still represent a relatively small piece of the investment world. For comparison, the market capitalization of Apple, Inc. (NASDAQ: AAPL) was approximately $530 billion at the end of 2015. As the industry has grown, particularly in the last 10 years, REITs have gained traction in the minds and portfolios of an increasing number of investors, though some still view them as alternative investments. In any given year, the total returns of REITs have to be all the more compelling to attract and retain investors. The industry's smaller relative size magnifies the effects of investor rotations into or out of REITs. A $100 million swing of funds into or out of the $939 billion REIT market has a more material impact on REIT returns than it would on the Dow Jones Industrial Average, whose 30 constituent companies had a combined market capitalization of $5.1 trillion at the end of 2015.

As the shaded areas in Table 7.1 show, REITs delivered strong total returns in 1995–1997, from 2000 to 2006, and again from 2009 to 2012. The disappointing total returns in 1998–1999 illustrate what happened to REIT returns when fund flows rotated to the higher growth NASDAQ. During the 2007–2008 global financial crisis,

Table 7.1   Total Returns of REITs vs. Major Indices

	REITs[a]	S&P 500	NASDAQ	DJIA	Russell 2000	10-Year Ty Yield[b]	10-Year CMBS[c]
1990	−17.3%	−3.1%	−17.8%	−4.3%	−21.5%	8.1%	NA
1991	35.7%	30.5%	56.8%	20.3%	46.0%	6.7%	NA
1992	12.2%	7.6%	15.5%	4.2%	16.4%	6.7%	NA
1993	18.5%	10.1%	14.8%	17.0%	17.0%	5.8%	NA
1994	0.8%	1.3%	−3.2%	5.0%	−3.2%	7.8%	NA
1995	18.3%	37.6%	39.9%	36.9%	26.2%	5.6%	NA
1996	35.8%	23.0%	22.7%	28.9%	16.6%	6.4%	115
1997	18.9%	33.4%	22.2%	24.9%	22.2%	5.7%	140
1998	−18.8%	28.6%	40.2%	18.1%	−2.2%	4.6%	270
1999	−6.5%	21.0%	86.1%	27.2%	21.4%	6.4%	210
2000	25.9%	−9.1%	−39.2%	−4.7%	−3.0%	5.1%	235
2001	15.5%	−11.9%	−20.8%	−5.4%	2.5%	5.0%	220
2002	5.2%	−22.1%	−31.2%	−15.0%	−20.5%	3.8%	181
2003	38.5%	28.7%	50.8%	28.3%	47.3%	4.3%	129
2004	30.4%	10.9%	9.2%	5.3%	18.3%	4.2%	127
2005	8.3%	4.9%	2.1%	1.7%	4.6%	4.4%	180
2006	34.4%	15.8%	10.4%	19.0%	18.4%	4.7%	123
2007	−17.8%	5.5%	10.7%	8.9%	−1.6%	4.0%	790
2008	−37.3%	−37.0%	−40.0%	−31.9%	−33.8%	2.2%	5,362
2009	27.4%	26.5%	45.4%	22.7%	27.2%	3.8%	7,315
2010	27.6%	15.1%	16.9%	14.1%	26.9%	3.3%	5,932
2011	7.3%	2.1%	−1.8%	5.5%	−4.2%	1.9%	725
2012	20.1%	16.0%	15.9%	7.3%	16.4%	1.8%	400
2013	3.2%	32.4%	38.3%	26.5%	38.8%	3.0%	370
2014	27.2%	13.7%	13.4%	7.5%	4.9%	2.2%	355
2015	2.3%	1.4%	5.7%	−2.2%	−4.4%	2.3%	545
1991–2015, 25-year CAGR	12.1%	9.8%	10.9%	7.9%	10.5%	–	–

Shaded areas represent years in which REITs outperformed most major indexes.
Source: NAREIT; S&P Global Market Intelligence; Yahoo! Finance; Bloomberg & Wells Fargo Securities, LLC
[a]Annual total returns on the FTSE NAREIT All REITs Index.
[b]Represents the yield on 10-year U.S. treasury notes at the end of each year.
[c]10-year CMBS yield for BBB notes in excess of 10-year U.S. Treasuries (CMBS "spreads"), in basis points.

REITs significantly underperformed other indexes in 2007, strongly rebounded (like other indexes) in 2009, and then significantly outperformed other indexes in 2010. Real estate fundamentals, changes in interest rates, and many other market forces all play a role in determining REIT performance. Understanding the evolution of the marketplace for REIT shares is instructive for predicting how the companies may perform in future circumstances. The following sections highlight the major milestones in the evolution of the modern REIT market—which in 25 years, has emerged from obscurity and grown into an industry that, effective September 1, 2016, will largely compose S&P's eleventh Global Industry Classification Standards (GICS) sector: Real Estate.

Factors Influencing Demand for REIT Shares

A basic economic principle is that the price of something equals where supply of that item intersects with demand for it. Although current stock prices reflect investor expectations about future company earnings, the fundamental laws of supply and demand also matter. Because the REIT industry is small relative to other industries, REIT returns can be negatively affected when too many REITs issue too many new shares, creating a temporary market situation of oversupply. As Figure 7.1 shows, the FTSE NAREIT Equity REITs (FNER) index returns declined after 1997 and 2006. Although other market forces also played a role in declining REIT values, both years were preceded by multiple years of heavy new equity issuance. When other forces caused demand for REIT shares to soften, the greater supply of REIT equity likely compounded those declines. What is encouraging is that, after five years of record equity issuance from 2009 through 2013, the FNER continued to rise in 2014 and in 2015. Demand for REITs appears to have kept up with new supply of REIT shares.

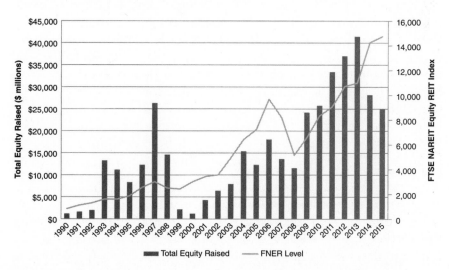

Figure 7.1   Supply of New Equity versus REIT Performance, 1990–2015

Source: NAREIT.

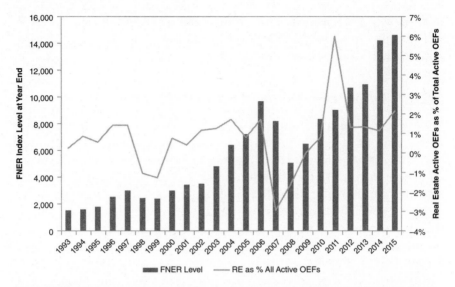

Figure 7.2   Real estate-dedicated mutual fund flows through, 1993–2015. (Note: Total Fund Flows based on all actively managed open-end funds (OEFs) for all U.S. OE Morningstar Categories excluding Money Market & Funds of Funds. Total Fund Flows for U.S. Real Estate based on actively managed funds in the Morningstar U.S. OE Real Estate Category. The percent of real estate active OEFs as a percent of all active OEFs is calculated using annual fund-flow data.)

Source: Morningstar Direct; Cohen & Steers; NAREIT.

Demand for REIT shares plays a larger and multifaceted role in REIT performance. It can be measured by observing the weekly flow of funds into (or out of) real estate–dedicated mutual funds. As Figure 7.2 shows, the strong performance of REITs from 2000 through 2006 corresponded to a sustained flow of funds into real estate mutual funds. Similarly, REIT returns were negative in 2007 and 2008, years in which funds flowed out of REITs. Fund-flow data is expensive to access, and, therefore, not available to all investors. Some REIT research teams at investment banks produce weekly or monthly fund flow reports but, again, these are not accessible to all investors. The data shown in Figure 7.2 was provided by Cohen & Steers, Inc. (NYSE: CNS).

Events That Increased Demand for REIT Shares

What Figure 7.2 also shows is that fund flows into REITs—though volatile from year to year—have increased from around 25 basis points of total fund flows in the early 1990s to over 2 percent in 2015. From 1993 through 2015, real estate fund flows as a percent of total fund flows averaged 80 basis points. What Figure 7.2 does not show is that REITs existed for three-and-a half decades, from 1960 through 1995, before the industry gained meaningful traction with investors.

Until the mid-1990s, the percent of real estate assets as a percent of total mutual fund assets was less than 25 basis points. Prior to 1990, the supply of REIT shares was too small and the marketplace for REITs was too illiquid to attract meaningful institutional investor interest. Though REITs offered attractive yields and strong portfolio diversification benefits discussed in Chapter 2, their thin average daily trading volumes (see Figure 7.3) relegated them to a subset of income-seeking individual investors. In 1990, for example, there were 58 equity REITs with a combined average trading volume of $114 million, implying an average trading dollar volume per REIT of less than $2 million. By contrast, in 1990, The Walt Disney Company (NYSE: DIS) average daily dollar trading volume was $58 million (source: NYSE).

In the past 25 years, however, the REIT industry has grown dramatically. Since 2005 alone, the industry's average daily dollar trading volume has increased at a compounded average rate of 12.5 percent, from $1.7 billion in 2005 to $$6.2 billion in 2015

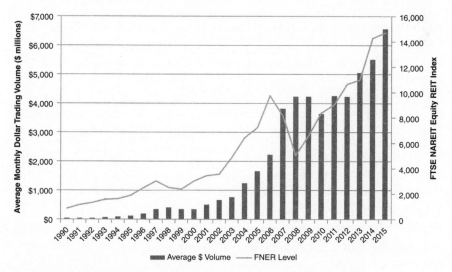

Figure 7.3   Annual Dollar Trading Volume of the FNER, 1990–2015

Source: NAREIT.

(source: NAREIT). In the 1990s, the REIT industry went through a period of tremendous growth, both in terms of the number of REITs that came public and in terms of the market capitalization of the REIT industry itself. Recall Table 1.1 in Chapter 1, which summarizes the industry's growth since the early 1970s. In 1990, there were 58 equity REITs, 43 mortgage REITs, and 18 hybrid REITs, for a total of 119 companies with a combined equity market capitalization of $8.7 billion. At the end of 2015, there were 182 equity REITs and 41 mortgage REITs, for a total of 223 companies with a combined equity market capitalization of $939 billion. Several distinct events supported the REIT industry's rapid growth since 1990. The following pages address the major milestones that punctuated the REIT industry's growth.

S&L Crisis of 1980s Was a Unique Buying Opportunity

During the savings and loan crisis (the S&L crisis), approximately one-third of the 3,234 savings and loan associations in the United States failed between 1986 and 1995. Two government organizations were created to close or otherwise resolve the failed associations: the Federal Savings and Loan Insurance Corporation (FSLIC) and the Resolution Trust Corporation (RTC). A major tactic used by these organizations was to sell the commercial real estate holdings of S&Ls, often for pennies on the dollar. Real estate companies and REITs purchased high-quality assets from the RTC for deeply discounted prices, a rare buying opportunity that positioned the REIT industry for tremendous growth in the 1990s. As the U.S. economy and commercial real estate markets recovered, REITs began leasing up vacancy and capturing higher market rents in their RTC properties. As a result, REITs were able to generate average annual total returns of 17 percent from 1992 through 1996, which significantly outperformed the returns of other investments (see Table 7.1).

REIT Returns Attract Tsunami of New Capital, 1992–1996

The REIT industry's strong performance from 1992–1996 attracted significant amounts of new capital. Taking advantage of the strong demand for REIT shares, dozens of private companies and portfolios were able to complete the initial public offering (IPO) process, swelling the ranks of publicly traded REITs from 138 at the end of 1991 to 199 companies at the end of 1996. By the same token, the size of the REIT industry also expanded rapidly. According to NAREIT, REITs issued $49.7 billion in equity (both through IPOs and follow-on stock offerings) from 1990 through 1996. The industry's equity market capitalization increased from $13.0 billion at the end of 1991 to $88.8 billion at the end of 1996, representing a compound annual increase of 37.7 percent.

Professional Money Managers Discover REITs

The advent of professional money managers into the REIT market was a critical component of the industry's growth and evolution. In 1985, Cohen & Steers, Inc. (NYSE: CNS) created the first real estate–"dedicated" mutual fund, and was the sole real estate–dedicated mutual fund until 1989. As Figure 7.2 demonstrated earlier in this chapter, investors have increased their allocations to real estate–dedicated mutual funds dramatically since the late 1980s. Today, hundreds of institutional money managers invest in a vast array of REIT-dedicated mutual funds.

Improvements to the REIT Structure Aligned Management with Shareholders

Part of the reason REITs were small and micro-cap companies prior to the 1990s was that the REIT structure was flawed. In the late 1980s and through the 1990s, the structural impediments that hampered REIT growth were resolved. *The Tax Reform Act of 1986* (the "1986 Tax Act") often is cited for giving the U.S. economy a nasty case of whiplash when it eliminated certain tax deductions, such as the ability to recognize passive losses generated by real estate limited partnership (RELP) investments, which are discussed in Chapter 6. However, it also dramatically improved the corporate structure and governance of REITs. Prior to the 1986 Tax Act, REITs were required to be externally advised and managed by third parties; as a result, REITs were mutual fund–like, passively managed pools of properties. Managers were paid a percent of the book value of assets owned by the REIT, rather than according to profitability. The 1986 Tax Act empowered REITs with the right to self-manage, self-advise, and to provide basic "landlord" services to tenants. Accordingly, REIT management teams became more active managers of their assets, enabling companies to differentiate themselves from other REITs by delivering above-average growth.

The REIT Simplification Act of 1994 further streamlined the REIT structure so that companies could operate as fully integrated businesses run by professional managers who were compensated for creating shareholder value, rather than amassing large portfolios. *The REIT Modernization Act of 1999* (the "RMA") became effective January 1, 2001, and further increased REITs' ability to provide tenant services through the use of taxable REIT subsidiaries (TRSs). The result of these Acts was to align the economic interests of REIT management teams with those of the shareholders, making REITs more appealing investments.

Inclusion in Major Stock Indexes Boosted Market Capitalizations and Liquidity

The structural improvements to REITs discussed in the preceding paragraphs, combined with the sector's attractive total returns, continued to attract an increasing level of capital to the REIT industry in the 1990s. As the average market capitalization of REITs and trading volumes increased, it became cost efficient for a broader array of money managers and pension funds to build and maintain a position in REITs as part of their portfolios. Then in 2001, Standard & Poor's admitted the first equity REIT to its 500 Index. During the past 14 years, several REITs have been added and, at the end of 2015, the S&P 500 Index included 24 equity REITs (see Table 1.2 in Chapter 1 for more detail). The inclusion of an increasing number of REITs to broader market indexes that money managers use as benchmarks, combined with a strong investor appetite for the safety and yield offered by REITs, sparked a second sustained inflow of funds into REIT-dedicated mutual funds, from 2000 to 2006. REIT generally outperformed other indexes again from 2009 to 2015, years of slow economic growth and lackluster performance from the broader stock market that followed the Great Recession of 2008–2009.

Changes to FIRPTA Tax Law Should Boost Demand for REITs, Beginning in 2016

Congress enacted the Foreign Investment in Real Property Act (FIRPTA) in 1980 in order to tax the gains on sales that non-U.S.

residents realized when selling U.S. real estate, and also to limit the amount of U.S. property and REITs that foreign investors can purchase. In December 2015, the *Protecting Americans from Tax Hikes Act of 2015* (the "PATH Act"), affected three significant reforms to FIRPTA that should increase foreign investor demand for U.S. REITs. According to NAREIT's analysis, the PATH Act:

1. Increased from 5 percent to 10 percent the ownership stake that a foreign investor can take in a publicly traded REIT without triggering FIRPTA liability (i.e., a tax).
2. Removed the tax penalty that FIRPTA imposes on foreign pension funds that invest in U.S. real estate.
3. Clarified when a listed REIT can be considered "controlled" by U.S. persons so that sales of its stock are not subject to FIRPTA.

The PATH Act also eliminated the tax advantages previously associated with spinoff activity, effectively ending the ability of non-REIT corporations to spin off their real estate holdings into REITs. (REITs' ability to continue spinning off new REITs, such as Vornado [NYSE: VNO] recently did with its retail properties into a new REIT, Urban Edge [NYSE: UE], remains intact and fundamentally unchanged.) REIT spinoffs by non-REITs became increasingly popular in recent years as corporations sought to maximize their valuations by monetizing their real estate holdings in what was a tax-efficient manner. Such spinoffs, however, violated the spirit of the law that supports REITs, which are not intended to provide a legal means for tax avoidance. If the trend toward real estate spinoffs by non-REITs had continued, it very likely would have damaged the REIT industry's reputation for good corporate governance, among other things, and tainted the industry in general. It also would have been a massive step backward to the days before 1986, when many REITs existed because they essentially served as financing vehicles for banks that funded real estate projects. By taking away the tax incentives for non-REITs to divest their real estate holdings into make-a-REIT spinoffs, the PATH Act strengthened the overall integrity of the REIT industry and validated it in the eyes of investors.

Creation of Real Estate GICS Sector in 2016 Should Increase Demand for REITs

On September 1, 2016, S&P and MSCI will create a new Global Industry Classification Standard (GICS) sector called *Real Estate*, which should be a watershed event for REITs. In the industry's initial decades, mortgage REITs outnumbered equity REITs. First impressions linger and, while the number of equity REITs and their combined market capitalizations have been greater than those of mortgage REITs since the 1970s, many money managers viewed REITs as being a type of financial institution. In 1999, when S&P established its ten GICS classifications, they formally categorized REITs into the Financials code, cementing this impression. Real Estate will be the eleventh such investment sector; its formation should materially increase investor awareness of REITs, and further broaden the industry's appeal to individual and institutional investors. (Note that mortgage REITs will remain in S&P's Financials sector.)

REITs versus the Attractiveness of Other Investments (Lessons from History)

Demand for REIT shares is also affected by the availability of alternative investments that investors think may offer better returns. REITs periodically have underperformed other investments during certain time periods, not so much because of real estate fundamentals, but because of market forces that drove investor dollars into growth stocks (1998–1999), into U.S. Treasuries (2004–2005), and into people's mattresses (2007–2008). Conversely, when returns on the S&P500 index are uncertain, REITs generally outperform because investors tend to look for investments that offer safety (or certainty) and yield. The annual total returns presented in Table 7.1 at the beginning of this chapter illustrate these distinct trading periods.

Growth Stocks versus REITs, 1998–1999

REIT share prices have been and will continue to be vulnerable to shifts in investor sentiment toward higher-growth sectors. As shown in Table 7.1, from 1993 through 1997 REITs delivered average annual total returns of 18.5 percent, which kept pace with the similarly strong returns in both the S&P 500 Index and the NASDAQ (see area A of Figure 7.4). Investor sentiment—and their

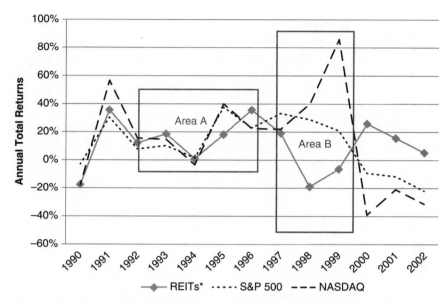

Figure 7.4   REIT Performance versus S&P 500 and NASDAQ, 1990–2002 (Note: Annual total returns on the FTSE NAREIT All REITs Index)

*Annual total returns on the FTSE NAREIT All REITs Index.
Source: NAREIT; S&P Global Market Intelligence.

funds—quickly shifted away from REITs in 1998, however, when the dot-com and tech frenzy accelerated. During this rotation-to-growth, which is also called a *risk-on* trade, investors pulled funds out of defensive investments, like bonds and REITs, and plowed them into the tech-heavy NASDAQ. As Area B in Figure 7.4 shows, REIT returns simply could not compete for investor dollars against the NASDAQ's 40 percent returns in 1998 and their eye-popping 86 percent total return in 1999. Even though fundamental demand for commercial real estate in 1998 and 1999 was strong across all property types, REITs delivered negative total returns of 18.8 percent and 6.5 percent in those respective years. Note that in the spring of 2000, when the dot-com investment bubble burst, investors rotated out of the NASDAQ. This *risk-off* trade by investors is reflected in the NASDAQ's negative 39.2 percent return in 2000 and the REIT industry's positive 25.9 percent total return that same year.

Treasury Yield versus REITs, 2004–2006

Although REITs outperformed the S&P500 and the NASDAQ hand-ily from 2004 to 2006, their returns were muted for several months from yield investors opting out of REITs in favor of U.S. government bonds. Because REITs offer attractive dividend income, investors will (and should) always compare REIT yields to those of fixed-income investments. Historically, REIT yields have been compared against the yield on 10-year U.S. Treasury notes. From March 2004 through June 2006, notable increases in the yield on 10-year U.S. Treasuries precipitated equally distinct declines in REIT valuations. The drop in valuations was short-term and sporadic. Typically, a decline in REIT valuations in reaction to rising interest rates or Treasury yields turns out to be a compelling buying opportunity for REIT investors, especially those that are patient. (Please refer to *REIT Performance in a Rising Interest Rate Environment* later in this chapter for a more detailed discussion of this topic.)

Safety and Yield, and the Big League of Benchmarks, 2000–2006

The bursting of the technology bubble in spring 2000; the accounting scandals at high-profile companies like Enron (formerly NYSE: ENE) in 2001 and 2002; the tragedy associated with events in the United States on September 11, 2001 (9/11). Each event shook investor confidence and negatively affected the broader stock market. Each event also helped fuel a seven-year rally in REITs, as investors increasingly looked to the group as a source of stable, more visible income. As Table 7.1 illustrated earlier in this chapter, REITs outperformed the broader markets from 2000 through 2006. As previously discussed, investors already were rotating from the NASDAQ into investments, like REITs, that offered safety and yield. From 2000 through 2006, REITs issued $200 billion of equity, preferred stock, and debt capital, $65.3 billion of which was common equity. The industry's market capitalization increased approximately 250 percent, from $124 billion at the beginning of 2000 to $438 billion at the end of 2006 (see Figure 7.5). The strong demand for REIT shares was driven both by the fundamental investor appetite for safer, higher-yielding investments, such as REITs, and also by a watershed event for REITs: the addition of the first equity REIT, Equity Office Properties (former NYSE: EOP), to the S&P 500 Index. REITs had made it to the big league of benchmarks, and the added visibility from inclusion in the S&P 500 Index supercharged market dynamics that already favored REIT investment.

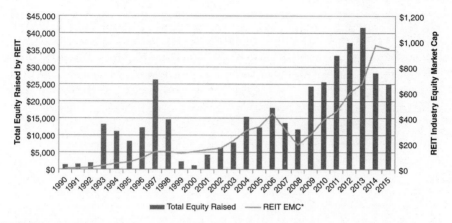

Figure 7.5   REIT Common Stock Issuance and Growth in Industry Market Cap, 1990–2015

Source: NAREIT.

REITs During the Financial Crisis of 2007–2008

One of the most reliable ways investors can gauge market risk is to observe the weekly rate of change in 10-year commercial mortgage-backed security (CMBS) spreads. (If investors do not have access to a Bloomberg terminal, they can request this information from their financial advisors.) When the CMBS spreads increase (or *widen*) over the prior week's level, then the market is factoring in more risk, such as the risk of recession or other events that would affect the broader markets.

Changes in the spreads on 10-year CMBS have proven to be a highly accurate predictor of short-term returns in the REIT market. For example, the 10-year CMBS spreads, which are expressed as a number of basis points above the yield on 10-year U.S. Treasury notes, dramatically widened by 540 percent throughout 2007, from 123 basis points at the beginning of the year, to 790 basis points. By the end of 2008, 10-year CMBS spreads had exploded to 5,362 basis points over Treasuries. As Figure 7.6 and Table 7.1 show, REIT share prices declined commensurately as the CMBS spreads increased. Even though the global financial crisis of 2007–2008 began in the overleveraged housing market, rather than in the commercial property markets, REITs delivered total returns of negative 17.8 percent in 2007 and negative 37.3 percent in 2008.

> ### Investment Tip
>
> If a credit crisis is possible, stocks associated with real estate, such as REITs, are likely to underperform the broader market due to investor fears—real and imagined—about the sustainability of corporate dividends and the risk of defaulting on loans scheduled to mature in the near term.

Investors feared that all companies, including REITs, would either refinance maturing debt at abnormally high interest rates or, worse, that they might not be able to refinance debt "at any price," in which case management may choose to dilute existing shareholders with an "emergency" equity issuance to raise capital. Any of these pricey refinancing alternatives would dampen future REIT profitability. As discussed in Chapter 3, between 2007 and 2009 only one publicly traded equity REIT entered bankruptcy to restructure its debt, but nearly a third cut or suspended their dividends to preserve capital during these highly uncertain market conditions. Once REITs began issuing new equity—at prices that were highly dilutive to existing shareholders and to future earnings—it became clear that the industry and its constituents would endure. REIT valuations recovered fairly rapidly in 2009, as a result.

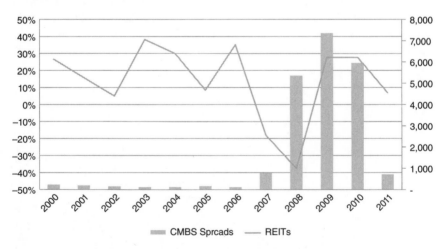

Figure 7.6   REITs Returns versus 10-Year CMBS Spreads, 2000–2011. (Note: REIT performance as measured by the annual total returns for the FTSE NAREIT All REITs Index. CMBS Spreads are for 10-year, BBB notes at year-end, in basis points.)

Source: NAREIT; Bloomberg & Wells Fargo Securities, LLC.

Company Attributes That Affect Performance

The REIT industry comprises an increasingly wide array of commercial real estate. Each REIT in every property sector is governed by three broad forces that affect their performance, both on an absolute basis and relative to other REITs: real estate fundamentals, lease structure and duration, and cost of capital. Real estate fundamentals, and especially the degree to which demand for a property type is consistent throughout different phases of the economic cycle, affect a REIT's profitability over the long term. A property sector like health care, for example, benefits from steady (or *inelastic*) demand for its product; regardless of economic growth, people need access to health-care services. Consistent demand translates into steady occupancy levels, which should translate into a consistently profitable REIT. Different lease structures and durations discussed in Chapter 4 result in different operating margins, which also affect operating profits. Lastly, how a management team finances its operations is an increasingly important factor in determining long-term total returns. When the economy slows or goes into recession, the profitability of any real estate will decline. But stock performance across property sectors and among companies can differ widely due to these three basic extrinsic and intrinsic factors, which the next several pages explain in more detail.

Real Estate Fundamentals and REIT Performance

Real estate is tangible, and investors often take comfort in the visible signs that indicate how the local economy is fairing. A full parking lot at an office building or at a retail center signals times are good; "For Rent" or "Space Available" signs can signal the beginning of an economic slowdown. Often, however, REIT share price performance does not reflect what investors observe. Retailers often go bankrupt during a recession, but retail REITs rarely do. In fact, REIT share prices frequently appear to perform without a direct relationship to what is happening in the underlying property markets. Such counterintuitive behavior typically occurs when the economy is in transition, either going into or coming out of recession. The explanation for this occasional disconnect between REITs and real estate fundamentals lies in understanding the tension that exists between the fact that real estate is a *lagging* economic indicator, whereas REIT share prices (like any publicly traded equity) are functions of *future* earnings expectations. The following pages address the periodic disconnect between real estate fundamentals and REIT share performance.

The Property Cycle and the Economic Cycle

Market forces discussed earlier in this chapter typically affect REIT performance in the short or medium term. Supply of and demand for commercial space, which are the two primary real estate fundamentals, affect REITs' longer-term operating performance and, by extension, returns for shareholders. When a property market is inundated with too much new construction (*supply*), vacancy rates increase and landlords decrease rental rates in an attempt to keep existing tenants in their spaces. Whether landlords experience increases in vacancy or declines in rental rates (or both), their profit margins decline.

Although assessing the supply of competitive buildings by each property type is an important component of selecting REITs that may outperform (or avoiding those that may underperform), it is difficult for most individuals to gauge new construction in multiple markets with much accuracy. Apart from subscribing to a data provider that tracks supply, most investors rely on anecdotal information gleaned from newspapers and conversations with local real estate brokers. More dedicated individuals may even count cranes they see in cities they visit to assess whether a market may be getting overbuilt. It is far easier to estimate and anticipate demand for property in each market by interpreting current economic data. By understanding how the real property cycle interacts with the economic cycle, it is possible to make smart and timely REIT investments.

The property cycle encompasses how occupancies and rents in a market fluctuate, and whether new construction "makes sense." Overbuilding of certain property types has precipitated economic declines in the past when demand was not sufficient to fill new buildings, leading to widespread defaults on debt, such as was seen during the S&L crisis. The "housing bubble" and related defaults are often cited for triggering the Great Recession of 2008–2009 in the United States. Setting aside periods of severe market dislocation, the real property cycle generally responds in predictable ways to what is occurring in the underlying economy. Figure 7.7 illustrates how the property cycle responds to the economic cycle. Each phase is then discussed.

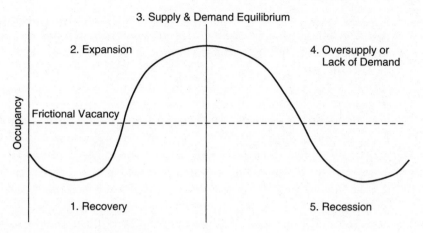

Figure 7.7   The Property Cycle

1. **Recovery**—After the economy emerges from recession, the recovery period for real estate is characterized by a lack of new construction because rental rates are not improved enough, generally, to merit the cost of new development. (Land prices, labor, and construction materials, such as steel, tend to appreciate or inflate over time, making new development more costly from one cycle to the next.) Because demand for space is recovering without the addition of new supply, occupancies rise. REITs with cash on hand (or low levels of debt) are able to buy assets at attractive discounts to replacement cost, enabling them to deliver outsized returns on their investment.

2. **Expansion**—During an economic expansion, occupancy continues to increase but at a decreasing rate from prior periods. Landlords are able to push for higher rents on new leasing to the point that assets can no longer be purchased at discounts to replacement costs. As rental rates rise, new construction begins to become profitable again.

3. **Supply-and-Demand Equilibrium**—This is a state of commercial property nirvana that is rarely achieved, in large part because private developers tend to overbuild their markets (at least slightly) during each cycle.

4. **Oversupply or Lack of Demand**—As the economy begins to slow, property markets continue to add new supply, albeit at

a reduced pace. This is because new construction started during the late phase of the economic expansion frequently is delivered into a softening economy. A "construction cycle" is the time it takes to erect a building, usually expressed in months or years. The longer the construction cycle is for a property type, the greater the risk that the property sector will experience periods of oversupply. High-rise office buildings, for example, can take two or more years to construct, and that is after the developer receives all the zoning and necessary approvals, and then breaks ground on the site. During construction time, the economy may change for the worse, resulting in some office buildings being delivered to a market that no longer has sufficient demand to fill the new space. During periods of oversupply or declining demand, vacancies increase. However, rents may still increase for a period of time because not all tenants' business will feel the effects of a slowing economy at the same time.

5. **Recession**—An extension of the oversupply phase, property markets can slip into recession if too much supply is delivered into an economy that is in recession. The lack of demand for space, compounded by the new square feet coming onto the market initially, causes some tenants to sublease their unused space. Investors should watch for signs of increasing levels of subleased space, also called "shadow supply," to signal a market's decline. Then direct vacancies begin to rise as tenants choose not to renew some or all of their previously leased space. In such an environment, landlords will offer concessions and lower rental rates to maintain as much occupancy as possible. The magnitude of such concessions varies by property type and by market.

Performance by Property Type

As discussed in Chapter 5, in addition to the "basic foods groups" of office, industrial, retail, and apartment buildings, REITs own and operate nearly every type of property imaginable. The drivers of demand for each property type also differ. Table 7.2 summarizes how the different property types of REITs have performed over time. Before discussing how different economic news is likely to affect the performance of different REITs, there are two broad-based factors that influence tenant demand for all types of space.

Table 7.2 Historical Total Returns by Property Sector

Annual Total Returns (a)

Property Sector	1994	1995	1996	1997	1998	1999	2000	2001	2002	2003	2004	2005	2006	2007	2008	2009	2010	2011	2012	2013	2014	2015	Average
Industrial/Office	16.6%	25.8%	44.4%	27.5%	−14.4%	3.4%	33.4%	7.1%	0.9%	33.3%	25.2%	12.9%	39.4%	−14.9%	−50.3%	29.2%	17.0%	−1.5%	19.1%	6.0%	24.3%	–	13.5%
Office	2.9%	38.8%	51.8%	29.0%	−17.4%	4.3%	35.5%	6.7%	−6.8%	34.0%	23.3%	13.1%	45.2%	−19.0%	−41.1%	35.5%	18.4%	−0.8%	3.3%	5.6%	25.7%	0.3%	13.1%
Industrial	18.7%	16.2%	37.2%	19.0%	−11.7%	3.9%	28.6%	7.4%	17.3%	33.1%	34.1%	15.4%	28.9%	0.4%	−67.5%	12.2%	18.9%	−5.2%	31.3%	7.4%	21.0%	2.6%	12.2%
Office & Other	NA	NA	40.8%	27.9%	−8.9%	−0.7%	32.0%	8.2%	8.6%	31.3%	19.6%	7.4%	28.3%	−33.1%	−34.0%	34.9%	8.8%	2.7%	20.8%	5.6%	23.1%	–	11.7%
Retail	3.0%	5.1%	34.6%	16.9%	−4.9%	−11.8%	18.0%	30.4%	21.1%	46.8%	40.2%	11.8%	29.0%	−15.8%	−48.4%	27.2%	33.4%	12.2%	26.7%	1.9%	27.6%	4.6%	14.1%
Shopping Centers	1.3%	7.4%	33.5%	21.4%	−7.0%	−10.7%	15.1%	29.9%	17.7%	43.1%	36.3%	9.3%	34.9%	−17.7%	−38.8%	−1.7%	30.8%	−0.7%	25.0%	5.0%	30.0%	4.7%	12.2%
Regional Malls	8.8%	3.0%	45.3%	13.7%	−2.6%	−4.9%	23.5%	31.9%	24.6%	52.2%	45.0%	16.5%	23.8%	−15.9%	−60.6%	63.0%	34.6%	22.0%	28.2%	−1.0%	32.6%	4.2%	17.2%
Free Standing	−5.5%	31.6%	30.9%	17.7%	−6.2%	−4.9%	8.9%	24.0%	21.8%	35.9%	32.9%	−0.5%	30.7%	−0.4%	−15.1%	25.9%	37.4%	0.4%	22.5%	7.3%	9.7%	5.9%	14.1%
Residential	2.3%	12.0%	29.5%	16.3%	−8.1%	9.5%	34.3%	9.0%	−6.0%	25.9%	32.7%	13.7%	38.9%	−25.2%	−24.9%	30.8%	46.0%	15.4%	6.9%	−5.4%	40.0%	17.1%	14.1%
Multifamily	2.2%	12.3%	28.9%	16.0%	−8.8%	10.7%	35.5%	8.7%	−6.2%	25.5%	34.7%	14.7%	39.9%	−25.4%	−25.1%	30.4%	47.0%	15.1%	6.9%	−6.2%	39.6%	16.5%	14.2%
Manufactured Homes	3.3%	10.7%	34.9%	18.6%	−0.9%	−2.8%	20.9%	13.7%	−4.1%	30.0%	6.4%	−2.6%	15.3%	−19.3%	−20.2%	40.9%	27.0%	20.4%	7.1%	10.5%	46.2%	25.7%	12.8%
Single Family Homes	–	–	–	–	–	–	–	–	–	–	–	–	–	–	–	–	–	–	–	–	–	1.8%	–
Diversified	−6.0%	21.1%	34.0%	21.7%	−22.1%	−14.4%	24.1%	12.5%	4.2%	40.3%	32.4%	9.9%	38.0%	−22.3%	−28.2%	17.0%	23.8%	2.8%	12.2%	4.3%	27.2%	−0.5%	10.5%
Hotels	−8.9%	30.8%	49.2%	30.1%	−52.8%	−16.1%	45.8%	−8.6%	−1.5%	31.7%	32.7%	9.8%	28.2%	−22.4%	−59.7%	67.2%	42.8%	−14.3%	12.5%	27.2%	32.5%	−24.4%	10.5%
Health Care	4.1%	24.9%	20.4%	15.8%	−17.4%	−24.8%	25.8%	51.9%	4.8%	53.6%	21.0%	1.8%	44.5%	2.1%	−12.0%	24.6%	19.2%	13.6%	20.4%	−7.1%	33.3%	−7.3%	14.2%
Self Storage	8.9%	34.4%	42.8%	3.4%	−7.2%	−8.0%	14.7%	43.2%	0.6%	38.1%	29.7%	26.6%	23.6%	−24.8%	5.0%	8.4%	19.2%	35.2%	19.9%	9.5%	31.4%	40.7%	19.2%
Triple-Net & Specialty	−5.2%	27.6%	46.1%	27.3%	−24.3%	−25.7%	−31.6%	7.6%	−5.4%	38.6%	26.9%	10.4%	23.6%	14.6%	−25.7%	31.5%	b	–	–	–	–	–	8.5%
Timber	NA	NA	–	–	–	–	–	–	–	–	–	NA	NA	NA	NA	NA	NA	7.7%	37.1%	7.9%	8.6%	−7.0%	10.8%
Infrastructure	NA	NA	–	–	–	–	–	–	–	–	–	NA	NA	NA	NA	NA	NA	NA	29.9%	20.2%	20.2%	3.7%	18.5%
Data Centers	–	–	–	–	–	–	–	–	–	–	–	–	–	–	–	–	–	–	–	–	–	1.5%	–
Specialty	–	–	–	–	–	–	–	–	–	–	–	–	–	–	–	–	–	–	–	–	–	1.7%	1.7%
FN Equity REIT Index	3.2%	15.3%	35.3%	20.3%	−17.5%	−4.6%	26.4%	13.9%	3.8%	37.1%	31.6%	12.2%	35.1%	−15.7%	−37.7%	28.0%	28.0%	8.3%	18.1%	2.5%	30.1%	3.2%	12.6%
FN Mortgage REIT Index	−24.3%	63.4%	50.9%	3.8%	−29.2%	−33.2%	16.0%	77.3%	31.1%	57.4%	18.4%	−23.2%	19.3%	−42.3%	−31.3%	24.6%	22.6%	−2.4%	19.9%	−2.0%	17.9%	−8.9%	10.3%
Hybrid REIT Index	4.0%	23.0%	29.4%	10.8%	−34.0%	−35.9%	11.6%	50.7%	23.3%	56.2%	23.9%	−10.8%	40.9%	−34.8%	−75.5%	41.3%	c	–	–	–	–	–	–
FN ALL REITs Index	0.8%	18.3%	35.8%	18.9%	−18.8%	−6.5%	25.9%	15.5%	5.2%	38.5%	30.4%	8.3%	34.4%	−17.8%	−37.3%	27.5%	27.6%	7.3%	20.1%	3.2%	27.2%	2.3%	12.1%

Source: NAREIT.

Shaded areas highlight top-performing property sector each year.

a Returns are based on monthly returns for 1994-1998, and daily returns for 1999 and thereafter.

b NAREIT discontinued tracking Triple-Net/Specialty REITs in 2010, and reclassified the constituent companies into other categories.

c NAREIT discontinued its FTSE NAREIT Hybrid and REIT Index in 2010.

Location and Efficiency Matter

Demand for a property is measured by how fully occupied a building is, especially when compared to similar, "competing" buildings in a market. If office building A is 90 percent occupied and office building B is only 80 percent occupied, it is likely that office building A is both more modern and functionally efficient for office tenants than building B, and/or building A may be in a better location than B. The average rents in place at a building also help investors gauge how desirable a property is, as better locations almost always garner higher rental rates. Regardless of whether the underlying economy is expanding or contracting, office building A has the competitive advantages of functionality and location, and should benefit from higher tenant demand throughout the economic cycle than building B.

"Defensive" Property Types Enjoy Steady Demand

Some types of property are considered defensive because they generate consistent earnings and/or maintain fairly high occupancy rates regardless of the economic or business cycle. For example, triple-net REITs (see Chapters 4 and 5) employ long-term leases that provide predictable earnings streams in any economic condition. The only disruptions to the landlord's cash flows are when a tenant goes bankrupt or does not renew a lease when it expires. Neighborhood or community shopping centers also tend to be defensive assets, owing to the fact that they usually are anchored by a grocery or drugstore, both of which enjoy fairly inelastic demand for their goods. In contrast, hotels have no leases with their customers, and experience higher vacancies when consumers cut back business and leisure travel when the economy slows. Investors, therefore, may enhance their returns by accurately assessing the direction of the economy and aligning that view with REITs in property sectors that are likely to benefit from current and expected economic conditions.

If the economy has a high probability of slipping into recession, property sector returns from the recent global financial crisis are instructive. As Figure 7.8 demonstrates, the more defensive property sectors (net-lease REITs, health-care, self-storage, and industrial REITs) significantly outperformed less defensive asset types (malls, office apartments, and hotels).

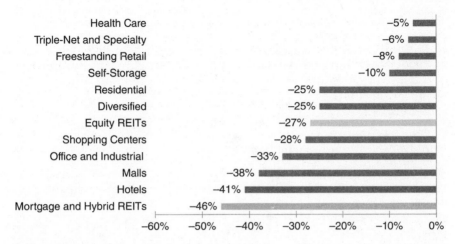

Figure 7.8   Total Returns of Different Property Types During the 2007–2008 Global Financial Crisis

Source: NAREIT.

Recall that Table 7.2 provides historical total return data by property type, and highlights which sectors delivered the higher total return each year. Table 7.3 summarizes how different economic statistics that are in the news typically affect demand for different types of commercial property. Investors can use the information contained in both tables to observe how different property types performed in past economic recessions and recoveries. To facilitate such an analysis, there is a more detailed discussion of how different types of REITs perform during certain economic conditions.

To illustrate the information in Table 7.3, assume the economy is likely to go into recession within the next year, that unemployment will rise, and corporate and consumer spending will decline. Assume for now that interest rates remain stable. (The last section of this chapter addresses *REIT Performance in a Rising Interest Rate Environment.*) The following information is a generalization about how REIT shares in different property sectors are likely to trade in advance of an economic downturn:

- Hotel REITs are likely to underperform because investors will expect reduced spending to result in less travel, or demand for hotel rooms. Because hotel REITs generally have no leases, their stock prices immediately reflect lower expected future profits.

Table 7.3   Economic Drivers of Demand for Real Estate

Economic Indicator	Impact on Demand for Space		
	Direct	Indirect	None
Rising Unemployment	Office (–) Apartments (–)(+)[a]	Industrial (–) Retail (–) Hotels (–) Self-Storage (+)	Health Care
Decreased Corporate Spending	Hotels (–) Office (–)	Industrial (+)[b] Apartments (–)	Health Care Retail Self-Storage
Decreased Consumer Spending	Industrial (–) Hotels (–) Retail (–)	Apartments (–) Office (–) Self-Storage (–)	Health Care
Rising Interest Rates	Mortgage REITs (–)[c]	Apartments (+)(–)[d e] Industrial (–)[e] Hotels (–)[e] Health Care (–)[e] Office (–)[e] Retail (–)[e] Self-Storage (–)[e]	

[a]If unemployment is high for an extended period of time, demand for apartments may increase as some homeowners will need to sell their homes (or be foreclosed upon) and become renters.

[b]While a prolonged recession likely would result in decreased demand for industrial space to accommodate a smaller volume of goods flowing to market, in the short term, inventories typically accumulate, causing a modest, short-lived increase in demand for industrial space.

[c]Rising interest rates would lower the positive spreads most mortgage REITs could lock in on investments. The "spread" is the difference between where a REIT can invest capital versus the cost of that capital.

[d]A rise in long-term interest rates would make home buying less affordable, which would generate incremental demand for apartments.

[e]An increase in interest rates would negatively affect any REIT that needed to refinance debt, provided that the interest rate on new debt is higher than the rate on the debt that is maturing. However, any such dilution to future cash flow would be limited to specific debt maturities that need to be refinanced, rather than the REIT's entire debt profile.

- Apartment REITs are likely to outperform because demand for rental properties may remain steady or actually increase, making them a defensive asset class. There are three sources of demand for apartments in a market: (1) newly hired workers who typically rent for a period of time before buying a house, (2) homeowners who need to re-enter the rental market again because they cannot afford the costs of home ownership and maintenance, and (3) "empty-nesters" who decide to sell their houses and move into rental units (usually in more densely populated cities or town centers) in order to avoid the hassles of homeownership. As long as a market has not become overbuilt with too many new residential units, apartment REIT landlords are likely to fare better than landlords of some other property types.

- Shopping center REITs are likely to outperform other sectors during a slow or soft economic environment because they are also defensive asset classes. Many shopping centers are anchored by grocery stores and/or pharmacies. The essential nature of the goods sold at these stores generates steady traffic at such centers, regardless of the broader economic trends.
- Self-storage REITs are another defensive property type. Demand for space tends to be steady as long as people are moving from one location or household to another, whether it is part of taking a new job or downsizing into a smaller household after children have graduated college, for instance. Stable households also use self-storage to store seasonal and other items that may not fit into their attics and other home storage areas.
- Industrial REITs are a defensive asset class because goods need to be stored and distributed to retailer and consumers throughout the economic cycle. Demand for industrial space is driven by population growth and the associated growth in consumer spending, including the increasing use of shopping online with the Internet. At the onset of a recession, demand for industrial space may actually increase because manufacturers are not selling their goods as quickly, and have not yet adjusted to the lower demand for product. Industrial space demand is not completely inelastic, however, and vacancies do rise modestly during a recession, causing the industrial REITs to sometimes underperform other sectors.
- Office REITs actually perform well for the first year or two of an economic slowdown, which is counterintuitive because demand for office space is correlated to job growth. A decrease in nonfarm payrolls (or office-using jobs) translates into lower demand for office space, but the tenants cannot give back unneeded space until their lease expires. As a result, the inevitable increase in office vacancy during a recession takes a few years to materialize. Once landlords (REITs) begin

experiencing "roll-down" in their rents (meaning the new market rents they negotiate on expiring space is below the rent that was being paid), their stock prices tend to underperform other sectors for two or three years until they have worked through their rent roll-down.

- Health-care REITs are a very defensive asset class because people always use health and medical services, regardless of what the economy is doing. As the population grows, there is more demand for health-care services and, by extension, more need for new, efficient, well-located health-care real estate.

How Lease Length and Structure Affect REIT Returns

Most investors have heard or read that "real estate is a lagging indicator." Whatever the economy is doing, it takes a number of months or years for an office building or shopping mall to reflect economic changes in the form of higher/lower rents and occupancy levels. The longer the leases the landlord has negotiated with tenants, the longer it will take a property's cash flows to reflect any change—good or bad—in the local economy. In other words, real estate lags because it has leases.

Existing leases generate revenues even when there is no new leasing or demand for property in the market. As a result, landlords (REITs) can deliver relatively solid 4 to 8 percent earnings growth even as the economy slips into recession. Similarly, when the economy begins expanding again, existing leases cannot be marked to higher current market rents until they expire. So it takes varying amounts of time for changes in the economy to trickle through different property types. Knowing the average lease length and type of lease used by a REIT, therefore, is helpful in determining when to buy or sell its stock.

Real estate performance lags economic conditions, depending on the leases in place. The longer the lease length, the longer the property's cash flow takes to reflect what's happening in the economy. Knowing the average lease length and the type of lease structure a REIT employs helps predict how a REIT's shares may trade during times of economic expansion and contraction.

For example, the longer average lease term associated with office space is the main reason why office REITs often outperform in the early phases of a recession. Their multiyear average lease term delays the effects of current employment trends from manifesting in their rents and occupancies for several years. Assuming the landlord prudently staggers lease expirations throughout the portfolio, five-year leases would translate into approximately one-fifth, or 20 percent of leases expiring (or rolling) each year. Office landlords mark the expiring leases to current market rents, and they try to lease any vacancy their portfolio contains. During the early phase of an economic decline, office REIT returns are buffered by the existence of in-place leases, and the sector tends to outperform the average REIT. Conversely, office REITs tend to underperform the REIT industry during the early stages of an economic recovery, as rents that were negotiated in better economic times expire and roll to potentially lower market rents.

Lease Length and Volatility (Risk)

As a general rule, REITs that own commercial properties with shorter initial lease lengths tend to trade with more volatility—meaning they experience greater percentage change in their daily stock price—than REITs that employ longer leases. Figure 7.9 graphically presents where REITs focused on different types of property rank in terms of trading volatility, which is a proxy for risk. The nature of the demand for each property type, which was discussed earlier in this chapter, also plays a part in a stock's trading volatility. For example, demand for hotels is more cyclical, or dependent on broader economic trends, than demand for warehouse space. People do not have to travel, but goods have to be stored and/or distributed to grocery stores and other vendors regardless of the economic state.

In Figure 7.9, property types in quadrant 1 generally are appropriate for investors who have a higher risk tolerance. REITs in quadrant 4 are focused on property types that are less volatile, making these types of REITs more appropriate for risk-averse investors.

Shares of REITs that own properties with shorter-term leases tend to trade with more volatility than those with longer lease lengths.

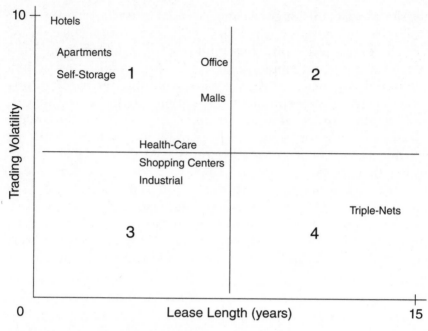

Figure 7.9   Riskiness of Different Property Types. (Note: Quadrant #1 = highest volatility/risk; quadrant #4 = lowest volatility/risk.)

Long-Term Leases = Low Volatility

As discussed in Chapters 4 and 5, REITs that use triple-net leases typically rent their properties to tenants for 10 years or longer. During times of economic expansion, the triple-net landlord is not able to mark existing leases to market and misses out on potential windfalls from rent increases. Similar to how municipal bonds and other fixed-income investments generally underperform equities during an economic expansion, REITs that use long-term triple-net leases also tend to underperform other REIT sectors when investors seek growth over safety. However, during tough economic times, long-term leases produce steady, highly visible lease revenue. When investors are uncertain about the economy, they tend to invest in defensive assets—ones that will produce steady returns and/or cash dividends, regardless of the economic environment. During uncertain or recessionary economic times, triple-net REITs tend to outperform other property types. (Note that NAREIT does not have a triple-net REIT classification; as Chapter 5 discusses, REITs that use triple-net leases tend to be those companies in the freestanding retail, health-care, and diversified property types.)

Short-Term Leases = High Volatility

Hotel REIT cash flows are more like those of an operating company than of other REITs. Unlike most traditional REITs that receive contractual rents from leases with tenants, hotel REITs do not have "guest leases." Guests stay at hotels for business or leisure, and usually only for a night or two. Though advanced bookings by large groups for conventions or weddings can provide a margin of visibility for room demand, hotel operators essentially need to lease up their properties from scratch each day. During flush economic times, hotel landlords can increase prices and achieve strong, double-digit earnings growth. Therefore, when it looks like the economy is coming out of recession, hotel REITs tend to outperform other REIT-asset classes, because investors will pay a higher premium today to participate in the expected strong rent growth they will enjoy. In a down economy, however, hotel operators often have to cut their daily rates (and a portion of their employees) to maintain profitability. Unsurprisingly, hotel REITs tend to underperform when the economy is slowing down and/or at risk of slipping into recession.

Hotel REITs' Higher Volatility Is an Investment Opportunity

The cyclical nature of demand for lodging is a major reason why hotel REITs trade with greater levels of volatility than the average REIT. This volatility lends itself to greater risks for would-be investors but also to greater potential returns. As Table 7.4 illustrates, hotel REIT annual total returns tend to diverge from that of the broader REIT industry. For example, in 2008 when the U.S. economy was sliding into recession, the average REIT declined 41 percent and hotel REITs fell 63 percent. Conversely, in 2009, when the economy stabilized and started to recover, the average REIT rebounded 27 percent, which was impressive but still paled in comparison to the 63 percent price appreciation enjoyed by hotel REITs.

Because they trade with greater volatility, hotel REITs are one of the few property types investors may want to buy opportunistically when they are at depressed levels, and sell when the stocks—and the underlying economy—are recovered. There is an old expression that the only people who can time the stock market are fools and liars. However, using a contrarian trading strategy with hotel REITs, over time, does seem to be possible and should help investors avoid "buying high and selling low."

Table 7.4 Hotel REIT performance vs. US GDP

	1990	1991	1992	1993	1994	1995	1996	1997	1998	1999	2000	2001	2002	2003	2004	2005	2006	2007	2008	2009	2010
Hotel REITs[a]	−74%	−14%	−9%	105%	−4%	21%	43%	25%	−54%	−29%	31%	−13%	−5%	25%	29%	6%	23%	−27%	−63%	63%	38%
All Equity REITs[b]	−28%	25%	6%	13%	−4%	7%	26%	13%	−22%	−12%	17%	6%	−3%	28%	24%	7%	30%	−19%	−41%	21%	23%
U.S. GDP[c]	2%	0%	3%	3%	4%	3%	4%	5%	4%	5%	4%	1%	2%	3%	4%	3%	3%	2%	0%	−3%	3%

[a] Source: SNL Financial; Price-only.
[b] Source: FTSE NAREIT Equity REIT Index; Price-only.
[c] Source: Bureau of Economic Analysis.
Recessions years are shaded.

126

Weighted Average Cost of Capital and REIT Performance

Chapter 1 highlighted the fact that REITs with above-average lever-age do not have as much financial flexibility as REITs that operate with lower levels of debt. As a result, the more highly leveraged REITs often are not able to take advantage of opportunistic investments. Research has demonstrated that REIT management teams who oper-ate with more leverage typically underperform their lower-leveraged peers. This section discusses the perils of debt and the overall impor-tance of a REIT's cost of capital.

Debt as a Four-Letter Word

The global financial crisis of 2007–2008 illustrated somewhat dramatically that balance sheets matter. According to an analysis by S&P Global Market Intelligence, of the 128 REITs that were paying a dividend in 2007, 84—or roughly two-thirds—cut their dividend over the following two years. The portfolio of 44 REITs that did not cut their dividends (Keepers) delivered a 135 percent return from the beginning of 2008 through 2015, whereas the cutter portfolio returned only 78 percent. Figure 7.10 plots the performance of these Keeper versus Cutter REITs. Furthermore, studies by numerous reputable firms such as Green Street Advisors have demonstrated how REITs that operate their business with lower levels of debt tend to outperform other, more leveraged REITs.

The 44 Keeper REITs were those that had relatively lower levels of debt going into 2007, before the crisis took hold of the markets. Specifically, the median 2007 debt-to-EBITDA multiples of Keepers was 5.67 times, and for the Cutters it was 7.23 times, clearly demon-strating how higher leverage levels lead to dividend cuts during the global financial crisis. (Debt-to-EBITDA is defined and discussed in Chapter 8.)

Competitive Advantage or Disadvantage—Why Cost of Capital Matters

One of the main reasons why REITs with more highly leveraged balance sheets tend to underperform is that they miss opportunities to acquire assets at deeply discounted prices during times of market dislocation, such as we saw during 2007 through 2009. REITs with too much debt going into a recession or market crisis simply don't have the financial flexibility to capitalize on market opportunities.

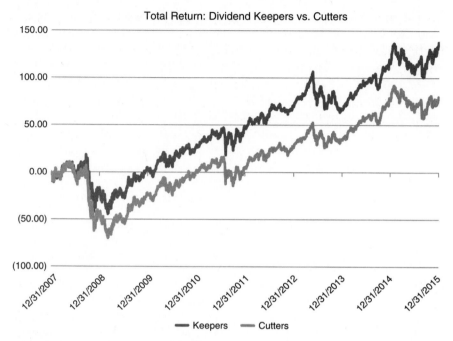

Figure 7.10   Returns of REITs That Cut versus Those That Did Not Cut Dividends, 2007–2009

Source: S&P Global Market Intelligence.

By contrast, REITs with lower leverage can and do, thereby meriting a higher relative valuation from investors.

Even in normal market conditions, a REIT's weighted average cost of capital (WACC) affects stock price performance. As Chapter 8 discusses in more detail, WACC is calculated by adding up a company's debt, preferred stock, and common equity, weighting each portion of capital by the average cost of each piece. Using an oversimplified example, if Rockland REIT has $50 million of debt outstanding with a weighted average interest rate of 5 percent, $10 million of preferred stock with a 6.5 percent coupon rate, and $100 million of common equity with an estimated cost of 9 percent, then Rockland REIT's WACC is 7.6 percent, which essentially is this company's cost of doing business. In order to make a profit on new investments, Rockland REIT needs to invest its capital into opportunities that return more than 7.6 percent. When competing for an acquisition property or development opportunity, REITs that have a

WACC that is less than 7.6 percent will have a competitive advantage over Rockland REIT. Lastly, Rockland REIT's management, if they feel they are under pressure to grow, may commit "unforced errors," such as investing in high-yielding but low-quality assets. Ultimately, a poor allocation of capital into subpar assets will translate into a lower stock valuation for Rockland REIT. Rather than chase growth through questionable investments, Rockland REIT's management would serve shareholders better by paying down debt, which will help lower its WACC to more competitive levels.

REIT Performance in a Rising Interest Rate Environment

Perhaps one of the greatest misunderstandings about REITs is how rising interest rates will affect their future profitability. By extension, some of the most attractive buying opportunities in REITs have resulted when investors erroneously drove down REIT share prices because they expected interest rates to increase. The likely root of confusion is the fact that S&P historically has included REITs in the Financials sector. As discussed in Chapters 1 and 5, mortgage REITs are more like banks and may suffer lower profitability during periods of rising interest rates. In contrast, economics of the leases in place at equity REITs are not affected by rising rates. Equity REIT profitability should only be affected on the margin to the extent they refinance maturing debt at higher interest rates. After S&P launches the Real Estate GICS sector on September 1, 2016, equity REIT stock price performance should progressively de-couple from that of Financials (which will continue to include mortgage REITs) as investors become more educated about how real estate performs in a rising rate environment.

Cohen & Steers (NYSE: CNS) periodically publishes research on REIT industry topics, including how REITs have performed in past interest-rate cycles. The following observations are reproduced with their permission from *REIT Opportunities in a Rising-Rate Market (June 2015)*:

> We believe interest-rate-driven corrections may present buying opportunities for long-term investors .... Share prices of REITs have become increasingly sensitive to bond yields, more often rising as yields fall and falling as yields rise. Since the first hints in 2013 that the Federal Reserve could taper quantitative easing

("QE"). Correlations between REITs and the broad stock market have declined ..., while correlations with bonds have risen above historical levels .... Periods of rising rates may cause earnings multiples to contract—like they did in April [of 2015]—due to fears that higher yields will negatively impact property values. Ultimately, however, we believe REIT performance will be driven by fundamental factors such as cash flows, competitive positioning and the value of a company's property holdings relative to the private market.

Their report expands on the following conclusions:

- Rising bond yields may cause negative market reactions (among REITs) in the short term. However, REITs tend to recover as time goes on, as higher yields are often a byproduct of improving economic growth, which can lead to stronger demand for real estate.
- U.S. REITs have delivered 19 percent returns on average in the 12 months following corrections that pushed REIT prices below their net asset value (see Table 7.5).

Table 7.5   U.S. REIT Returns After Trading Discounts to NAV

Months When REITs Began Trading at Discounts to NAV After 6+ Months at Premiums to NAV	Discounts to NAV at End of Month	12 Months Later[a]	
		Total Return	Premium or Discount to NAV
October 1994	−0.7%	12.2%	−1.7%
November 1995	−0.1%	29.2%	19.0%
August 1998	−7.7%	2.7%	−9.2%
September 2002	−0.7%	25.2%	11.8%
December 2005	−10.8%	35.1%	3.8%
May 2007	−3.7%	−11.9%	−3.3%
September 2011	−6.0%	32.6%	5.5%
August 2013	−5.1%	24.1%	5.0%
September 2014	−1.1%	–	–
April 2015	−1.6%	–	–
Simple Average	−3.8%	18.7%	3.9%

At May 31, 2015. Source: UBS and Cohen & Steers.
Performance data quoted represents past performance. Past performance is no guarantee of future results.
[a]There is no entry when less than 12 months of data is available.

Conclusion

Since 1990, REITs have evolved into a liquid, institutional invest-ment class. With greater liquidity comes greater volatility, which when harnessed and interpreted appropriately, can lead to greater returns. As the industry has evolved, company-specific character-istics, rather than broad-brush industry trends, increasingly have driven REIT stock performance. Property type, WACC, and lease structure collectively determine total returns in different economic environments, with property type (that is, fundamental demand) being the dominant governor. Investors can choose REITs based on their outlook for the economy and in accordance with their individual tolerance for risk.

CHAPTER 8

Analyzing REITs

This chapter is designed to provide investors with an understanding of the performance and valuation metrics required to evaluate REITs. When used in combination, these measurements provide insight into the financial flexibility, dividend safety, and long-term growth prospects of companies.

One of the more enduring challenges in analyzing REITs—individually and for comparison purposes—is the lack of standardized reporting. Each publicly traded REIT files quarterly Form 10-Q and annual Form 10-K reports with the SEC. These reports provide information about a company's history and summarize its latest financial performance. Although REITs report results in accordance with GAAP, each company reports slightly differently. For example, one company may detail the line items needed to adjust funds from operation (FFO) to Adjusted FFO (AFFO), whereas another REIT may not disclose its AFFO calculation.

In addition to reading a company's earnings releases, and SEC filings, investors should also obtain the supplemental information package that most REITs provide (often filed as a Form 8-K with the SEC). REITs provide non-GAAP, supplemental calculations and metrics that may or may not be in accordance with GAAP, but which are helpful for understanding and forecasting their businesses. Most companies post all their SEC filings, along with their press releases, on their company websites; Appendix C provides website addresses for the 223 REITs in the FTSE NAREIT All REITs Index as of December 31, 2015.

Operating Metrics

There are a number of metrics used to assess the relative strength (or weakness) of a REIT's operations. The following pages provide key operating metrics that are germane to understanding REITs.

Net Operating Income (NOI)

Net operating income, or NOI, is similar to an operating company's gross profit margin. As shown in Table 8.1, NOI equals the sum of rental revenues from properties plus any tenant reimbursement revenue, less all property operating expenses, including fees paid to any third-party property managers, taxes, and insurance. (Please refer to Chapter 4 for an overview of leasing terminology.) Said another way, NOI measures the property-level profit on a stand-alone basis, excluding the REIT's corporate overhead or the effects of financing.

Same-Store (Organic) Earnings

Borrowed from the retail industry, the term *same-store* generally refers to revenues, operating expenses, and net operating income from assets the REIT has owned and operated for 12 or more months. Isolating the profitability of assets owned for at least 12 months from earnings generated by recently acquired or developed properties enables investors to gauge how competent the REIT management team is at operating their properties. An increase in same-store NOI is also referred to as "organic" or "internal" growth (though these descriptions are not technically precise); an increase generated from newly acquired or developed buildings is often referred to as "external growth." Each company may have slight variations about how they classify properties into (or out of) their same-store portfolio; generally, once a company has owned and

Table 8.1 Calculating Net Operating Income (NOI)

Rental revenues	$30.00
+ Tenant reimbursement revenue (including CAM)	15.00
Total property revenues	45.00
– Property operating expenses (including property management fee)	–15.00
– Taxes and insurance	–5.00
Net operating income (NOI)	$25.00

operated an asset or for 12 months, that asset is added to the same-store portfolio.

Growth in a REIT's same-store NOI measures a REIT management team's ability to grow earnings internally, or "organically"—without buying or building new assets. Contractual increases built into tenant rents, the expiration and re-leasing of space at higher (or lower) market rents, and changes in occupancy levels generate increases or decreases in same-store NOI. Among these variables, a change in occupancy is the dominant driver of fluctuations in same-store NOI because, in addition to no longer receiving rental revenue on the vacated space, the landlord also has to pay the basic operating expenses that no longer get reimbursed by a tenant. These expenses are basic electricity to keep the space's temperature ambient (too cold, and drywall cracks and/or pipes burst; too hot or moist, and mold can infiltrate), plus property taxes and insurance. The basic operating costs are not as high as the full expenses incurred when the space is occupied, but the inability to pass them through to a tenant significantly impedes a landlord's operating margin on the building. The one-two combination punch that vacancy has on landlord's operating margins—the loss of revenue, plus increased operating expenses—is why the demand profile for a property sector is a dominant factor in determining long-term performance.

> The one–two combination punch that vacancy has on landlord's operating margins—the loss of revenue, plus increased operating expenses—is why the demand profile for a property sector is a dominant factor in determining long-term performance.

(Please also refer to Chapter 7.) In short, vacancy is not profitable, and property sectors for which demand remains steady during economic downturns tend to outperform other sectors.

'Earnings Growth' for REITs Is 'FFO Growth'

REITs calculate earnings growth like any company: as the percentage change in earnings for the most current reporting period, versus results from the prior year's comparable period, as follows:

REIT earnings growth

$$= \left[\left(\frac{\textit{Current period FFO per share}}{\textit{FFO per share for same period a year ago}} \right) - 1 \right] \times 100$$

Unlike C-corporations, whose growth is measured as a change in earnings per share (EPS), REITs' growth is measured by the year-over-year change in funds from operations (FFO). In 2003, the SEC officially recognized NAREIT's definition of FFO as a supplemental earnings measure. Accordingly, when referring to a REIT's earnings, analysts and investors are referring to FFO, not EPS.

A REIT increases its FFO by combining same-store growth with external growth derived from properties the REIT acquired or developed, less the FFO from any properties sold. Many REITs also have "other income" that is separate from the profit generated by their buildings. Since the *REIT Modernization Act of 1999*, REITs have had more flexibility to provide tenant services through taxable REIT subsidiaries (TRSs). (Please refer to Chapters 6 & 7 for more information.) Since that legislation went into effect, many REITs now also derive small amounts of additional income from real estate–related services and businesses. FFO also includes the REIT's general and administrative (G&A) costs. Comparing the G&A as a percent of real estate revenues across different REITs in the same property type is a quick way to compare the relative efficiency with which respective management teams operate their real estate. Lastly and similar to EPS, FFO per share also accounts for the effects of any changes to a REIT's capital structure in the form of higher (or lower) interest expense and/or a different diluted share count.

As with any industry, higher earnings growth generally merits a higher valuation, provided that the quality of earnings is sound. For REITs, investors typically ascribe a higher multiple to "better quality" earnings, namely those derived from the business of owning and leasing real estate. Investors generally ascribe a lower valuation to earnings generated from areas of the business that are less predictable, such as income from merchant development or third-party property management activities.

Management's Track Record as a Screening Tool

There are over 200 publicly traded REITs. Screening companies using meaningful, easy-to-find performance results will help narrow the list of investment prospects. Over time, better senior-management teams should generate above-average same-store NOI growth and superior annual total returns for shareholders. Assessing management's performance by comparing the last five or more years of reported same-store NOI growth and annual total returns against what that company's peers produced should help investors quickly assess if the REIT they are evaluating tends to perform on, below, or above-par versus REITs in the same property sector. S&P Global Market Intelligence, whose website is listed in the Further Resources section of this book's conclusion, has one of the more robust databases of historical same-store and other data on individual REITs dating back to the mid-1990s. NAREIT's website, www.reit.com, also provides a host of historical company data, including annual total returns.

Profitability Metrics

Like C-corporations, REITs report net income and EPS calculated in accordance with GAAP. According to GAAP, however, REITs must depreciate the cost of their properties (excluding the amount allocated to the cost of land) over the useful life of an asset. Yet well-located and -maintained buildings tend to appreciate in value over time. In 1991, to address the discrepancy between GAAP rules and current market values for real estate, the REIT community adopted FFO as a supplemental measure of earnings per share. FFO and two additional supplemental performance metrics—adjusted FFO (AFFO) and cash (or funds) available for distribution (CAD or FAD)—are described in the paragraphs that follow, and Table 8.2 illustrates the adjustments that need to be made to reconcile "Net income available to shareholders" to an estimate of CAD.

Funds from Operation

Funds from operation is a supplemental though more broadly used measurement of REIT earnings, created by the REIT industry in 1991 and recognized by the SEC in 2003. According to NAREIT's latest whitepaper on the topic, FFO equals:

- Net income, as computed in accordance with GAAP, excluding:
  - Real estate depreciation and amortization
  - Gains (or losses) on the sales of previously depreciated operating properties
  - Impairment write-offs on previously depreciated operating properties
- Adjust to include the REITs share of FFO (or losses) in unconsolidated entities

NAREIT's definition of FFO excludes preferred dividends. If net income reflects dividends paid to preferred share (or unit) holders, then add the preferred dividends back, as well. Note that the gains

Table 8.2   Reconciliation of GAAP Net Income to CAD

Net income (loss) available to common shareholders[a]
+ Preferred stock dividends paid to preferred share & unit holders

---

Net income[a]
+ Real estate depreciation and amortization
− Gains on the sale of previously depreciated operating properties sold, net of income taxes
+ Impairment write-offs on previously depreciated operating properties
± Reconciling FFO related to noncontrolling interests[b]

Funds from Operation (FFO) attributable to the Company—per NAREIT
− Recurring capital expenditures[c]
± Adjustment for straight-lining of rents[d]
+ Impairment charges on undepreciated property, net of income taxes[e]
− Gain on sale of undepreciated property, net of income taxes[e]
+ Amortization of stock compensation
+ Amortization of deferred financing costs
± One-time items, such as the losses on the early extinguishment of debt

---

Adjusted FFO (AFFO)
− Capitalized interest expense
− Scheduled principal amortization payments on debt[f]

Cash Available for Distribution (CAD)

---

[a] As defined by GAAP. If starting with net income available to common shareholders, adjust back to "Net income" to begin calculating FFO in accordance with NAREIT's definition.

[b] These generally are partnerships and joint ventures in which the REIT owns less than a controlling interest.

[c] Includes non–revenue enhancing items, such as new carpeting or painting the walls of a space, as well as leasing commission paid to a leasing agent. In contrast, non-recurring capital expenditures add value to or extend the life of a property and include major structural items, such as expanding a property or constructing a parking deck. Both recurring and non-recurring items can be capitalized. However, only recurring capital expenditures are deducted in calculating AFFO.

[d] In accordance with GAAP, REITs "straight line" the rental income they are contractually entitled to receive for each lease. This is done by reporting the average rent (the sum of the total rent to be received, divided by the length of the lease), as opposed to the actual cash rent paid by the tenant. The straight-lined adjustment REITs report is the aggregate amount to be added to or subtracted from the GAAP rents reported on the income statement to arrive billable rent received in a reporting period.

[e] Undepreciated property includes land and recently developed but not yet stabilized buildings (i.e., buildings that were not yet included in a REIT's operating portfolio).

[f] Excludes balloon or maturing principal payments.

and losses on undepreciated property—such as land or recent development projects that were not part of the REIT's in-service (or *operating*) portfolio—and any impairments on undepreciated property are included in calculating FFO.

> Many REITs also report a 'core' FFO that better reflects their specific operations than NAREIT's White Paper definition. When comparing companies, investors need to be aware of (and adjust for) major differences.

Table 8.3   Adjusting NAREIT-Defined FFO to Account for Preferred Dividends

Net income[a]
+ Real estate depreciation and amortization
− Gains on the sale of previously depreciated operating properties sold, net of income taxes
+ Impairment write-downs on previously depreciated operating properties
± Reconciling FFO related to noncontrolling interests[b]

Funds from Operation (FFO) attributable to the Company—per NAREIT
− Preferred stock dividends paid to preferred share & unit holders

Diluted FFO available to common share and common OP unit holders[c]

[a] As defined by GAAP, and before payment of dividends to preferred share and preferred unit holders.
[b] These generally are partnerships and joint ventures in which the REIT owns less than a controlling interest.
[c] This will be the numerator for calculating diluted FFO per share.

As just mentioned, NAREIT's definition of FFO does not include the effect of dividends paid to holders of a REIT's preferred stock and preferred OP units. If a REIT has preferred stock or preferred OP units outstanding, its Net Income will be higher than its Net Income Available to Common Share & Unit Holders. In such instances, subtract the preferred dividends paid to these investors in order to calculate the numerator used to compute diluted FFO per share, as shown in Table 8.3. (The denominator will be the sum of the REIT's common shares and common OP units outstanding at the end of the reporting period.)

Adjusted Funds from Operations (AFFO)

Adjusted funds from operations (AFFO) is a more precise measure of a REIT's earnings than FFO because it adjusts for GAAP accounting conventions and for recurring capitalized expenditures (see footnotes *c* and *d* of Table 8.2, as well as the Glossary). As such, AFFO represents a more normalized or recurring form of FFO. AFFO is calculated by adding any amortized expenses (which are noncash items) to FFO, then subtracting a "normalized level" of recurring capital expenditures, and adjusting for straight-lined rents. (Recurring capital expenditures and straight-lined rent are also defined in the Glossary.)

Examples of recurring capital expenditures include leasing commissions and tenant improvement paid to lease a space, both of which are capitalized and then amortized (that is, *averaged*) over the life of the lease. Observing the last three-to-five years of historical data is helpful in estimating a reasonable level of recurring capital expenditures for each REIT. Recurring capital expenditure information typically can be found in the AFFO reconciliations REITs provide in their quarterly supplemental packages. To estimate future spending, divide the average annual recurring capital expenditures by the average square feet leased in each year, then multiply the resulting "CapEx per square foot" number by the amount of occupied square feet forecasted for future years. Note that square feet in this calculation should only include space associated with a REIT's in-service portfolio. Development square footage should not be included.

Lastly, the effects of any one-time items should be reversed. For example, it is customary to add back charges that get written off when REITs redeem preferred shares. These charges are the original underwriting costs incurred when the REIT issued the preferred stock. They are noncash expenses associated with the redemption, and are nonrecurring. Therefore, it makes sense to exclude them when calculating AFFO.

Cash Available for Distribution (CAD)

Cash available for distribution (CAD) estimates the cash a REIT has available to pay dividends and is the most meaningful indicator of dividend safety. Not every analyst or investor goes the extra mile to calculate CAD, and NAREIT offers no opinion on it. CAD is calculated by subtracting capitalized interest expense and principal amortization payments due on secured debt—excluding any principal amounts that are maturing; these "balloon payments" are accounted for in the financing activities section of a company's Statement of Cash Flows and typically get refinanced with new debt when they mature.

Balance Sheet Metrics and Analysis

A REIT's balance sheet can also provide important information about dividend safety or a REIT's ability to grow FFO. The following metrics enable investors to assess a REITs' financial flexibiltiy.

Leverage

The REIT industry has progressively de-levered over the decades. Prior to 1990 it was not unusual for real estate companies to finance 80 percent or more of their property values with debt. Using large amounts of leverage ("levering up") to acquire or develop buildings results in impressive FFO per share growth; however, it also adds significant risk and, historically, when combined with an economic slowdown, has been the root cause of many private real estate company bankruptcies. In the 2000s, leverage came back in vogue, only to end poorly for many overleveraged private landlords when the global financial crisis began to unfold in 2007.

> When assessing the financial health of any real estate company or REIT, investors may want to remember one truism:
>
> "Debt" is a four-letter word

In contrast to the private property market, REITs historically have maintained a more disciplined, conservative approach to financing operations with debt. To wit, as of December 31, 2006, the REIT industry's average debt-to-gross book ratio was 57 percent. Out of the 130 REITs that composed the FTSE NAREIT All REITs Index going into 2007, only one REIT, General Growth Properties (NYSE: GGP), ended up reorganizing under Chapter 11 bankruptcy law. As discussed in Chapter 3, General Growth's debt-to–gross book ratio at the end of 2006 was 74 percent, or 17 percentage points greater than the industry average.

Debt-to–Total Market Capitalization Ratio

As of December 31, 2015 and according to NAREIT, equity REITs average debt-to–total market capitalization ratio was 36.0 percent. This ratio is calculated by dividing a company's total debt outstanding by its total market capitalization, which is the sum of the following:

- Total debt outstanding
- The liquidation value of any preferred stock outstanding, calculated as the liquidation value per share (typically $25) times the number of preferred shares outstanding; a company's supplemental package and/or the footnotes to its periodic SEC filings typically contain the liquidation values of preferred shares
- The REIT's Equity Market Capitalization (EMC or *equity market cap*), calculated as the current stock price times the sum of all common shares and OP units outstanding:

$$EMC = (\text{Common shares} + \text{OP units}) \times \text{current stock price}$$

The combined formula for calculating debt-to–total market capitalization is as follows:

Debt-to–total market capitalization

$$= \frac{\text{total debt outstanding}}{\text{total debt} + \text{preferred stock at liquidation value} + \text{equity market capitalization}}$$

As discussed in Chapter 3, a debt-to–total capitalization ratio changes depending on a REIT's current stock price, resulting in leverage being over- or understated. To obtain a more accurate idea about how leveraged a REIT is, calculate its debt-to–gross book value ratio.

Debt-to–Gross Book Value Ratio

Gross book value, which is often called *gross asset value,* can be calculated by taking total assets listed on the balance sheet of the REIT's financial statements, less any goodwill or intangibles, plus any accumulated depreciation and amortization (generally listed in the footnotes to the financial statements), as shown in the following equation.

Debt-to–gross asset value

$$= \frac{\text{total debt outstanding}}{(\text{total assets} - \text{intangibles}) + \text{accumulated depreciation}}$$

As of December 31, 2015, the average debt-to–gross asset ratio of REITs in the FTSE NAREIT All REITs index was 46.4 percent.

Debt-to-EBITDA Ratio

REITs that are investment-grade rated have to operate their businesses within the leverage limits (or *covenants*) imposed on them by the ratings agencies. The largest three such agencies in the United States are Fitch, Moody's, and Standard & Poor's. One of the most critical ratios the investment community focuses on is a REIT's debt-to-EBITDA, which measures how many years it would take a company, in theory, to pay off its leverage using the most recent quarter's earnings before interest, taxes, depreciation, and amortization (EBITDA). For example, a debt-to-EBITDA ratio of

4.5× implies it would take the REIT four-and-a-half years to repay its debt, assuming the most recent quarter's EBITDA is recurring.

Calculating a REIT's debt-to-EBITDA sounds straightforward: Divide total debt outstanding by the most recently reported quarter's EBITDA, annualized. However, in practice, there are many adjustments that need to be made to the denominator to ensure the EBITDA is *recurring*. Many (but not all) REITs that have investment-grade ratings disclose their debt-to-EBITDA ratio in the "debt analysis" pages of their quarterly supplemental information packages. A lower ratio equates to lower levels of debt and, implicitly, a more secure common dividend.

Weighted Average Cost of Capital (WACC)

Often referred to as a company's "cost of capital," the weighted average cost of capital (WACC) is the average return a company expects to pay all its stakeholders: lenders, preferred shareholders, and common shareholders. WACC is calculated by proportionately weighting the cost of each of the three types of capital—debt, preferred, and common shares—as a percentage of the company's total market capitalization (defined earlier in this chapter). The formula for calculating WACC is as follows:

$$\text{WACC} = \frac{D}{\text{TMC}} \times D_c + \frac{P}{\text{TMC}} \times P_c + \frac{E}{\text{TMC}} \times E_c$$

or simply:

$$\text{WACC} = \frac{(D \times D_C) + (P \times P_c) + (E \times E_c)}{\text{TMC}}$$

where:

D is the total amount of debt outstanding
D_c is the average interest rate on total
P is the liquidation value of all preferred stock*
P_c is the average dividend rate on all preferred stock
E is the equity market capitalization*
E_c is the cost of equity
TMC is the total market capitalization*

*These calculations are discussed in Chapter 7.

Determining the cost of equity for the preceding calculation is not as easy as looking something up in the company's SEC filings or supplemental package. Technically, common stock does not have an explicit cost associated with it the way that loans and preferred stock issuances do with their respective interest rates and dividend coupon rates. One accepted method is to use the average expected total return for the industry, which for REITs is 10–12 percent (please refer to Table 2.1 in Chapter 2). To be more precise, use the average total returns specific to each property sector, as shown in Table 7.1 of Chapter 7. Another method for calculating a company's cost of equity is to use the following formula:

$$E_c = \frac{\text{Current Dividend, Annualized}}{\text{Current Share Price}} + \text{Average Dividend Growth}$$

There are other methods for calculating the cost of equity, some of which are more scientific, some of which are more subjective. As long as the approach for estimating the cost of equity is consistently applied, then the relative WACCs should be meaningful for comparing across different REITs.

> A higher WACC could signal a company's capital allocation is out-of-whack.

Companies with a higher WACC implicitly are riskier than companies with lower costs of capital. Before investing, be sure to understand if a company's WACC is higher than its peers because the company is newer to the public market and, as a result, perhaps has a less institutional quality balance sheet. Provided investors and analysts believe management is allocating capital wisely, a company can lower its WACC over time by refinancing maturing debt with new debt that has a lower interest rate, or by redeeming existing preferred stock by issuing new, lower-cost preferred stock, and also by increasing its common share price. Each of these tactics will lower a company's WACC, but they are only possible if management consistently executes a growth strategy that investors deem to be a good balance between risk and returns.

Alternatively, a company may have a higher WACC than its peers because its management team does not allocate capital well. A company that grows FFO by levering up its balance sheet with short-term, variable rate debt—which carries a lower interest rate than long-term debt—may fool investors for a little while; ultimately, when that company has to refinance debt at higher rates, or, more likely, if investors chose to sell their shares because they are uncomfortable with the increased leverage, the REIT's stock price will decline, further increasing the company's WACC.

Valuation Metrics

Valuation is a critical step in selecting which REITs to buy, hold, or sell. The following metrics provide different ways to measure a REIT's relative value versus a group of peer companies or on an absolute basis.

Price/Earnings Multiple

As was discussed at the beginning of this chapter, REITs trade off expected FFO per share estimates rather than EPS. Accordingly, REIT earnings multiples are expressed as FFO multiples, calculated simply as the current stock price divided by current or next year's FFO per share estimates, depending on how forward looking your analysis is. The equation to calculate price/earnings (P/E) is:

A REIT's P/E

$$= P/FFO = \frac{\text{current stock price}}{\text{the current or next year's estimate of FFO per share}}$$

A lower FFO multiple may indicate a REIT is trading at a bargain price. So if Rockland REIT trades at 10.0× next year's estimate FFO, and REIT ABC with a similar portfolio of assets trades at 12.5×, Rockland REIT may be a good value relative to REIT ABC. If there is no fundamental problem with Rockland REIT's markets and operations, then its shares probably represent a good value. Looking at other metrics, such as FFO growth and leverage, will help determine the answer.

PEG Ratios

Investors look at FFO multiples as a simple calculation of the relative valuation of REITs within their sectors. Although FFO multiples are helpful indicators for assessing relative value, price multiple-to-earnings growth, or PEG ratios, are a better indicator of how much an investor is paying today for a company's expected earnings growth. PEG ratios for REITs are calculated by dividing the price/FFO multiple by expected future growth in FFO. For example, if a REITs FFO multiple on next year's estimated FFO is 9.5×, and the REIT's FFO per share is expected to increase 8 percent next year, the PEG ratio is 9.5 divided by 8, which equals 1.2×. This can be calculated using the following equation:

$$\text{A REIT's PEG ratio} = \frac{\text{next year's FFO multiple}}{\text{next year's expected growth in FFO per share}}$$

Because PEG ratios isolate the growth component of value, they provide investors with a clearer understanding of how much they are paying today for future earnings. Assuming comparable risk profiles among companies, lower PEG ratios represent better relative values for investors. One caveat regarding PEG ratios is that in years when companies are expected to deliver flat or modestly negative earnings growth, PEG ratios should be calculated using a longer-term (three–five-year) estimate of earnings potential for each company.

Dividend Yield

At December 31, 2015, the average equity REIT offered investors a current return, or dividend yield, of 4.3 percent, which was 200 basis points above the yield on 10-year U.S. Treasury notes, and 210 basis points greater than the S&P 500 Index's yield. Unsurprisingly, many investors choose to invest in REITs solely for their current yield. Chapter 3 discussed REIT dividends at length, so this section will simply restate two points. First, a REIT's current yield is calculated as the current dividend annualized (multiplied by four, in most cases), divided by the current stock price:

$$\text{Current Yield} = \frac{\text{Current quarterly dividend} \times 4}{\text{Current price per share}}$$

Second, because many investors hold investments for several years, it is also important to understand the concept of yield on cost, which is calculated by dividing the current dividend annualized by the investor's cost basis in the REIT's stock:

$$\text{Yield on Cost} = \frac{\text{Current quarterly dividend} \times 4}{\text{Shareholder's per share cost basis}}$$

> ## Three General Rules about Dividend Safety
>
> 1. REITs that own property types with short-term lease revenues carry more risk of cutting their dividends than those with longer-term leases.
> 2. Dividends tend to be more at-risk in companies whose management teams incur too much leverage. A debt-to–gross asset value of 50 percent generally should be the absolute maximum amount of leverage (and even that level may prove to be too high, depending on the property sector).
> 3. REITs with dividend yields that materially exceed the industry's average tend to be companies with significantly more corporate risk and less secure dividends. (Please see the discussion of sucker yield in Chapter 3.)
>
> Bottom line: If a REIT's yield looks too good to be true, it probably is.

Dividend Safety

Although Chapter 3 addressed dividend safety, the point bears repeating. Although the contractual nature of leases makes most property sector dividends reasonably secure, REITs have cut or suspended their dividends in times of financial crisis—both in the wake of the S&L crisis of the late 1980s/early 1990s, and more recently in response to the global financial crisis of 2007–2008.

Putting aside these two extreme economic times, REIT dividends tend to be sustainable. By calculating a REIT's dividend payout ratio, discussed next, investors can assess how secure the dividend is, at least in the near term.

Dividend Coverage, or Payout Ratios

FFO, AFFO, and CAD payout ratios are a common means of evaluating the relative security of a company's dividend. FFO is quoted more broadly because stock analysts provide Thomson First Call, Bloomberg, and S&P Global Market Intelligence with their estimates of FFO per share for companies. Increasingly, analysts are also furnishing AFFO per-share estimates on REITs they analyze, but the practice is not yet uniform. As discussed in Chapter 7, FFO payout ratios indicate the relative ability of a REIT to meet its dividend obligation, in that, if the payout ratio is less than 1.0, the dividend is reasonably secure:

$$\text{Dividend payout ratio} = \frac{\text{current quarterly dividend}^* \times 4}{\text{next year's FFO}^\dagger \text{ per share estimate}}$$

Note: *If the REIT pays a monthly dividend, multiply the most recent dividend by 12.
†Use AFFO or CAD per-share estimates, if available, instead of FFO.

Dividing the annualized dividend by the next year's estimate of AFFO or CAD per share is a better method for gauging dividend safety than using FFO estimates; however, investors may need to do the spadework to create their own estimates of both metrics, if stock analysts providing research on the REIT do not provide these estimates.

Dividend Discount Model

Investors who are interested in owning REITs primarily for dividend income should also employ the dividend discount model to evaluate whether a REIT's shares are fairly priced. The following formula will calculate the present value of a REIT's expected future dividends, using a discount rate and a reasonable expected annual growth rate for the current dividend. If the fair value for a REIT calculated using the dividend discount model is higher than the price at which the stock is trading, then the stock most likely is a good value.

$$\text{Fair stock price} = \frac{\text{Annualized dividend per share}}{\text{Discount Rate} - \text{Dividend Growth Rate}}$$

Dividend Discount Model Example

To illustrate the dividend discount model with a practical example, assume that Rockland REIT:

- Pays a dividend of $0.25 per share per quarter
- Has increased its annualized dividend 3 percent, on average, for the past five years
- Has a cost of equity (or *discount rate*) of 12 percent

Based on the dividend discount model, $11.11 is a fair value for Rockland REIT's shares:

$$\$11.11 = (\$0.25 \times 4) \div [12\% - 3\%]$$

If Rockland REIT's shares are trading below $11.11, then the stock most likely is a good investment from a valuation standpoint.

In terms of the inputs, you can use a company's historical annualized growth rate in its dividend, which often is cited in an annual report to shareholders or company presentation posted on the company's website. Determining which discount rate, or cost of equity, to use is more difficult. In addition to the methods discussed earlier in this chapter related to WACC, some investors simply add an equity risk premium of 500 basis points to the 10-year U.S. Treasury bond rate (the *risk-free* rate).

Net Asset Valuation (NAV)

One way to assess if the managers of a REIT are prudent allocators of shareholder capital it to observe the investment tactics they use when their stock is trading significantly above or below net asset value (NAV). NAV estimates the current market value of a REIT's properties, net of other non–real estate assets and liabilities. Investors prefer NAV per share over gross book value per share because the latter does not account for changes in the value of the underlying land on which properties are built, or the future earnings potential (and associated change in market value) of real estate assets.

REITs whose shares trade at a premium to NAV have a cost of capital advantage and should continue buying and/or developing to grow their portfolios (assuming they issue enough common stock to maintain their prior debt ratios, discussed earlier). In contrast, if a REIT's shares are trading at a significant discount to NAV, management should shrink its portfolio by selling the lowest performing or lowest growth assets and use the proceeds to pay down debt (or redeem any callable preferred shares). If the discount persists for several quarters, management should also consider buying back common stock—but only if they can do so without increasing their total debt.

REITs whose stocks trade at premiums to estimated NAV per share might have some specific reason, such as their property

Stock Price Above NAV = Green Light on Growth

Stock Price Below NAV = Red Light on Growth

sector or markets may be in favor with investors. Alternatively, the premium may indicate the shares are overvalued. Conversely, if a stock is trading at a steep discount to NAV per share, then either the market is undervaluing the business, in which case investors can buy shares at an attractive sale price; or the investment community believes management is destroying shareholder value, in which case the shares are cheap for a reason and should be avoided.

According to analyses published by Green Street Advisors, historically, REITs trade at a modest premium to NAV per share, as the market generally prescribes some premium for liquidity and an even greater premium to REITs with management teams that have consistently added value through rigorous property management and asset allocation tactics. That said, according to an analysis provided by S&P Global Market Intelligence, REITs traded at an average 2.7 percent discount to NAV at the end of 2015. Investor concerns about slowing global economic growth and the potential for higher interest rates from Federal Reserve actions caused most REIT property types to finish that year below NAV (see Figure 8.1). Because NAV increasingly dominates investor buy-and-sell decisions,

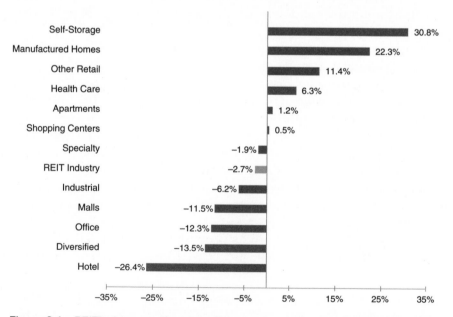

Figure 8.1   REIT's Average Premium (Discount) to NAV at December 31, 2015 (Includes U.S. REITs with at least three NAV per-share estimates. Property sectors are weighted by market capitalization.)

Source: S&P Global Market Intelligence.

Table 8.4   Basic Calculation of NAV per Share

Cash NOI "run rate" for recent quarter	$10,000
× 4 to annualize	× 4
Annualized adjusted cash NOI	$40,000
× (1 + 3 percent annual same-store growth assumption)	×1.03
Annualized adjusted cash NOI	$41,200
÷ Cap rate	5.5%
Fair market value of a REIT's in-service properties*	$749,100
Adjusted for:	
+ Accounts receivable, cash, and other tangible assets, net of current liabilities	1,500
+ Fair value of properties held for sale, net of related debt	50,000
+ Properties under development at costs invested to date	20,000
Total	
− debt	−250,000
− Preferred stock, at liquidation value	−150,000
Net asset value (NAV)	$420,600
Shares and OP units outstanding at the end of the quarter	25,000
NAV per share (rounded to nearest dollar)	$16.82

*Number is rounded for presentation purpose.

the remainder of this chapter demonstrates how it may be calculated for Rockland REIT.

Calculating NAV

Although there are several calculations involved in estimating a REIT's NAV, the basic concept is simple: estimate the current market value of the REIT's portfolio, then add any other tangible assets, subtract all liabilities, and divide the sum by the shares and OP units outstanding. Table 8.4 provides a simplified example of an NAV calculation, after which the five major components of NAV are broken down in more detail.

Step 1: Estimating a Quarterly Run Rate for "Cash" NOI

The first step in calculating NAV is to calculate a REIT's billable NOI (as opposed to GAAP NOI) for the most recently reported earnings period. (NOI was discussed at the beginning of this chapter.) Note that billable (or *contractual*) NOI is often referred to as "cash" NOI. The goal of step 1 is to isolate the cash NOI due from a REIT's in-service portfolio and adjust it for any assets bought, sold, or placed into service during the most recent reporting period. In-service properties are ones that are not under development. Other assets, such as income from a business services TRS or properties still under construction, are valued in a later step.

Cash NOI Estimation

Estimate Cash NOI for most recently reported quarter:	First Approach	Second Approach	Likely Source
Rental revenues + tenant recoveries reported for Q	$15,000	–	Income statement
– Property operating expenses for Q	–6,550	–	Income statement
Net operating income (NOI) reported for Q	8,450	–	
± Straight-lined rent adjustment	–1,000	–	AFFO calculation (supplemental)
Cash NOI for Q	$7,450	$7,500	

- The first approach represents financials of a REIT that does not disclose cash NOI, in which case investors need to use line items from the income statement and the straight-lined rent adjustment disclosed in the reconciliation from FFO to AFFO (likely in the supplemental information package).

- The second approach shows the shortcut investors can take advantage of in instances where REITs report their cash NOI (most likely in the supplemental information package available on their websites).

- HFS vs. Discontinued Operations—The $50 difference between the two cash NOI numbers exists because in the first approach, the REIT has assets held for sale (HFS) that qualify for discontinued operations treatment; as a result, their NOI is not in continuing operations. In the second approach, the HFS assets do not qualify for discontinued operations treatment, so their NOI is still reported in continuing operations.

Properties that are in-service but not collecting rent because they are vacant are not directly valued by NAV. One of the fastest ways a REIT can grow its NAV per share is to re-lease vacant space.

Straight-Lined Rent   In compliance with GAAP, REITs *straight-line* the rental income they receive by reporting the average annual rent to be received over the life of a lease instead of the contractual rent due each period. The straight-lining of rent adjustment a REIT reports is the amount to be added to or subtracted from GAAP rents (reported on the income statement) to arrive at "cash" rents. The following example demonstrates the straight-lining of rents:

Example of Straight-Lining Rents	Year 1	Year 2	Year 3	Year 4
Contractual rent per square foot	$15.00	$16.50	$18.00	$19.50
× Square feet leased	5,000	5,000	5,000	5,000
Cash rent to be received ("A")	$75,000	$82,500	$90,000	$97,500
Total cash rent to be received	$345,000			
÷ Lease length (in years)	4			
Average rent reported annually for GAAP ("B")	$86,250			
Therefore:				
GAAP rent reported on financial statements	$86,250	$86,250	$86,250	$86,250
− Straight-lined rent adjustment (A − B)*	(11,250)	(3,750)	3,750	11,250
Cash rent due	$75,000	$82,500	$90,000	$97,500

*Note in this example that after the halfway point in the lease, the straight-lined rent adjustment becomes positive, meaning that the NOI calculated from the REIT's income statement will need to be *increased* by the straight-line adjustment amount.

Step 2: Estimating a Quarterly Run Rate for Cash NOI

Very few REITs provide good disclosure on what their quarterly cash NOI "run rate" from in-service properties is. Run-rate cash NOI is the cash NOI calculated in step 1, adjusted for the estimated addition (or deletion) of cash NOI in the period related to the REIT's investment activity. The following example demonstrates how to adjust a REIT's cash NOI to a run-rate that can serve as the basis of the NAV calculation:

Step #2 – Adjustments to Cash NOI from Step #1 to estimate "run rate" for the in-service portfolio:		First Approach	Second Approach
Cash NOI for Q, calculated in Step #1		$7,450	$7,500
+ Unaccounted NOI from:			
• Acquisitions made during Q	(A)	17	17
• Developments placed into service in the Q	(B)	58	58
− NOI from assets sold during the Q	(C)	−20	−20
− NOI from assets held for sale ("HFS")	(D)	–	−50
Net adjustment to cash NOI from investment activity in the Q		56	6
Cash NOI "run rate" for Q		$7,506	$7,506

Explanations of footnotes A through D in Step 2 are as follows:

[A]The company acquired a building in the middle of the quarter. The purchase price was $2,500 and the property has a stabilized return (or 'yield') of 5.5%. Accordingly, only half of the asset's NOI was included in the most recent reported quarter.

[B]The company developed a building for $5,000 that has a stabilized yield of 7.0% and placed it into service on the 60th day of the 90-day quarter. Therefore, only one month (30 days) of NOI was in the latest quarter's NOI; two month's NOI needs to be added.

[C]On the 30th day of the 90-day quarter, the company sold an asset for $3,000 and at an exit cap rate of 8%. One month of NOI from this asset was in the most recent quarter's NOI and needs to be subtracted.

The table below calculates the amount of cash NOI that needs to be added to or subtracted from cash NOI to get to a run-rate:

Adjustment	Total Cost	Cap Rate	Total NOI	Qtly NOI	Months of NOI to Adjust	Adjustment to Cash NOI
A—Acquisition	$2,500	5.5%	$138	$34	$+45/90 = 1/2$	$17
B—Development	$5,000	7.0%	350	88	$+60/90 = 2/3$	58
C—Asset sold	($3,000)	8.0%	−240	−60	$-30/90 = (1/3)$	−20
Total estimated adjustments from investment activity in the Q						$56

[D]If a company has assets held for sale ("HFS"), investors need to understand if the assets also qualify for discontinued operations treatment. If they do, then no adjustment is required. The Second Approach reflects a scenario where HFS assets do not qualify as discontinued operations. Accordingly, their NOI needs to be deducted to arrive at a run rate for NOI. This scenario assumes the assets HFS have a book value of $2,500 and generate an 8.0% cash NOI yield, resulting in quarterly NOI of $50 (calculated as $2,500 × 8%, divided by 4).

Step 3: Annualize the Quarterly Run Rate for Cash NOI & Adjust for Same-Store Growth

The third step is to annualize the cash NOI run rate calculated in Step 2, plus make a reasonable assumption about what degree these earnings will grow (or contract) over the next 12 months:

Annualized cash NOI, assuming 2% same-store growth	First Approach	Second Approach
Cash NOI Run Rate for Q (from Step #2)	$7,506	$7,506
× 4	× 4	× 4
Cash NOI Run Rate, annualized	30,022	30,022
× 2% same-store growth assumption	× 1.02	× 1.02
Cash NOI annualized, with growth	$30,623	$30,623

Same-Store Growth Assumption   As Table 8.5 shows, each property sector exhibits certain growth or contraction during times of economic expansion or decline. Investors should make a reasonable assumption, based on the historical same-store growth a company has achieved, tempered by the investors' outlook on the broader economy.

Step 4: Calculate Fair Market Value of the In-Service Portfolio

The fourth step uses the annualized cash NOI calculated in Step 3 to estimate the fair market value of the REIT's in-service properties. As the example below shows, divide the annualized cash NOI calculated in Step 3 by an appropriate cap rate.

Table 8.5   Historical Same-Store NOI Growth Rates for Major Property Types

	1999–2008	2009–2010	2011–2015
Apartments	2.4%	−2.8%	6.0%
Industrial	2.0%	−4.4%	3.2%
Malls	3.3%	−0.6%	3.0%
Office	0.0%	−1.1%	1.5%
Self-Storage	3.8%	−1.4%	8.3%
Shopping Centers	2.3%	−2.3%	2.9%

Source: S&P Global Market Intelligence.

Calculate Fair Market Value of in-service portfolio:	First Approach	Second Approach
Annualized cash NOI (from Step #3)	$30,623	$30,623
÷ Cap rate	6.50%	6.50%
Fair market value of in-service properties	$471,116	$471,116

Fair market value is the price a buyer would pay today for the REIT's assets, before taking into consideration the assumption of any debt and preferred shares the REIT has used to finance their purchase. In an actual transaction, the buyer would analyze each property and calculate the present value of expected cash NOI from the portfolio over 5 or 10 years. A short-hand way of expressing the resulting value is to use a capitalization rate, or *cap rate.*

The cap rate is expressed as the quotient of the portfolio's annualized adjusted cash NOI divided by the purchase price a buyer is willing to pay. In the analytical world, there is always a lot of debate about which cap rate is appropriate for calculating a REIT's NAV. Although there is no "right answer," knowledge of the debate should help investors adopt one that is defensible.

Capitalization Rates – *Capitalization rates* (or more commonly, *cap rates*) are a measure of the expected unleveraged return on assets. Another way to think about cap rates is that they are the inverse of a P/E ratio, where "price" is the fair market value (or purchase price) of the asset, and "earnings" are the property's cash NOI. Cap rates for the same type of property may differ vastly based on the general quality of the physical assets, as well as the quality of its locations (based on the relative strength of the markets' supply-and-demand fundamentals), and buyer or seller motivation to complete the trade.

$$\text{Cap rate} = \frac{\text{"Earnings"}}{\text{"Price"}} = \frac{\text{Property's Cash NOI}}{\text{Market value or price paid for a property}}$$

In theory, the cap rate should approximate a price at which the assets of the REIT could be sold in the direct property markets. Investors can estimate which cap rates to use for their NAV calculations by looking at the cap rates at which similar assets (or portfolios of assets) have traded recently. Ultimately, however, cap rates are subjective. If a seller is motivated by some extenuating circumstance, such as the inability to refinance debt on the property that may be maturing, the seller may be willing to sell the asset below what the fair market value would be without extenuating circumstances. The lower the price, the higher the cap rate. The amount of money one buyer is willing to pay for an asset may differ widely from what another buyer would pay. Differences among buyers' bids are a function of multiple factors, including divergent views on the economic outlook, or tenant relationships that one buyer possesses that would enable him to lease the assets better/worse than other potential buyers, or differing plans to redevelop the asset over time.

Step 5: Adjust Fair Market Value for Other Investments and Financing

The final step in calculating NAV is to adjust the fair market value calculated in Step 4 to include values for assets that are not currently generating NOI, and to subtract the REIT's total debt and preferred stock outstanding:

Adjust Fair Market Value for Other Investments and Financing:		First Approach	Second Approach
Fair market value of in-service properties		$471,116	$471,116
± Accounts receivable, cash, and other tangible assets, net of current liabilities	(E)	−15,000	−15,000
+ Properties HFS, net of associated debt	(F)	2,500	2,500
+ Properties under development:	(G)		
• 1st Approach: development shown at cost		100,000	
• 2nd Approach: development shown at 110 percent of cost			110,000
+ Land for development at book value	(H)	25,000	25,000
+ Construction management business (5× net income, annualized)	(I)	4,000	4,000
− Total debt	(J)	−200,000	−200,000
− Preferred stock, at liquidation value	(J)	−75,000	−75,000
Net asset value (NAV)		$312,616	$322,616
Shares and OP units outstanding at the end of Q		25,000	25,000
NAV per share		$12.50	$12.90
- vs. -			
Closing current stock price		$10.00	$10.00
Premium (discount) to NAV per share		−20.0%	−22.5%

(*continued*)

Explanations of the footnotes to Step 5's are as follows:

[E]Using information from the REIT's balance sheet, add tangible assets not accounted for as in-service properties, such as cash and restricted cash, accounts receivable, and prepaid expenses. Tangible assets do not include deferred items, such as deferred leasing and financing costs or deferred rent receivable.

[F]Assets held for sale—Because the NOI from assets HFS was not included in the cash NOI in the First Approach, and because the Second Approach deducted the cash NOI from assets HFS as part of calculating the run rate NOI, the assets HFS are not yet valued for NAV purposes. They will be listed on the balance sheet at book value, and should be added.

[G]If a REIT has properties under development, they most likely are not accounted for in NOI. The industry values developments two ways. First, if the REIT's disclosure is adequate, investors can project the estimated cash flows from the development projects and calculate their net present value. However, this calculation is complicated and usually not materially better than the more simplified method of adding the costs incurred to-date for any development or redevelopment project, including land being used in the development. If the developments appear to be low risk in nature (e.g., they are pre-leased), a premium of 10 percent (or more) can be added.

[H]Add land at book value (generally listed on the balance sheet or in a schedule in the supplemental).

[I]Value business services by adding their last four quarters of net income, and multiply the sum by five, which is the equivalent of applying a 20 percent cap rate. Such services are viewed as being variable, so a high cap rate typically is appropriate.

[J]Next, subtract all debt outstanding and the liquidation value of any preferred stock or preferred units (preferred stock "issued" at the OP level).

This resulting sum is the REIT's NAV. Divide the NAV by the sum of the REIT's total shares and OP units outstanding to calculate NAV per share.

Implied Capitalization Rate

A REIT's implied capitalization rate (implied cap rate) is analogous to an unlevered internal rate of return (IRR) in that it is the unleveraged return an investor locks-in if he or she buys the REIT at the current price. Since a cap rate is equal to the inverse of a company's earnings multiple, a REIT with a higher implied cap rate generally is considered a better relative value than a comparable REIT trading at a lower implied cap rate, especially if similar quality properties have recently been sold in similar markets at lower cap rates.

A second way to apply implied cap rates in analyzing REITs is to compare them to cap rates being paid for similar assets in the direct

> If a REIT's implied cap rate > cap rates on similar assets for sale in the direct property market, the REIT's shares are an attractive value.

property markets. For example, if the implied cap rate of an industrial REIT is higher than cap rates on recent, comparable industrial assets that recently traded owners, then buying the industrial REIT's shares is the better value.

To calculate the implied cap rate at which a REIT is trading, enter the current stock price as the REIT's NAV per share and solve for the cap rate. Table 8.6 illustrates these steps, which are simply the reverse of the major steps used to calculate NAV.

Table 8.6   Implied Cap Rate Calculation

Step 1:	REIT's current share price	$10.00
	× shares and OP units outstanding	25,000
	Implied net asset value	$250,000
Step 2:	Adjust for non-income-producing items & financing:	
	Implied net value of Rockland REIT (from above)	250,000
	+ Preferred stock, at liquidation value	75,000
	+ Total debt	200,000
	− Construction management business	−4,000
	− Land for development at book value	−25,000
	− Properties under development	−100,000
	− Properties HFS, net of associated debt	−2,500
	± Accounts receivable, cash, and other tangible assets, net of current liabilities	15,000
	Implied fair market value	$408,500
Step 3:	Divide the annualized cash NOI calculated in Step #3 in calculating NAV by the implied fair market value:*	
	Annualized adjusted cash NOI	$30,623
	÷ Implied gross asset value	$408,500
	Implied Cap Rate	7.5%

*Based on information presented in the First Approach in Step #3 of calculating NAV.

Conclusion

Many investors make the mistake of investing in a REIT because they "like the buildings" or know someone who works there. Although these two stock picking strategies can work out, they usually do not. As discussed in Chapter 7, if a REIT has a superior portfolio of properties, a conservatively leveraged balance sheet, and a management team with a proven track record of allocating capital prudently, it is likely to be a good investment, even if the price at which you buy it is not "cheap" or deeply discounted at the time.

Most investors do not have the opportunity to assess management's character directly. They also may not be skilled at gauging the direction in which the U.S. economy is headed—although 24/7 news stations make it easier to stay current. One thing every investor can do is to understand the risks and rewards inherent in each of the different property types. As discussed in Chapters 4 and 5, the risks and benefits of different property types are related to how short or long a REIT's leases are with tenants, as well as the durability of demand for that property type in times of economic growth or contraction.

Longer leases generate steady, more predictable earnings, whereas earnings from shorter leases can be more volatile. REIT share prices and, by extension, P/FFO multiples (see Chapter 8) reflect this fundamental difference in earnings volatility. Table C.1 indicates typical lease durations used by each property type and ranks the sectors by their *betas*. According to Investopedia.com, beta is a measure of a stock's volatility in relation to the stock market, where the stock market has a beta of 1.0. A "high-beta stock" is one that exhibits price swings greater than the market over time

Investors who simply buy shares in a REIT "because they like the buildings" may face frustration as REITs in other property types outperform their selection.

Table C.1   Lease Length and Stock Beta by Property Type

Property Sector	Typical Lease Duration	Average of Beta	
		1 Year	3 Years
Hotel	N/A	0.99	0.98
Regional Mall	3–7 years	0.86	0.82
Industrial	3–7 years	0.81	0.83
Shopping Center	3–7 years	0.76	0.76
Office	3–7 years	0.76	0.78
Multi-Family	1 year	0.73	0.65
Self-Storage	Monthly	0.73	0.75
Specialty	Varies by Company	0.72	0.86
Other Retail (triple-net)	10-plus years	0.66	0.67
Health Care	10-plus years	0.66	0.63
Manufactured Home	Monthly	0.61	0.63
Diversified	Varies by Company	0.58	0.66
Grand Total		0.74	0.77

Source: S&P Global Market Intelligence.

and has a beta above 1.0. Conversely, stocks that trade with less volatility than the market ("low-beta stocks") have a beta that is less than 1.0. Stocks with higher betas carry more risk, but can also deliver greater returns. Hotel REITs, which have no leases, trade with greater volatility than health-care REITs, which typically employ long-term, triple-net leases. While some property types are higher beta than others, every REIT sector shown in Table C.1 trades with less volatility than the market. Investors should understand which REITs are appropriate, given each investor's risk tolerance.

Which REITs Are Right for Your Portfolio?

Understanding how REITs in different property sectors have traded in the past is instructive for setting expectations as to how they may perform in similar trading environments in the future. Table 7.2 in Chapter 7 provides total returns by property sector from 1994–2015. However, developing a sense of *when* to buy *which* REITs is complicated by the fact that real estate fundamentals lag the economy, but REIT shares (as stocks) reflect future expectations.

Real estate fundamentals lag the general economy; by how much depends on the type of property (office, warehouse, hotel, etc.), the structure and average lease length in place in existing buildings, and how balanced the demand for commercial space is with supply. There is no hard, fast rule to determine when the time is right to buy or

Predicting REIT returns is more complicated than for other industries. The difficulty arises from the fact that commercial property is a defensive, lagging indicator for the economy. However, stock prices represent investors' present value of future expected earnings. As a result, REIT stock prices often do not reflect what investors physically see as they go to work, shop, or enjoy recreational activities.

sell which sectors. Each economic cycle is different with regard to how long and how strong a recovery phase will last, or how long and deep the trough of a recession will endure. There is an adage about investing that still holds true:

The only people who can time the market are fools and liars.

The point being, there is not a best time to buy or sell any stocks, including REITs. Applying the guidelines, data, and historical information, as well as the analytical tools provided in this book, will help investors choose REITs that are appropriate for their portfolios. Reading the information that is available on company websites will also yield a wealth of information that an investor and financial advisors can use to decide if a REIT fits the investor's risk tolerance and return goals. Investors who do not like to see the prices of their stocks gyrate wildly may want to avoid investing in hotel or office REITs. If an investor is more interested in buying REITs for the dividend income, he or she should focus on REITs that use long-term triple-net leases, such as the freestanding retail REITs, most health-care REITs, and many of the specialty REITs.

Whatever the case, individuals would be well served to discuss the appropriateness of their investment with an informed financial advisor—preferably one who has also read this book! Ultimately, the most sound investment strategy for investing in REITs is to go for quality: quality real estate, quality balance sheet, and quality management. Identifying REITs whose senior management teams have successfully navigated their companies through at least one recession is a good screening technique (though there are many skilled teams running newly formed REITs). Assess the strength of the balance sheet and the safety of the dividend using the simple equations provided in Chapter 8, and read about the quality of their properties in research reports and in the REIT's public information. *The Intelligent REIT Investor* has given you the tools and guidelines you need to choose the right REITs, and to avoid investing in the wrong ones. So keep your copy handy and go enjoy the wealth-building power of investing in real estate investment trusts.

Further Resources

The Intelligent REIT Investor can be used in several ways. Individuals who simply want to have more informed discussions about REITs with their financial advisors should focus on Chapters 1–5. Chapters 6–8 are more technical in nature and are geared for professional money managers and analysts who may be investing other people's money in the sector. Financial advisors, depending on the quality of REIT research they have access to within their firms, may want to read every chapter, even if their firm employs a research team to analyze REITs.

REIT.com is NAREIT's website and contains news, articles, and data on REITs and the industry. Investors can access nearly all information for free, including the basics of REIT investment in real estate, lists of REIT funds, detailed company-specific information, and detailed industry research.

SPGlobal.com is the website for S&P Global Market Intelligence, an organization that provides the information that's essential for companies, governments, and individuals to make decisions with conviction. Previously known as SNL Financial, S&P Global Market Intelligence has provided specialized data and news on the REIT industry since 1994.

GreenStreetAdvisors.com is the website for Green Street Advisors. Founded in 1985, Green Street Advisors is the preeminent independent research and advisory firm concentrating on the commercial real estate industry in North America and Europe. The company is a leading provider of real estate analytics, research, and data on both the listed and private markets. Green Street also offers investment research on REITs and trading services to equity investors.

TheIntelligentREITInvestor.com is a reasonably priced, web-based research platform operated by Forbes and R. Brad Thomas.

Other books on REITs have been written that delve more deeply into certain subject matter discussed in this book, including the following:

- *Watch that Rat Hole: And Witness the REIT Revolution,* by Kenneth D. Campbell, 2016
- *Getting Started in Real Estate Investment Trusts* by Richard Imperiale, 2006
- *Investing in REITs: Real Estate Investment Trusts* by Ralph L. Block
- *The Complete Guide to Investing in REITS—Real Estate Investment Trusts: How to Earn High Rates of Returns Safely* by Mark Gordon
- *REITs: Building Profits with Real Estate Investment Trusts* by John A. Mullaney, 1998
- *Real Estate Investment Trusts: Structure, Performance, and Investment Opportunities* (Financial Management Association Survey and Synthesis Series) by Su Han Chan, John Erickson, and Ko Wang

APPENDIX A

REITs Listed Alphabetically by Company Name

Company Name	Ticker Symbol	Type
Acadia Realty Trust	AKR	Equity
AG Mortgage Investment Trust	MITT	Mortgage
Agree Realty Corporation	ADC	Equity
Alexander's, Inc.	ALX	Equity
Alexandria Real Estate Equities	ARE	Equity
Altisource Residential	RESI	Mortgage
American Assets Trust, Inc.	AAT	Equity
American Campus Communities, Inc.	ACC	Equity
American Capital Agency Corp	AGNC	Mortgage
American Capital Mortgage Investment	MTGE	Mortgage
American Farmland Company	AFCO	Equity
American Homes 4 Rent[a]	AMH	Equity
American Residential Properties, Inc.[a]	ARPI	Equity
American Tower Corp	AMT	Equity
Annaly Capital Management	NLY	Mortgage
Anworth Mortgage Asset	ANH	Mortgage
Apartment Investment and Management Company[b]	AIV	Equity
Apollo Commercial Real Estate Finance[c]	ARI	Mortgage
Apollo Residential Mortgage[c]	AMTG	Mortgage
Apple Hospitality REIT, Inc.	APLE	Equity

Company Name	Ticker Symbol	Type
Arbor Realty Trust	ABR	Mortgage
Ares Commercial Real Estate	ACRE	Mortgage
Armada Hoffler Properties	AHH	Equity
ARMOUR Residential REIT	ARR	Mortgage
Ashford Hospitality Prime, Inc.	AHP	Equity
Ashford Hospitality Trust, Inc.	AHT	Equity
AvalonBay Communities, Inc.	AVB	Equity
BioMed Realty Trust, Inc.[d]	BMR	Equity
Blackstone Mortgage Trust	BXMT	Mortgage
Bluerock Residential Growth REIT, Inc.	BRG	Equity
Boston Properties, Inc.	BXP	Equity
Brandywine Realty Trust	BDN	Equity
Brixmor Property Group, Inc.	BRX	Equity
BRT Realty Trust	BRT	Equity
Camden Property Trust	CPT	Equity
Campus Crest Communities, Inc.[e]	CCG	Equity
Capstead Mortgage	CMO	Mortgage
Care Capital Properties, Inc.	CCP	Equity
CareTrust REIT, Inc.	CTRE	Equity
CatchMark Timber Trust, Inc.	CTT	Equity
CBL & Associates Properties, Inc.	CBL	Equity
Cedar Realty Trust, Inc.	CDR	Equity
Chatham Lodging Trust	CLDT	Equity
Cherry Hill Mortgage Investment	CHMI	Mortgage
Chesapeake Lodging Trust	CHSP	Equity
Chimera Investment	CIM	Mortgage
City Office REIT, Inc.	CIO	Equity
Colony Capital	CLNY	Mortgage
Colony Starwood Homes[f]	SFR	Equity
Columbia Property Trust, Inc.	CXP	Equity
Communications Sales & Leasing	CSAL	Equity
Community Healthcare Trust Incorporated	CHCT	Equity

Company Name	Ticker Symbol	Type
Condor Hospitality Trust, Inc.	CDOR	Equity
CorEnergy Infrastructure Trust	CORR	Equity
CoreSite Realty Corporation	COR	Equity
Corporate Office Properties Trust[g]	OFC	Equity
Corrections Corporation of America	CXW	Equity
Cousins Properties Incorporated[h]	CUZ	Equity
Crown Castle International Corp	CCI	Equity
CubeSmart	CUBE	Equity
CyrusOne, Inc.	CONE	Equity
CYS Investments	CYS	Mortgage
DCT Industrial Trust, Inc.	DCT	Equity
DDR Corp.	DDR	Equity
DiamondRock Hospitality Company	DRH	Equity
Digital Realty Trust, Inc.	DLR	Equity
Douglas Emmett, Inc.	DEI	Equity
Duke Realty Corporation	DRE	Equity
DuPont Fabros Technology, Inc.	DFT	Equity
Dynex Capital	DX	Mortgage
Easterly Government Properties, Inc.	DEA	Equity
EastGroup Properties, Inc.	EGP	Equity
Education Realty Trust, Inc.	EDR	Equity
Ellington Residential Mortgage REIT	EARN	Mortgage
Empire State Realty Trust, Inc.	ESRT	Equity
EPR Properties	EPR	Equity
Equinix	EQIX	Equity
Equity Commonwealth	EQC	Equity
Equity LifeStyle Properties, Inc.	ELS	Equity
Equity One, Inc.	EQY	Equity
Equity Residential	EQR	Equity
Essex Property Trust, Inc.	ESS	Equity
Extra Space Storage, Inc.	EXR	Equity
Farmland Partners, Inc.	FPI	Equity
Federal Realty Investment Trust	FRT	Equity
FelCor Lodging Trust Incorporated	FCH	Equity

Company Name	Ticker Symbol	Type
First Industrial Realty Trust, Inc.	FR	Equity
First Potomac Realty Trust	FPO	Equity
Five Oaks Investment Corp	OAKS	Mortgage
Franklin Street Properties Corporation	FSP	Equity
Gaming and Leisure Properties, Inc.	GLPI	Equity
General Growth Properties, Inc.	GGP	Equity
GEO Group, Inc.	GEO	Equity
Getty Realty Corp.	GTY	Equity
Gladstone Commercial Corp	GOOD	Equity
Gladstone Land Corporation	LAND	Equity
Global Net Lease	GNL	Equity
Government Properties Income Trust	GOV	Equity
Gramercy Property Trust, Inc.[i]	GPT	Equity
Great Ajax	AJX	Mortgage
Hannon Armstrong Sustainable Infrastructure	HASI	Mortgage
Hatteras Financial	HTS	Mortgage
HCP, Inc.	HCP	Equity
Healthcare Realty Trust Incorporated	HR	Equity
Healthcare Trust of America, Inc.	HTA	Equity
Hersha Hospitality Trust	HT	Equity
Highwoods Properties, Inc.	HIW	Equity
HMG/Courtland Properties	HMG	Equity
Hospitality Properties Trust	HPT	Equity
Host Hotels & Resorts, Inc.	HST	Equity
Hudson Pacific Properties, Inc.	HPP	Equity
Independence Realty Trust, Inc	IRT	Equity
InfraREIT, Inc.	HIFR	Equity
Inland Real Estate Corporation[j]	IRC	Equity
InnSuites Hospitality Trust	IHT	Equity
Invesco Mortgage Capital	IVR	Mortgage
Investors Real Estate Trust	IRET	Equity
Iron Mountain Incorporated	IRM	Equity
iStar, Inc.	STAR	Mortgage

Company Name	Ticker Symbol	Type
JAVELIN Mortgage Investment[†]	JMI	Mortgage
Jernigan Capital	JCAP	Mortgage
Kilroy Realty Corporation	KRC	Equity
Kimco Realty Corporation	KIM	Equity
Kite Realty Group Trust	KRG	Equity
Ladder Capital Corp[k]	LADR	Mortgage
Lamar Advertising	LAMR	Equity
LaSalle Hotel Properties	LHO	Equity
Lexington Realty Trust	LXP	Equity
Liberty Property Trust	LPT	Equity
LTC Properties, Inc.	LTC	Equity
Macerich Company	MAC	Equity
Mack-Cali Realty Corporation	CLI	Equity
Medical Properties Trust, Inc.	MPW	Equity
MFA Financial	MFA	Mortgage
Mid-America Apartment Communities, Inc.[l]	MAA	Equity
Monmouth Real Estate Investment Corporation	MNR	Equity
Monogram Residential Trust, Inc.	MORE	Equity
National Health Investors, Inc.	NHI	Equity
National Retail Properties, Inc.	NNN	Equity
National Storage Affiliates Trust	NSA	Equity
New Residential Investment Corp	NRZ	Mortgage
New Senior Investment Group, Inc.	SNR	Equity
New York Mortgage Trust	NYMT	Mortgage
New York REIT, Inc.	NYRT	Equity
Newcastle Invt Corp	NCT	Mortgage
NexPoint Residential Trust, Inc.	NXRT	Equity
NorthStar Realty Europe	NRE	Equity
NorthStar Realty Finance	NRF	Equity
Omega Healthcare Investors, Inc.	OHI	Equity
One Liberty Properties	OLP	Equity
Orchid Island Capital	ORC	Mortgage
Outfront Media	OUT	Equity

Company Name	Ticker Symbol	Type
Owens Realty Mortgage, Inc.	ORM	Mortgage
Paramount Group, Inc.	PGRE	Equity
Parkway Properties, Inc.[h]	PKY	Equity
Pebblebrook Hotel Trust	PEB	Equity
Pennsylvania REIT	PEI	Equity
PennyMac Mortgage Investment Trust	PMT	Mortgage
Physicians Realty Trust	DOC	Equity
Piedmont Office Realty Trust, Inc.	PDM	Equity
Plum Creek Timber Company, Inc.[m]	PCL	Equity
Post Properties, Inc.	PPS	Equity
Potlatch Corporation	PCH	Equity
Power REIT	PW	Equity
Preferred Apartment Communities, Inc.	APTS	Equity
Prologis, Inc.	PLD	Equity
PS Business Parks, Inc.	PSB	Equity
Public Storage	PSA	Equity
QTS Realty Trust, Inc.	QTS	Equity
RAIT Financial Trust	RAS	Mortgage
Ramco-Gershenson Properties Trust	RPT	Equity
Rayonier, Inc.	RYN	Equity
Realty Income Corporation	O	Equity
Redwood Trust	RWT	Mortgage
Regency Centers Corporation	REG	Equity
Resource Capital	RSO	Mortgage
Retail Opportunity Investments Corp.	ROIC	Equity
Retail Properties of America, Inc.	RPAI	Equity
Rexford Industrial Realty, Inc.	REXR	Equity
RLJ Lodging Trust	RLJ	Equity
Rouse Properties, Inc.[†]	RSE	Equity
Ryman Hospitality Properties, Inc.	RHP	Equity
Sabra Health Care REIT, Inc.	SBRA	Equity
Saul Centers, Inc.	BFS	Equity
Select Income REIT	SIR	Equity
Senior Housing Properties Trust	SNH	Equity

Company Name	Ticker Symbol	Type
Seritage Growth Properties	SRG	Equity
Silver Bay Realty Trust Corp.	SBY	Equity
Simon Property Group, Inc.	SPG	Equity
SL Green Realty Corp.	SLG	Equity
SoTHERLY Hotels, Inc.	SOHO	Equity
Sovran Self Storage, Inc.	SSS	Equity
Spirit Realty Capital, Inc.	SRC	Equity
STAG Industrial, Inc.	STAG	Equity
Starwood Property Trust, Inc.	STWD	Mortgage
STORE Capital Corporation	STOR	Equity
Summit Hotel Properties, Inc.	INN	Equity
Sun Communities, Inc.	SUI	Equity
Sunstone Hotel Investors, Inc.	SHO	Equity
Tanger Factory Outlet Centers, Inc.	SKT	Equity
Taubman Centers, Inc.	TCO	Equity
Terreno Realty Corporation	TRNO	Equity
TIER REIT, Inc.	TIER	Equity
Two Harbors Investment	TWO	Mortgage
UDR, Inc.	UDR	Equity
UMH Properties, Inc.	UMH	Equity
Universal Health Realty Income Trust	UHT	Equity
Urban Edge Properties	UE	Equity
Urstadt Biddle Properties, Inc.	UBA	Equity
Ventas, Inc.	VTR	Equity
VEREIT, Inc.[n]	VER	Equity
Vornado Realty Trust	VNO	Equity
W. P. Carey, Inc.	WPC	Equity
Washington REIT	WRE	Equity
Weingarten Realty Investors	WRI	Equity
Welltower, Inc.	HCN	Equity
Western Asset Mortgage Capital	WMC	Mortgage
Weyerhaeuser Company	WY	Equity
Wheeler Real Estate Investment Trust, Inc.	WHLR	Equity

Company Name	Ticker Symbol	Type
Whitestone REIT	WSR	Equity
Winthrop Realty Trust	FUR	Equity
WP Glimcher, Inc.	WPG	Equity
Xenia Hotels & Resorts, Inc.	XHR	Equity
ZAIS Financial Corp	ZFC	Mortgage

[†]This REIT is in the process of being acquired and is not likely to remain public.

[a]In February 2016, American Homes 4 Rent merged with American Residential Properties, Inc. (former NYSE: ARPI).

[b]This company is often referred to as "Aimco."

[c]AMTG agreed to be acquired by ARI in February 2016.

[d]In January 2016, BioMed Realty Trust (former NYSE: BMR) was taken private.

[e]In January 2016, Campus Crest Communities (former NYSE: CCG) was taken private.

[f]In January 2016, Starwood Waypoint Residential Trust (former NYSE: SWAY) merged with Colony American Homes.

[g]This company is often referred to as "COPT."

[h]In April 2016, Parkway Properties and Cousins Properties announced they will merge; the transaction is expected to be complete before the end of 2016.

[i]In December 2015, Gramercy acquired Chambers Street Properties (former NYSE: CSG).

[j]In 2016, Inland Real Estate (former NYSE: IRC) was taken private.

[k]LADR was not included in the FTSE NAREIT All REITs Index at December 31, 2015, but was added in 2016.

[l]This company is often referred to as "MAA."

[m]Plum Creek Timber was acquired by Weyerhauser in February 2016.

[n]Former name: American Realty Capital Properties (NYSE: ARCP).

REITs Listed Alphabetically by Ticker Symbol

Symbol	Company Name	Type
AAT	American Assets Trust, Inc.	Equity
ABR	Arbor Realty Trust	Mortgage
ACC	American Campus Communities, Inc.	Equity
ACRE	Ares Commercial Real Estate	Mortgage
ADC	Agree Realty Corporation	Equity
AFCO	American Farmland Company	Equity
AGNC	American Capital Agency Corp	Mortgage
AHH	Armada Hoffler Properties	Equity
AHP	Ashford Hospitality Prime, Inc.	Equity
AHT	Ashford Hospitality Trust, Inc.	Equity
AIV	Apartment Investment and Management Company[a]	Equity
AJX	Great Ajax	Mortgage
AKR	Acadia Realty Trust	Equity
ALX	Alexander's, Inc.	Equity
AMH	American Homes 4 Rent[b]	Equity
AMT	American Tower Corp	Equity
AMTG	Apollo Residential Mortgage[c]	Mortgage
ANH	Anworth Mortgage Asset	Mortgage
APLE	Apple Hospitality REIT, Inc.	Equity
APTS	Preferred Apartment Communities, Inc.	Equity
ARE	Alexandria Real Estate Equities	Equity
ARI	Apollo Commercial Real Estate Finance[c]	Mortgage

Symbol	Company Name	Type
ARPI	American Residential Properties, Inc.[b]	Equity
ARR	ARMOUR Residential REIT	Mortgage
AVB	AvalonBay Communities, Inc.	Equity
BDN	Brandywine Realty Trust	Equity
BFS	Saul Centers, Inc.	Equity
BMR	BioMed Realty Trust, Inc.[d]	Equity
BRG	Bluerock Residential Growth REIT, Inc.	Equity
BRT	BRT Realty Trust	Equity
BRX	Brixmor Property Group, Inc.	Equity
BXMT	Blackstone Mortgage Trust	Mortgage
BXP	Boston Properties, Inc.	Equity
CBL	CBL & Associates Properties, Inc.	Equity
CCG	Campus Crest Communities, Inc.[e]	Equity
CCI	Crown Castle International Corp	Equity
CCP	Care Capital Properties, Inc.	Equity
CDOR	Condor Hospitality Trust, Inc.	Equity
CDR	Cedar Realty Trust, Inc.	Equity
CHCT	Community Healthcare Trust Incorporated	Equity
CHMI	Cherry Hill Mortgage Investment	Mortgage
CHSP	Chesapeake Lodging Trust	Equity
CIM	Chimera Investment	Mortgage
CIO	City Office REIT, Inc.	Equity
CLDT	Chatham Lodging Trust	Equity
CLI	Mack-Cali Realty Corporation	Equity
CLNY	Colony Capital	Mortgage
CMO	Capstead Mortgage	Mortgage
CONE	CyrusOne, Inc.	Equity
COR	CoreSite Realty Corporation	Equity
CORR	CorEnergy Infrastructure Trust	Equity
CPT	Camden Property Trust	Equity
CSAL	Communications Sales & Leasing	Equity
CTRE	CareTrust REIT, Inc.	Equity
CTT	CatchMark Timber Trust, Inc.	Equity
CUBE	CubeSmart	Equity
CUZ	Cousins Properties Incorporated[f]	Equity
CXP	Columbia Property Trust, Inc.	Equity

Symbol	Company Name	Type
CXW	Corrections Corporation of America	Equity
CYS	CYS Investments	Mortgage
DCT	DCT Industrial Trust, Inc.	Equity
DDR	DDR Corp.	Equity
DEA	Easterly Government Properties, Inc.	Equity
DEI	Douglas Emmett, Inc.	Equity
DFT	DuPont Fabros Technology, Inc.	Equity
DLR	Digital Realty Trust, Inc.	Equity
DOC	Physicians Realty Trust	Equity
DRE	Duke Realty Corporation	Equity
DRH	DiamondRock Hospitality Company	Equity
DX	Dynex Capital	Mortgage
EARN	Ellington Residential Mortgage REIT	Mortgage
EDR	Education Realty Trust, Inc.	Equity
EGP	EastGroup Properties, Inc.	Equity
ELS	Equity LifeStyle Properties, Inc.	Equity
EPR	EPR Properties	Equity
EQC	Equity Commonwealth	Equity
EQIX	Equinix	Equity
EQR	Equity Residential	Equity
EQY	Equity One, Inc.	Equity
ESRT	Empire State Realty Trust, Inc.	Equity
ESS	Essex Property Trust, Inc.	Equity
EXR	Extra Space Storage, Inc.	Equity
FCH	FelCor Lodging Trust Incorporated	Equity
FPI	Farmland Partners, Inc.	Equity
FPO	First Potomac Realty Trust	Equity
FR	First Industrial Realty Trust, Inc.	Equity
FRT	Federal Realty Investment Trust	Equity
FSP	Franklin Street Properties Corporation	Equity
FUR	Winthrop Realty Trust	Equity
GEO	GEO Group, Inc.	Equity
GGP	General Growth Properties, Inc.	Equity
GLPI	Gaming and Leisure Properties, Inc.	Equity
GNL	Global Net Lease	Equity
GOOD	Gladstone Commercial Corp	Equity
GOV	Government Properties Income Trust	Equity

Symbol	Company Name	Type
GPT	Gramercy Property Trust, Inc.[g]	Equity
GTY	Getty Realty Corp.	Equity
HASI	Hannon Armstrong Sustainable Infrastructure	Mortgage
HCN	Welltower, Inc.	Equity
HCP	HCP, Inc.	Equity
HIFR	InfraREIT, Inc.	Equity
HIW	Highwoods Properties, Inc.	Equity
HMG	HMG/Courtland Properties	Equity
HPP	Hudson Pacific Properties, Inc.	Equity
HPT	Hospitality Properties Trust	Equity
HR	Healthcare Realty Trust Incorporated	Equity
HST	Host Hotels & Resorts, Inc.	Equity
HT	Hersha Hospitality Trust	Equity
HTA	Healthcare Trust of America, Inc.	Equity
HTS	Hatteras Financial	Mortgage
IHT	InnSuites Hospitality Trust	Equity
INN	Summit Hotel Properties, Inc.	Equity
IRC	Inland Real Estate Corporation[h]	Equity
IRET	Investors Real Estate Trust	Equity
IRM	Iron Mountain Incorporated	Equity
IRT	Independence Realty Trust, Inc.	Equity
IVR	Invesco Mortgage Capital	Mortgage
JCAP	Jernigan Capital	Mortgage
JMI	JAVELIN Mortgage Investment[†]	Mortgage
KIM	Kimco Realty Corporation	Equity
KRC	Kilroy Realty Corporation	Equity
KRG	Kite Realty Group Trust	Equity
LADR	Ladder Capital Corp[i]	Mortgage
LAMR	Lamar Advertising	Equity
LAND	Gladstone Land Corporation	Equity
LHO	LaSalle Hotel Properties	Equity
LPT	Liberty Property Trust	Equity
LTC	LTC Properties, Inc.	Equity
LXP	Lexington Realty Trust	Equity
MAA	Mid-America Apartment Communities, Inc.[j]	Equity
MAC	Macerich Company	Equity

Symbol	Company Name	Type
MFA	MFA Financial	Mortgage
MITT	AG Mortgage Investment Trust	Mortgage
MNR	Monmouth Real Estate Investment Corporation	Equity
MORE	Monogram Residential Trust, Inc.	Equity
MPW	Medical Properties Trust, Inc.	Equity
MTGE	American Capital Mortgage Investment	Mortgage
NCT	Newcastle Invt Corp	Mortgage
NHI	National Health Investors, Inc.	Equity
NLY	Annaly Capital Management	Mortgage
NNN	National Retail Properties, Inc.	Equity
NRE	NorthStar Realty Europe	Equity
NRF	NorthStar Realty Finance	Equity
NRZ	New Residential Investment Corp	Mortgage
NSA	National Storage Affiliates Trust	Equity
NXRT	NexPoint Residential Trust, Inc.	Equity
NYMT	New York Mortgage Trust	Mortgage
NYRT	New York REIT, Inc.	Equity
O	Realty Income Corporation	Equity
OAKS	Five Oaks Investment Corp	Mortgage
OFC	Corporate Office Properties Trust[k]	Equity
OHI	Omega Healthcare Investors, Inc.	Equity
OLP	One Liberty Properties	Equity
ORC	Orchid Island Capital	Mortgage
ORM	Owens Realty Mortgage, Inc.	Mortgage
OUT	Outfront Media	Equity
PCH	Potlatch Corporation	Equity
PCL	Plum Creek Timber Company, Inc.[l]	Equity
PDM	Piedmont Office Realty Trust, Inc.	Equity
PEB	Pebblebrook Hotel Trust	Equity
PEI	Pennsylvania REIT	Equity
PGRE	Paramount Group, Inc.	Equity
PKY	Parkway Properties, Inc.[f]	Equity
PLD	Prologis, Inc.	Equity
PMT	PennyMac Mortgage Investment Trust	Mortgage
PPS	Post Properties, Inc.	Equity
PSA	Public Storage	Equity
PSB	PS Business Parks, Inc.	Equity

Symbol	Company Name	Type
PW	Power REIT	Equity
QTS	QTS Realty Trust, Inc.	Equity
RAS	RAIT Financial Trust	Mortgage
REG	Regency Centers Corporation	Equity
RESI	Altisource Residential	Mortgage
REXR	Rexford Industrial Realty, Inc.	Equity
RHP	Ryman Hospitality Properties, Inc.	Equity
RLJ	RLJ Lodging Trust	Equity
ROIC	Retail Opportunity Investments Corp.	Equity
RPAI	Retail Properties of America, Inc.	Equity
RPT	Ramco-Gershenson Properties Trust	Equity
RSE	Rouse Properties, Inc.[†]	Equity
RSO	Resource Capital	Mortgage
RWT	Redwood Trust	Mortgage
RYN	Rayonier, Inc.	Equity
SBRA	Sabra Health Care REIT, Inc.	Equity
SBY	Silver Bay Realty Trust Corp.	Equity
SFR	Colony Starwood Homes[m]	Equity
SHO	Sunstone Hotel Investors, Inc.	Equity
SIR	Select Income REIT	Equity
SKT	Tanger Factory Outlet Centers, Inc.	Equity
SLG	SL Green Realty Corp.	Equity
SNH	Senior Housing Properties Trust	Equity
SNR	New Senior Investment Group, Inc.	Equity
SOHO	SoTHERLY Hotels, Inc.	Equity
SPG	Simon Property Group, Inc.	Equity
SRC	Spirit Realty Capital, Inc.	Equity
SRG	Seritage Growth Properties	Equity
SSS	Sovran Self Storage, Inc.	Equity
STAG	STAG Industrial, Inc.	Equity
STAR	iStar Inc	Mortgage
STOR	STORE Capital Corporation	Equity
STWD	Starwood Property Trust, Inc.	Mortgage
SUI	Sun Communities, Inc.	Equity
TCO	Taubman Centers, Inc.	Equity
TIER	TIER REIT, Inc.	Equity
TRNO	Terreno Realty Corporation	Equity

Symbol	Company Name	Type
TWO	Two Harbors Investment	Mortgage
UBA	Urstadt Biddle Properties, Inc.	Equity
UDR	UDR, Inc.	Equity
UE	Urban Edge Properties	Equity
UHT	Universal Health Realty Income Trust	Equity
UMH	UMH Properties, Inc.	Equity
VER	VEREIT, Inc.[n]	Equity
VNO	Vornado Realty Trust	Equity
VTR	Ventas, Inc.	Equity
WHLR	Wheeler Real Estate Investment Trust, Inc.	Equity
WMC	Western Asset Mortgage Capital	Mortgage
WPC	W. P. Carey, Inc.	Equity
WPG	WP Glimcher, Inc.	Equity
WRE	Washington REIT	Equity
WRI	Weingarten Realty Investors	Equity
WSR	Whitestone REIT	Equity
WY	Weyerhaeuser Company	Equity
XHR	Xenia Hotels & Resorts, Inc.	Equity
ZFC	ZAIS Financial Corp	Mortgage

[†]This REIT is in the process of being acquired and is not likely to remain public.

[a]This company is often referred to as "Aimco. "

[b]In February 2016, American Homes 4 Rent merged with American Residential Properties, Inc. (former NYSE: ARPI).

[c]AMTG agreed to be acquired by ARI in February 2016.

[d]In January 2016, BioMed Realty Trust (former NYSE: BMR) was taken private.

[e]In January 2016, Campus Crest Communities (former NYSE: CCG) was taken private.

[f]In April 2016, Parkway Properties and Cousins Properties announced they will merge; the transaction is expected to be complete before the end of 2016.

[g]In December 2015, Gramercy acquired Chambers Street Properties (former NYSE: CSG).

[h]In 2016, Inland Real Estate (former NYSE: IRC) was taken private.

[i]LADR was not included in the FTSE NAREIT All REITs Index at December 31, 2015, but was added in 2016.

[j]This company is often referred to as "MAA. "

[k]This company is often referred to as "COPT. "

[l]Plum Creek Timber was acquired by Weyerhauser in February 2016.

[m]In January 2016, Starwood Waypoint Residential Trust (former NYSE: SWAY) merged with Colony American Homes.

[n]Former name: American Realty Capital Properties (NYSE: ARCP).

APPENDIX C

REITs by Sector

Table C.1   Diversified REITs

Company Name	Ticker Symbol	Headquarters City	State	Website Address
Alexander's, Inc.	ALX	Paramus	NJ	www.alx-inc.com
American Assets Trust	AAT	San Diego	CA	www.americanassetstrust.com
Armada Hoffler Properties	AHH	Virginia Beach	VA	www.armadahoffler.com
BRT Realty Trust	BRT	Great Neck	NY	www.brtrealty.com
Gladstone Commercial Corp	GOOD	McLean	VA	www.GladstoneCommercial.com
Global Net Lease	GNL	New York	NY	www.globalnetlease.com
HMG/Courtland Properties	HMG	Coconut Grove	FL	www.hmgcourtland.com
Investors Real Estate Trust	IRET	Minot	ND	www.iret.com
Lexington Realty Trust	LXP	New York	NY	www.lxp.com
NorthStar Realty Finance	NRF	New York	NY	www.nrfc.com
One Liberty Properties	OLP	Great Neck	NY	www.onelibertyproperties.com
VEREIT, Inc.[a]	VER	Phoenix	AZ	www.vereit.com
Vornado Realty Trust	VNO	New York	NY	www.vno.com
W. P. Carey Inc.	WPC	New York	NY	www.wpcarey.com
Washington REIT	WRE	Washington	DC	www.washreit.com
Whitestone REIT	WSR	Houston	TX	www.whitestonereit.com
Winthrop Realty Trust	FUR	Boston	MA	www.winthropreit.com

[a]Former name: American Realty Capital Properties (NYSE: ARCP)
Source: NAREIT, S&P Global Market Intelligence.

Table C.2   Specialty REITs

Company Name	Ticker Symbol	REIT Subproperty Type	Headquarters City	State	Website Address
American Farmland Company	AFCO	Land	New York	NY	www.americanfarmland company.com
Corrections Corporation of America	CXW	Prison	Nashville	TN	www.cca.com
EPR Properties	EPR	Cineplex Theater	Kansas City	MO	www.eprkc.com
Farmland Partners Inc.	FPI	Land	Denver	CO	www.farmlandpartners .com
Gaming and Leisure Properties, Inc.	GLPI	Casino	Wyomissing	PA	www.glpropinc.com
GEO Group, Inc.	GEO	Prison	Boca Raton	FL	www.geogroup.com
Gladstone Land Corporation	LAND	Land	McLean	VA	www.gladstoneland .com
Iron Mountain, Inc.	IRM	Data Center	Boston	MA	www.ironmountain.com
Lamar Advertising	LAMR	Billboards	Baton Rouge	LA	www.lamar.com
Outfront Media	OUT	Billboards	New York	NY	www.outfrontmediab .com

Source: NAREIT, S&P Global Market Intelligence.

Table C.3   Data Center REITs

Company Name	Ticker Symbol	Headquarters City	State	Website Address
CoreSite Realty Corp	COR	Denver	CO	www.CoreSite.com
CyrusOne, Inc.	CONE	Carrollton	TX	www.cyrusone.com
Digital Realty Trust, Inc.	DLR	San Francisco	CA	www.digitalrealty.com
DuPont Fabros Technology, Inc.	DFT	Washington	DC	www.dft.com
Equinix	EQIX	Redwood City	CA	www.equinix.com
QTS Realty Trust, Inc.	QTS	Overland Park	KS	www.qtsdatacenters.com

Source: NAREIT, S&P Global Market Intelligence.

Table C.4   Infrastructure REITs

Company Name	Ticker Symbol	Headquarters City	State	Website Address
American Tower Corp	AMT	Boston	MA	www.americantower.com
Communications Sales & Leasing	CSAL	Little Rock	AR	www.cslreit.com
CorEnergy Infrastructure Trust	CORR	Kansas City	MO	www.corenergy.corridortrust.com
Crown Castle International Corp	CCI	Houston	TX	www.crowncastle.com
InfraREIT, Inc.	HIFR	Dallas	TX	www.infrareitinc.com
Power REIT	PW	Old Bethpage	NY	www.pwreit.com

Source: NAREIT, S&P Global Market Intelligence.

Table C.5   Timber REITs

Company Name	Ticker Symbol	Headquarters City	State	Website Address
CatchMark Timber Trust, Inc.	CTT	Atlanta	GA	www.catchmark.com
Plum Creek Timber Company, Inc.[a]	PCL	--	--	N/A
Potlatch Corporation	PCH	Spokane	WA	www.potlatchcorp.com
Rayonier, Inc.	RYN	Jacksonville	FL	www.rayonier.com
Weyerhaeuser Co.	WY	Federal Way	WA	www.weyerhaeuser.com

[a]Plum Creek Timber was acquired by Weyerhauser in February 2016.
Source: NAREIT, S&P Global Market Intelligence.

Table C.6   Health-Care REITs

Company Name	Ticker Symbol	Headquarters City	State	Website Address
Care Capital Properties, Inc.	CCP	Chicago	IL	www.carecapitalproperties.com
CareTrust REIT, Inc.	CTRE	San Clemente	CA	www.caretrustreit.com
Community Healthcare Trust Incorporated	CHCT	Franklin	TN	www.communityhealthcaretrust.com
HCP, Inc.	HCP	Irvine	CA	www.hcpi.com
Healthcare Realty Trust Incorporated	HR	Nashville	TN	www.healthcarerealty.com
Healthcare Trust of America, Inc.	HTA	Scottsdale	AZ	www.htareit.com
LTC Properties, Inc.	LTC	Westlake Village	CA	www.ltcreit.com

Table C.6   Health Care REITs (*continued*)

Company Name	Ticker Symbol	Headquarters City	State	Website Address
Medical Properties Trust, Inc.	MPW	Birmingham	AL	www.medicalpropertiestrust .com
National Health Investors, Inc.	NHI	Murfreesboro	TN	www.nhireit.com
New Senior Investment Group, Inc.	SNR	New York	NY	www.newseniorinv.com
Omega Healthcare Investors, Inc.	OHI	Hunt Valley	MD	www.omegahealthcare.com
Physicians Realty Trust	DOC	Milwaukee	WI	www.docreit.com
Sabra Health Care REIT	SBRA	Irvine	CA	www.sabrahealth.com
Senior Housing Properties Trust	SNH	Newton	MA	www.snhreit.com
Universal Health Realty Income Trust	UHT	King of Prussia	PA	www.uhrit.com
Ventas, Inc.	VTR	Chicago	IL	www.ventasreit.com
Welltower, Inc.	HCN	Toledo	OH	www.welltower.com

Source: NAREIT, S&P Global Market Intelligence.

Table C.7   Industrial REITs

Company Name	Ticker Symbol	Headquarters City	State	Website Address
DCT Industrial Trust, Inc.	DCT	Denver	CO	www.dctindustrial.com
Duke Realty Corp	DRE	Indianapolis	IN	www.dukerealty.com
EastGroup Properties	EGP	Jackson	MS	www.eastgroup.net
First Industrial Realty Trust, Inc.	FR	Chicago	IL	www.firstindustrial.com
Liberty Property Trust	LPT	Malvern	PA	www.libertyproperty.com
Monmouth Real Estate Investment Corp	MNR	Freehold	NJ	www.mreic.com
Prologis, Inc.	PLD	San Francisco	CA	www.prologis.com
PS Business Parks, Inc.	PSB	Glendale	CA	www.psbusinessparks.com
Rexford Industrial Realty, Inc.	REXR	Los Angeles	CA	www.rexfordindustrial.com
STAG Industrial, Inc.	STAG	Boston	MA	www.stagindustrial.com
Terreno Realty Corp	TRNO	San Francisco	CA	www.terreno.com

Source: NAREIT, S&P Global Market Intelligence.

Table C.8   Lodging/Resorts REITs

Company Name	Ticker Symbol	Headquarters City	State	Website Address
Apple Hospitality REIT, Inc.	APLE	Richmond	VA	www.applehospitalityreit.com
Ashford Hospitality Prime, Inc.	AHP	Dallas	TX	www.ahpreit.com
Ashford Hospitality Trust, Inc.	AHT	Dallas	TX	www.ahtreit.com
Chatham Lodging Trust	CLDT	West Palm Beach	FL	www.chathamlodgingtrust.com
Chesapeake Lodging Trust	CHSP	Annapolis	MD	www.chesapeakelodgingtrust.com
Condor Hospitality Trust, Inc.	CDOR	Norfolk	NE	www.condorhospitality.com
DiamondRock Hospitality Company	DRH	Bethesda	MD	www.drhc.com
FelCor Lodging Trust	FCH	Irving	TX	www.felcor.com
Hersha Hospitality Trust	HT	Philadelphia	PA	www.hersha.com
Hospitality Properties Trust	HPT	Newton	MA	www.hptreit.com
Host Hotels & Resorts	HST	Bethesda	MD	www.hosthotels.com
InnSuites Hospitality Trust	IHT	Phoenix	AZ	www.innsuitestrust.com
LaSalle Hotel Properties	LHO	Bethesda	MD	www.lasallehotels.com
Pebblebrook Hotel Trust	PEB	Bethesda	MD	www.pebblebrookhotels.com
RLJ Lodging Trust	RLJ	Bethesda	MD	www.rljlodgingtrust.com
Ryman Hospitality Properties, Inc.	RHP	Nashville	TN	www.rymanhp.com
SoTHERLY Hotels Inc.	SOHO	Williamsburg	VA	www.sotherlyhotels.com
Summit Hotel Properties, Inc.	INN	Austin	TX	www.shpreit.com
Sunstone Hotel Investors, Inc.	SHO	Aliso Viejo	CA	www.sunstonehotels.com
Xenia Hotels & Resorts	XHR	Orlando	FL	www.xeniareit.com

Source: NAREIT, S&P Global Market Intelligence.

Table C.9   Mortgage REITs

| Company Name | Ticker Symbol | Headquarters | | Website Address |
		City	State	
Home Financing mREITs:				
AG Mortgage Investment Trust	MITT	New York	NY	www.agmit.com
Altisource Residential	RESI	Chrisriansted	VI	www.altisourceresi.com
American Capital Agency Corp	AGNC	Bethesda	MD	www.agnc.com
American Capital Mortgage Investment	MTGE	Bethesda	MD	www.mtge.com
Annaly Capital Management	NLY	New York	NY	www.annaly.com
Anworth Mortgage Asset	ANH	Santa Monica	CA	www.anworth.com
Apollo Residential Mortgage[a]	AMTG	New York	NY	www.apolloresidential mortgage.com
ARMOUR Residential REIT	ARR	Vero Beach	FL	www.armourreit.com
Capstead Mortgage	CMO	Dallas	TX	www.capstead.com
Cherry Hill Mortgage Investment	CHMI	Moorestown	NJ	www.chmireit.com
Chimera Investment	CIM	New York	NY	www.chimerareit.com
CYS Investments	CYS	Waltham	MA	www.cysinv.com
Dynex Capital	DX	Glen Allen	VA	www.dynexcapital.com
Ellington Residential Mortgage REIT	EARN	Old Greenwich	CT	www.earnreit.com
Five Oaks Investment Corp	OAKS	New York	NY	www.fiveoaksinvestment .com
Great Ajax	AJX	Beaverton	OR	www.great-ajax.com
Hatteras Financial	HTS	Winston-Salem	NC	www.hatfin.com
Invesco Mortgage Capital	IVR	Atlanta	GA	www.invescomortgage capital.com
JAVELIN Mortgage Investment [†]	JMI	Vero Beach	FL	www.javelinreit.com
MFA Financial	MFA	New York	NY	www.mfafinancial.com
New Residential Investment Corp	NRZ	New York	NY	www.newresi.com
New York Mortgage Trust	NYMT	New York	NY	www.nymtrust.com
Orchid Island Capital	ORC	Vero Beach	FL	www.orchidislandcapital .com
PennyMac Mortgage Investment Trust	PMT	Moorpark	CA	www.pennymacmortgage investmenttrust.com
Redwood Trust	RWT	Mill Valley	CA	www.redwoodtrust.com
Two Harbors Investment	TWO	New York	NY	twoharborsinvestment .com
Western Asset Mortgage Capital	WMC	Pasadena	CA	www.westernassetmcc .com
ZAIS Financial Corp	ZFC	Red Bank	NJ	www.zaisfinancial.com

Table C.9   *(continued)*

Company Name	Ticker Symbol	Headquarters City	State	Website Address
Commercial Financing mREITs:				
Apollo Commercial Real Estate Finance[a]	ARI	New York	NY	www.apolloreit.com
Arbor Realty Trust	ABR	Uniondale	NY	www.arborrealtytrust.com
Ares Commercial Real Estate	ACRE	New York	NY	www.arescre.com
Blackstone Mortgage Trust	BXMT	New York	NY	www.blackstonemortgage trust.com
Colony Capital	CLNY	Los Angeles	CA	www.colonyinc.com
Hannon Armstrong Sustainable Infrastructure	HASI	Annapolis	MD	www.hannonarmstrong .com
iStar, Inc.	STAR	New York	NY	www.istar.com
Jernigan Capital	JCAP	Memphis	TN	www.jernigancapital.com
Ladder Capital Corp [b]	LADR	New York	NY	www.laddercapital.com
Newcastle Invt Corp	NCT	New York	NY	www.newcastleinv.com
Owens Realty Mortgage Inc	ORM	Walnut Creek	CA	www.owensmortgage.com
RAIT Financial Trust	RAS	Philadelphia	PA	www.rait.com
Resource Capital	RSO	New York	NY	www.resourcecapitalcorp .com
Starwood Property Trust, Inc.	STWD	Greenwich	CT	www.starwoodproperty trust.com

[a]AMTG agreed to be acquired by ARI on February 26, 2016.
[b]LADR was not included in the FTSE NAREIT All REITs Index at 12/31/2015, but was added in 2016.
[†]This company was in the process of being acquired and may no longer be public.
Source: NAREIT, S&P Global Market Intelligence.

Table C.10   Office REITs

Company Name	Ticker Symbol	Headquarters City	State	Website Address
Alexandria Real Estate Equities	ARE	Pasadena	CA	www.are.com
BioMed Realty Trust[a]	BMR	San Diego	CA	www.biomedrealty.com
Boston Properties, Inc.	BXP	Boston	MA	www.bostonproperties.com
Brandywine Realty Trust	BDN	Radnor	PA	www.brandywinerealty.com
City Office REIT, Inc.	CIO	Dallas	TX	www.cityofficereit.com
Columbia Property Trust, Inc.	CXP	Atlanta	GA	www.columbiapropertytrust .com

Table C.10   Office REITs (*continued*)

Company Name	Ticker Symbol	Headquarters		Website Address
		City	State	
Corporate Office Properties Trust	OFC	Columbia	MD	www.copt.com
Cousins Properties[b]	CUZ	Atlanta	GA	www.cousinsproperties.com
Douglas Emmett, Inc.	DEI	Santa Monica	CA	www.douglasemmett.com
Easterly Government Properties, Inc.	DEA	Washington	DC	easterlyreit.com
Empire State Realty Trust, Inc.	ESRT	New York	NY	www.empirestaterealtytrust.com
Equity Commonwealth	EQC	Chicago	IL	www.eqcre.com
First Potomac Realty Trust	FPO	Bethesda	MD	www.first-potomac.com
Franklin Street Properties Corporation	FSP	Wakefield	MA	www.franklinstreetproperties.com
Government Properties Income Trust	GOV	Newton	MA	www.govreit.com
Gramercy Property Trust, Inc.[c]	GPT	New York	NY	www.gptreit.com
Highwoods Properties	HIW	Raleigh	NC	www.highwoods.com
Hudson Pacific Properties, Inc.	HPP	Los Angeles	CA	www.hudsonpacificproperties.com
Kilroy Realty Corp.	KRC	Los Angeles	CA	www.kilroyrealty.com
Mack-Cali Realty	CLI	Edison	NJ	www.mack-cali.com
New York REIT, Inc.	NYRT	New York	NY	www.nyrt.com
NorthStar Realty Europe	NRE	New York	NY	www.nrecorp.com
Paramount Group, Inc.	PGRE	New York	NY	www.paramount-group.com
Parkway Properties[b]	PKY	Orlando	FL	www.pky.com
Piedmont Office Realty Trust, Inc.	PDM	Johns Creek	GA	www.piedmontreit.com
Select Income REIT	SIR	Newton	MA	www.sirreit.com
SL Green Realty Corp.	SLG	New York	NY	www.slgreen.com
TIER REIT, Inc.	TIER	Dallas	TX	www.tierreit.com

[a]BioMed was acquired in early 2016 and no longer is public.
[b]Cousins and Parkway are merging during 2016.
[c]In December 2015, Gramercy acquired Chambers Street Properties (former NYSE: CSG).
Source: NAREIT, S&P Global Market Intelligence.

Table C.11   Apartment REITs

Company Name	Ticker Symbol	Headquarters City	State	Website Address
American Campus Communities, Inc.‡	ACC	Austin	TX	www.americancampus.com
Apartment Investment and Management Company	AIV	Denver	CO	www.aimco.com
AvalonBay Communities, Inc.	AVB	Arlington	VA	www.avalonbay.com
Bluerock Residential Growth REIT, Inc.	BRG	New York	NY	www.bluerock residential.com
Camden Property Trust	CPT	Houston	TX	www.camdenliving.com
Campus Crest Communities, Inc.‡ ª	CCG	Charlotte	NC	N/A
Education Realty Trust‡	EDR	Memphis	TN	www.edrtrust.com
Equity Residential	EQR	Chicago	IL	www.equityapartments.com
Essex Property Trust	ESS	San Mateo	CA	www.essex.com
Independence Realty Trust, Inc	IRT	Philadelphia	PA	www.irtreit.com
Mid-America Apartment Communities, Inc.	MAA	Memphis	TN	www.maac.com
Monogram Residential Trust, Inc.	MORE	Plano	TX	www.MonogramResidential Trust.com.
NexPoint Residential Trust, Inc.	NXRT	Dallas	TX	www.nexpointliving.com
Post Properties, Inc.	PPS	Atlanta	GA	www.postproperties.com
Preferred Apartment Communities, Inc.	APTS	Atlanta	GA	www.pacapts.com
UDR, Inc.	UDR	Highlands Ranch	CO	www.udr.com

‡These REITs own student housing.
ªIn January 2016, Campus Crest was taken private.
Source: NAREIT, S&P Global Market Intelligence.

Table C.12   Manufactured Housing

Company Name	Ticker Symbol	Headquarters City	State	Website Address
Equity LifeStyle Properties, Inc.	ELS	Chicago	IL	www.equitylifestyle.com
Sun Communities, Inc.	SUI	Southfield	MI	www.suncommunities.com
UMH Properties, Inc.	UMH	Freehold	NJ	www.umh.com

Source: NAREIT, S&P Global Market Intelligence.

Table C.13   Single-Family Home REITs

Company Name	Ticker Symbol	Headquarters City	State	Website Address
American Homes 4 Rent[a]	AMH	Agoura Hills	CA	www.americanhomes4rent.com
American Residential Properties, Inc.[a]	ARPI	--	--	N/A
Colony Starwood Homes[b]	SFR	Scottsdale	AZ	www.colonystarwood.com
Silver Bay Realty Trust Corp.	SBY	Plymouth	MN	www.silverbayrealtytrustcorp.com

[a]These companies merged in February 2016.
[b]Late in 2015, Starwood Waypoint Residential Trust (former NYSE: SWAY) merged with Colony American Homes.
Source: NAREIT, S&P Global Market Intelligence.

Table C.14   Shopping-Center REITs

Company Name	Ticker Symbol	Headquarters City	State	Website Address
Acadia Realty Trust	AKR	Rye	NY	www.acadiarealty.com
Brixmor Property Group, Inc.	BRX	New York	NY	www.brixmor.com
Cedar Realty Trust, Inc.	CDR	Port Washington	NY	www.cedarrealtytrust.com
DDR Corp.	DDR	Beachwood	OH	www.ddr.com
Equity One, Inc.	EQY	North Miami Beach	FL	www.equityone.net
Federal Realty Investment Trust	FRT	Rockville	MD	www.federalrealty.com
Inland Real Estate Corporation [a]	IRC	Oak Brook	IL	N/A
Kimco Realty Corporation	KIM	New Hyde Park	NY	www.kimcorealty.com
Kite Realty Group Trust	KRG	Indianapolis	IN	www.kiterealty.com
Ramco-Gershenson Properties Trust	RPT	Farmington Hills	MI	www.rgpt.com
Regency Centers Corporation	REG	Jacksonville	FL	www.regencycenters.com
Retail Opportunity Investments Corp.	ROIC	San Diego	CA	www.roireit.net
Retail Properties of America, Inc.	RPAI	Oak Brook	IL	www.rpai.com
Saul Centers, Inc.	BFS	Bethesda	MD	www.saulcenters.com
Tanger Factory Outlet Centers, Inc.	SKT	Greensboro	NC	www.tangeroutlet.com
Urban Edge Properties	UE	New York	NY	www.uedge.com
Urstadt Biddle Properties	UBA	Greenwich	CT	www.ubproperties.com
Weingarten Realty Investors	WRI	Houston	TX	www.weingarten.com
Wheeler Real Estate Investment Trust, Inc.	WHLR	Virginia Beach	VA	www.whlr.us

[a]This REIT was taken private in 2016 and is no longer public.
Source: NAREIT, S&P Global Market Intelligence.

Table C.15   Mall REITs

Company Name	Ticker Symbol	Headquarters City	State	Website Address
CBL & Associates Properties, Inc.	CBL	Chattanooga	TN	www.cblproperties.com
General Growth Properties, Inc.	GGP	Chicago	IL	www.ggp.com
Macerich Company	MAC	Santa Monica	CA	www.macerich.com
Pennsylvania REIT	PEI	Philadelphia	PA	www.preit.com
Rouse Properties, Inc.[†]	RSE	New York	NY	www.rouseproperties.com
Simon Property Group, Inc.	SPG	Indianapolis	IN	www.simon.com
Taubman Centers, Inc.	TCO	Bloomfield Hills	MI	www.taubman.com
WP Glimcher, Inc.	WPG	Columbus	OH	www.wpglimcher.com

[†]This company is being or has recently been acquired and may no longer exist.
Source: NAREIT, S&P Global Market Intelligence.

Table C.16   Freestanding Retail REITs

Company Name	Ticker Symbol	Headquarters City	State	Website Address
Agree Realty Corporation	ADC	Bloomfield Hills	MI	www.agreerealty.com
Getty Realty Corp.	GTY	Jericho	NY	www.gettyrealty.com
National Retail Properties, Inc.	NNN	Orlando	FL	www.nnnreit.com
Realty Income Corporation	O	San Diego	CA	www.realtyincome.com
Seritage Growth Properties	SRG	New York	NY	www.seritage.com
Spirit Realty Capital, Inc. [a]	SRC	Dallas	TX	www.spiritrealty.com
STORE Capital Corporation	STOR	Scottsdale	AZ	www.storecapital.com

[a]This company recently moved its headquarters from Scottsdale, Arizona, to Dallas, Texas.
Source: NAREIT, S&P Global Market Intelligence.

Table C.17   Self-Storage REITs

Company Name	Ticker Symbol	Headquarters City	State	Website Address
CubeSmart	CUBE	Malvern	PA	www.cubesmart.com
Extra Space Storage, Inc.	EXR	Salt Lake City	UT	www.extraspace.com
National Storage Affiliates Trust	NSA	Greenwood Village	CO	www.nationalstorage affiliates.com
Public Storage	PSA	Glendale	CA	www.publicstorage.com
Sovran Self Storage, Inc.	SSS	Williamsville	NY	www.unclebobs.com

Source: NAREIT, S&P Global Market Intelligence.

APPENDIX D

REITs with Credit Ratings

Company Name	Ticker	Corporate Rating by Agency			REIT OP Rating	Senior Unsecured Rating by Agency		
		Fitch Ratings	Moody's	S&P	Moody's	Fitch Ratings	Moody's	S&P
INVESTMENT GRADE RATED								
Alexandria Real Estate	ARE		Baa2	BBB-			Baa2	BBB-
American Assets Trust Inc.	AAT	BBB	Baa3	BBB-				
American Campus Communities	ACC		Baa3	BBB	Baa3			
American Tower Corp.	AMT.REIT	BBB	Baa3	BBB-		BBB	Baa3	BBB-
Aimco	AIV	BBB-		BBB-				
AvalonBay Communities, Inc.	AVB		Baa1	A-			Baa1	A-
Boston Properties, Inc.	BXP	BBB+	(P)Baa2	A-	Baa2		(P)Baa2	
Brandywine Realty Trust	BDN	BBB-	Ba1	BBB-	Baa3			
Brixmor Property Group, Inc.	BRX	BBB-	(P)Ba1	BBB-	Baa3			
Camden Property Trust	CPT	BBB+	Baa1	BBB+	Baa3	BBB+	Baa1	BBB+
Care Capital Properties, Inc.	CCP	BBB-		BB+				
CBL & Associates Properties	CBL	BBB-	Baa3	BBB-	Baa3			
CIM Commercial Trust Corp.	CMCT		Baa3		Baa3			
Columbia Property Trust	CXP		Baa2	BBB	Baa2			
Corporate Office Properties Trust	OFC	BBB-		BBB-	Baa3			
Crown Castle International	CCI.REIT	BBB-	Ba1	BBB-	Baa3	BBB-	Ba1	BBB-
CubeSmart	CUBE	BBB	Baa3	BBB	Baa2			
DCT Industrial Trust, Inc.	DCT		Baa2	BBB-	Baa2			
DDR Corp.	DDR	BBB-	Baa2	BBB-	Baa2			
Digital Realty Trust, Inc.	DLR	BBB	Baa2	BBB	Baa2	BBB-	Baa2	BBB-
Duke Realty Corp.	DRE	BBB	(P)Baa3	BBB	Baa2			
EastGroup Properties, Inc.	EGP	BBB	Baa2			BBB		

Company Name	Ticker	Corporate Rating by Agency			REIT OP Rating	Senior Unsecured Rating by Agency		
		Fitch Ratings	Moody's	S&P	Moody's	Fitch Ratings	Moody's	S&P
Education Realty Trust, Inc.	EDR		(P)Ba1	BBB-	Baa3			
EPR Properties	EPR	BBB-	Baa2	BB+		BBB-	Baa2	BBB-
Equity Commonwealth	EQC		Baa3	BBB-			Baa3	BBB-
Equity One, Inc.	EQY		Baa2	BBB			Baa2	BBB
Equity Residential	EQR	A-	Baa2	A-	Baa1	A-		
Essex Property Trust, Inc.	ESS	BBB+	(P)Baa3	BBB	Baa2			
Federal Realty Investment	FRT	A-	A3	A-		A-	A3	A-
First Industrial Realty Trust	FR	BBB-		BBB-	Baa3			
Franklin Street Properties	FSP		Baa3					
Government Properties Income Trust	GOV		Baa3	BBB-	Baa3		Baa3	BBB-
Gramercy Property Trust, Inc.	GPT			BBB-	Baa3			
HCP, Inc.	HCP	BBB+	Baa1	BBB+		BBB+	Baa1	BBB+
Healthcare Realty Trust, Inc.	HR	BBB	Baa2	BBB-		BBB	Baa2	BBB-
Healthcare Trust of America	HTA			BBB	Baa2			
Highwoods Properties, Inc.	HIW		Baa3	BBB	Baa2			
Hospitality Properties Trust	HPT		Baa2	BBB-	Baa2		Baa2	BBB-
Host Hotels & Resorts	HST	BBB-	Baa2	BB+	Baa2		Baa2	
Hudson Pacific Properties, Inc.	HPP	BBB-	Baa3	BBB-	(P)Baa3			
Kilroy Realty Corp.	KRC		Baa3	BBB	Baa2			
Kimco Realty Corp.	KIM	BBB+	Baa1	BBB+		BBB+	Baa1	BBB+
Kite Realty Group Trust	KRG		Baa3	BBB-				
Lexington Realty Trust	LXP	BBB	Baa2	BB+		BBB	Baa2	BBB-
Liberty Property Trust	LPT	BBB	(P)Baa2	BBB	Baa1			
MAA	MAA	BBB		BBB	Baa2			

Company Name	Ticker	Corporate Rating by Agency			REIT OP Rating	Senior Unsecured Rating by Agency		
		Fitch Ratings	Moody's	S&P	Moody's	Fitch Ratings	Moody's	S&P
National Retail Properties	NNN	BBB+	Baa1	BBB+		BBB+	Baa1	BBB+
Omega Healthcare Investors	OHI	BBB−	Baa3	BBB−		BBB−	Baa3	BBB−
Parkway Properties, Inc.	PKY		Baa3	BBB−				
Physicians Realty Trust	DOC				Baa3			
Piedmont Office Realty Trust	PDM		(P)Baa3	BBB	Baa2			
Post Properties, Inc.	PPS		Baa3	BBB	Baa2			
Potlatch Corp.	PCH		Baa3	BB			Baa3	BB
Prologis, Inc.	PLD	BBB	Baa2	BBB+	Baa1			
PS Business Parks, Inc.	PSB		Baa2	A−				
Public Storage	PSA		(P)A2	A			(P)A2	
Rayonier, Inc.	RYN		Baa2	BBB−			Baa2	BBB−
Realty Income Corp.	O	BBB+	Baa1	BBB+	Baa1	BBB+	Baa1	BBB+
Regency Centers Corp.	REG	BBB	Baa2	BBB	Baa1			
Retail Opportunity Investments	ROIC		Baa2	BBB−	Baa2			
Retail Properties of America	RPAI		Baa3	BBB−			Baa3	BBB−
Rexford Industrial Realty, Inc.	REXR	BBB−						
Select Income REIT	SIR		Baa2	BBB−				BBB−
Senior Housing Properties	SNH		Baa3	BBB−			Baa3	BBB−
Simon Property Group	SPG	A	(P)A3	A	A2			
SL Green Realty Corp.	SLG	BBB−	(P)Baa3	BBB−	(P)Baa3	BBB−	(P)Baa3	BBB−
Sovran Self Storage, Inc.	SSS	BBB	Baa2	BBB	Baa2	BBB		BBB
STAG Industrial, Inc.	STAG	BBB						
STORE Capital Corp.	STOR	BBB−				BBB−		
Tanger Factory Outlet Centers	SKT		(P)Baa2	BBB+	Baa1			

Company Name	Ticker	Corporate Rating by Agency			REIT OP Rating	Senior Unsecured Rating by Agency		
		Fitch Ratings	Moody's	S&P	Moody's	Fitch Ratings	Moody's	S&P
Terreno Realty Corp.	TRNO	BBB-						
UDR, Inc.	UDR		Baa1	BBB+			Baa1	BBB+
Ventas, Inc.	VTR	BBB+	(P)Baa2	BBB+	Baa1			
Vornado Realty Trust	VNO	BBB	Baa3	BBB+	Baa2			
W. P. Carey, Inc.	WPC		Baa2	BBB			Baa2	BBB-
Washington REIT	WRE		Baa2	BBB			Baa2	BBB
Weingarten Realty Investors	WRI		Baa1	BBB			Baa1	BBB
Welltower, Inc.	HCN	BBB+	Baa2	BBB		BBB+	Baa2	BBB
Weyerhaeuser Co.	WY		Baa2	BBB-			Baa2	BBB-
WP Glimcher, Inc.	WPG	BBB-	Ba1	BBB-				

RATED, NONINVESTMENT GRADE

Company Name	Ticker	Corporate Rating by Agency			REIT OP Rating	Senior Unsecured Rating by Agency		
		Fitch Ratings	Moody's	S&P	Moody's	Fitch Ratings	Moody's	S&P
CareTrust REIT, Inc.	CTRE		B2	B				
Communications Sales & Leasing, Inc.	CSAL	BB-	B2	B+		BB-	Caa1	B-
Corrections Corp. of America	CXW	BB+	Baa3	BB+		BB+	Baa3	BB+
CyrusOne, Inc.	CONE			B+	B1			
DuPont Fabros Technology, Inc.	DFT		Ba1	BB-	Ba1			
Equinix, Inc. (REIT)	EQIX.REIT	BB	Ba3	BB		BB	B1	BB
FelCor Lodging Trust, Inc.	FCH		B3	B	B3			
Forest City Realty Trust, Inc.	FCE.A	BB-	B2				B2	
Gaming and Leisure Properties	GLPI		Ba1	BB				
GEO Group, Inc.	GEO		Ba3	BB-			Ba3	BB-
Iron Mountain, Inc.	IRM		Ba3	B+			Ba3	B+
iStar Inc.	STAR		B2	B+			B2	B+

Company Name	Ticker	Corporate Rating by Agency			REIT OP Rating	Senior Unsecured Rating by Agency		
		Fitch Ratings	Moody's	S&P	Moody's	Fitch Ratings	Moody's	S&P
Lamar Advertising Co.	LAMR .REIT		Ba2	BB–				
Mack-Cali Realty Corp.	CLI	BB+	(P)Ba1	BB+	Baa3			
Medical Properties Trust, Inc.	MPW		Ba1	BB+	Ba1			
New Residential Investment Corp.	NRZ		B1					
OUTFRONT Media, Inc.	OUT.REIT		Ba3	BB–				
PennyMac Mortgage Investment	PMT		B1					
QTS Realty Trust, Inc.	QTS		B2	B+				
Ryman Hospitality Properties	RHP		Ba3	B+				
Sabra Health Care REIT	SBRA	BB+	Ba3	BB–	Ba3			
Spirit Realty Capital, Inc.	SRC			BB+				
Starwood Property Trust, Inc.	STWD		Ba3	BB				BB–
VEREIT, Inc.	VER		(P)Ba1	BB			(P)Ba1	

As of December 31, 2015

Source: S&P Global Market Intelligence.

Glossary

The following is a glossary of terms referenced in the REIT industry and throughout this book. Some definitions are based on information provided by NAREIT and company-specific documents filed with the SEC; others were sourced from Barron's *Dictionary of Real Estate Terms* and from online resources such as Investopedia .com and Leasing Professionals.com.

adjusted funds from operations (AFFO) As explained more fully in Chapter 8, because it incorporates adjustments for noncash items and deducts recurring capital expenditures (defined later in this Glossary), AFFO represents a more normalized, recurring measurement of a REITS's FFO (i.e., earnings). Please also refer to Chapter 8.

basis point (bps) The daily, often tiny, percentage changes in financial instruments in a portfolio, such as the yield on a fixed-income security, are expressed in basis points. A basis point is equal to 1/100 of a percentage point, so 1 percent equals 100 basis points.

base rent The minimum rent due to a landlord, as defined in a lease. Please refer to the discussion of rent in Chapter 4.

base (expense) year As explained in Chapter 4, a base year typically is the first year of a lease, during which time the landlord determines the actual taxes and operating expenses associated with a tenant's occupying their space. After the base year, the landlord agrees to pay an expense amount based on base year expenses, and the tenant pays any increases in expenses over the base amount.

C-Corporations A C-Corporation is a legal entity that is separate and distinct from its owners. Corporations enjoy most of the rights and responsibilities that an individual possesses, such as the right to enter into contracts, loan and borrow money, hire employees, own assets, and pay taxes. The most important aspect of a corporation is limited liability; that is, shareholders of a corporation have the right to participate in the profits, through dividends and/or the appreciation of stock, but are not held personally liable for the company's debts.

capital expenses GAAP requires that certain expenditures be classified as capital expenses rather than operating expenses. There are two primary classifications of capital expenses, or "capex":

1. **Recurring capex** is money spent on improvements to a property that facilitate its leasing but that are nonstructural. Examples of such expenditures include leasing commissions and tenant improvement paid to lease a space, both of which are capitalized and then amortized over the life of the lease.

2. **Nonrecurring capex** is money invested in structural improvements that extend the life of a property, such as constructing a parking deck. Because they involve structural enhancements, nonrecurring capex dollars are not expensed; instead, they are capitalized into the basis of a property. So if a property was worth $25 million and the landlord builds a $5 million parking deck, all else being equal the new basis of the property would be $30 million.

capitalization rate A capitalization (or "cap") rate measures the expected unleveraged return of an asset. The cap rate for a property is determined by dividing the property's net operating income (NOI, defined later in the Glossary) by its purchase price. Thought of another way, cap rates are the inverse of a price/earnings ratio, where earnings are measured by property-level NOI. High cap rates generally indicate higher expected returns and/or greater perceived risk. Please refer to Chapter 8 for additional information.

cash available for distribution (CAD) Cash available for distribution better approximates a REIT's free cash flow than AFFO and, therefore, is a more meaningful denominator for determining a REIT's dividend safety. CAD is calculated by subtracting the following items from AFFO: capitalized interest expense and monthly principal and interest payments due on secured debt (excluding maturities). Please see Chapter 8 for more information.

cash NOI Cash NOI adjusts the NOI calculated from a REIT's statement of operations (also known as its income statement) to exclude the effects of straight-lined rent. Please see Chapter 8 for more information.

common area maintenance (CAM) "Common areas" are areas within a property that are used by all tenants, such as an office building's lobby, sidewalks, landscaping, parking lot lighting, and snow removal services. As explained in Chapter 4, certain lease structures allow a landlord to charge tenants for their proportionate shares of the additional cost to maintain a property's common areas. CAM charges therefore are additional rent charged for maintenance that benefits all tenants.

cost of capital Cost of capital is the cost a company bears to have a form of equity and debt capital issued and outstanding. The cost of common stock generally is considered to include the dividend rate paid to shareholders plus investors' expected equity growth rate, the two of which typically total between 8 and 12 percent annually. The cost of preferred stock equals the dividend or "coupon" payment associated with each preferred share. The cost of debt capital is the interest rate associated with each type of debt (e.g., mortgage loan or senior note) issued by a company. Please see Chapter 7 for additional information.

diversification See **portfolio diversification**.

EBITDA Earnings before interest, taxes, depreciation, and amortization.

economic cycle The natural fluctuation of an economy between periods of expansion (growth) and contraction (recession).

economic indicator According to Investopedia.com, an economic indicator is a piece of economic data, such as the weekly employment report, used by investors to interpret the overall health of the economy.

equity market capitalization (EMC) A company's equity market capitalization is calculated by multiplying the stock price times the number of common shares outstanding. If the REIT is an UPREIT or has a DownREIT structure, the number of operating partnership (OP) units outstanding should be added to the common share count before multiplying by the stock price. Please refer to Chapter 8 for additional information.

escalation clauses Provisions in a lease that allow a landlord to pass through increases in operating expenses subject to the first- or "base"-year expense levels. Rent escalations usually occur on an annual basis and tend to be tied to increases in the Consumer Price Index or are expressed as fixed periodic increases. Please refer to Chapter 4 for additional information.

exchange-traded fund (ETF) According to Investopedia.com, an exchange-traded fund (ETF) is a marketable security designed to track the performance of an index, a commodity, bonds, or a basket of assets. Unlike mutual funds, an ETF trades like a common stock on a stock exchange and experiences price changes throughout the day as they are bought and sold.

Fannie Mae The Federal National Mortgage Association (commonly known as Fannie Mae) was established as a federal agency in 1938. In 1968 Congress chartered Fannie Mae as a private shareholder-owned company. Fannie Mae is a government-sponsored enterprise that operates in the U.S. secondary mortgage market, rather than making home loans directly to consumers.

fee simple interest Also referred to as "fee simple absolute" and "fee simple estate," fee simple interest in a property indicates the owner has absolute ownership of a property and the unconditional right to dispose of it. For example, most homeowners have a fee simple interest in their homes and can sell the property at their convenience or transfer ownership to an heir upon their deaths.

Freddie Mac Created in 1970, the Federal Home Loan Mortgage Corporation (commonly known as Freddie Mac) is similar to Fannie Mae in that it is a government-sponsored enterprise whose mission is to provide liquidity to the secondary mortgage market.

FTSE NAREIT REIT indexes Indexes published by the National Association of REITs (NAREIT) to track the performance of REITs. The FTSE NAREIT REIT indexes are not publicly traded; they simply aggregate performance data on the component REITs.

full-service lease A lease in which the tenant pays the landlord a fixed monthly rent that includes an expense stop calculated off of a base year. The landlord then pays all the monthly expenses associated with operating the property, including utilities, water, taxes, janitorial, trash collection, landscaping, and so forth. The tenant gets "full service" in exchange for the monthly rent and does not have to contract with service providers directly. Please refer to Chapter 4 for additional information.

funds from operations (FFO) A supplemental though more broadly used measurement of REIT earnings, created by the REIT industry in 1991 and recognized by the SEC in 2003. FFO is the REIT equivalent of earnings. Please refer to Chapter 8 for more detail.

Garn–St. Germain Act of 1982 The federal law that deregulated the savings and loan industry.

generally accepted accounting principles (GAAP) The set of rules considered standard and acceptable by Certified Public Accountants.

Global Industry Classification Standard (GICS) According to the website www.msci.com/gics, MSCI and Standard & Poor's developed the GICS in 1999 to create an efficient investment tool that would capture the breadth, depth, and evolution of industry sectors. GICS is a four-tiered industry classification system that originally consisted of 10 investment sectors, 24 industry groups, 67 industries, and 156 subindustries. On September 1, 2016, Real Estate will become the 11th GICS sector.

gross absorption According to CBRE (www.cbre.us), the absorption rate is the rate at which rentable space is filled. Gross absorption is a measure of the total square feet leased over a specified period with no consideration given to space vacated in the same geographic area during the same time period. (See also **net absorption**.)

gross lease A lease wherein the tenant pays a fixed monthly rent to the landlord; the landlord pays the property expenses, which includes insurance, utilities, and repairs, and usually property taxes. Please refer to Chapter 4 for additional information.

hedging According to Investopedia.com, a hedge is an investment to reduce the risk of adverse price movements in an asset. Hedging is analogous to taking out an insurance policy. If you own a home in a flood-prone area, you will want to protect yourself financially from the risk of flood damage—to hedge, in other words—by taking out flood insurance.

Internal Revenue Service (IRS) The U.S. government agency responsible for the collection and enforcement of taxes.

Established in 1862 by President Lincoln, the IRS operates under the authority of the U.S. Department of the Treasury.

lease A lease is a legal agreement between a landlord (the *lessor*) and a tenant (the *lessee*) whereby the tenant agrees to pay a monthly sum for a defined period of time (*rent*) in exchange for the right to occupy the landlord's space. Please refer to Chapter 4 for additional information.

limited partnership (LP) interests A partnership between at least two partners, one of whom is passive and whose liability in the venture is limited to his amount invested, and the active partner, whose liability in the venture extends beyond his monetary investment. Please refer to Chapter 6 for additional information.

market rent The rate a landlord could charge a tenant to occupy space, based on the competing spaces and current market conditions. Please refer to Chapter 4 for additional information.

modified gross lease A lease in which the tenant pays rent plus the property taxes and insurance, and any increases in these items over the base year. Please refer to Chapter 4 for additional information.

MSCI® US REIT Index (RMZ and RMS) A real-time, price-only index, the ticker symbol for which is RMZ. At December 31, 2015, the RMZ tracked the price movements of approximately 150 equity REITs. Mortgage and hybrid REITs are not included in this index. MSCI® also publishes the RMS, a daily total return version of the RMZ, which encompasses the companies' dividend yields. The RMS is not a real-time index; total returns for the constituent REITs are published at the end of the day.

NAREIT The National Association of Real Estate Investment Trusts is the worldwide representative voice for REITs and publicly traded real estate companies with an interest in U.S. real estate and capital markets. Please see www.reit.com for more information.

net absorption Calculated as the amount of occupied square feet at the end of a period, less the amount of square feet leased at the beginning of a period, net absorption measures the square feet leased in a specific geographic area over a fixed period of time, after taking into account any space vacated in the same area during the same period. (See also **gross absorption**.)

net asset value (NAV) An estimate of the current market value of all of a company's tangible assets, including but not limited to its properties, less the sum of all of a company's liabilities and obligations. Please refer to Chapter 8 for additional information.

net, double-net, and triple-net lease As described in Chapter 4, there are three levels of "net" when referencing lease structures wherein expenses are paid by the tenant as part of total rent: (1) maintenance, which includes items like utilities, water, janitorial, trash collection, and landscaping; (2) insurance; and (3) taxes.

- A net lease generally implies that the tenant pays rent and the costs of maintaining the property; the landlord pays the insurance and taxes.
- In a double-net lease, the tenant pays rent, including the taxes and insurance; the landlord pays the maintenance costs.
- In a triple-net lease, the tenant pays rent to the landlord and pays all costs associated with maintenance, insurance, and taxes. The landlord essentially collects monthly "coupon" payments, as if he owned a bond.

net operating income (NOI) The owner's rental revenues from property less all property operating expenses, including taxes and insurance. The term ignores depreciation and amortization expenses as well as interest on loans incurred to finance the property. Please also refer to Chapter 8.

non-recurring capex See **Capital expenses**

operating partnership unit (OP unit) Units of ownership in a REIT that generally can be exchanged on a one-for-one basis into common stock of the REIT but that are not publicly traded. Please refer to Chapter 6 for more detail.

percentage rents Additional rent payable to the landlord, based on a percentage of the volume of tenant sales generated on a property. The percentage is usually based on base year sales volume. For example, a retailer's lease may require contractual rent plus percentage rents equal to 1 percent of sales revenue that exceed sales revenue achieved in the first year of operations. Please refer to Chapter 4 for additional information.

portfolio diversification The act of investing in different asset classes and securities (i.e., stocks and bonds) in order to reduce investment risk and to enhance the expected return from an invested amount.

positive spread investing The ability to raise capital at a cost significantly less than the initial returns that can be obtained on real estate transactions.

property cycle According to Wikipedia.com, the property cycle is a sequence of recurrent and predictable events reflected in demographic, economic, and emotional factors that affect supply and demand for property.

R&D property Industrial buildings in which research and development (R&D) processes are performed, including any assembly, manufacturing, or office space required to support them. R&D buildings typically have a parking ratio of at least three parking spaces per 1,000 square feet, are one to two stories high, and feature interior clear heights of less than 18 feet.

Real Estate Investment Trust Act of 1960 The federal law that authorized REITs. Its purpose was to allow small investors to pool their investments in real estate to get the same benefits as might be obtained by direct ownership while also diversifying their risks and obtaining professional management.

real estate investment trust (REIT) A REIT is essentially a corporation or business trust that combines the capital of many investors to own or provide financing for all forms of investment real estate. A REIT is generally not required to pay corporate income tax if it distributes at least 90 percent of its taxable income to shareholders each year.

REIT Modernization Act of 1999 (RMA) The federal law that further increased REITs' abilities to operate as fully integrated operating companies, primarily by allowing REITs to provide tenant services through taxable REIT subsidiaries (TRSs). The RMA became effective in 2001.

recurring capex See **Capital expenses**

REIT Simplification Act of 1994 Predecessor to the REIT Modernization Act, the REIT Simplification Act was the federal law that streamlined the REIT structure, enabling management teams to operate their companies as more fully integrated businesses.

revenue per available room (RevPAR) The product of a hotel's average daily room rate (ADR) and its daily occupancy rate.

RMZ and RMS See **MSCI® US REIT index**.

Securities and Exchange Commission (SEC) A government commission created by Congress to regulate the securities markets and protect investors. In addition to regulation and protection, it also monitors the corporate takeovers in the United States. The SEC is composed of five commissioners appointed by the U.S. President and approved by the Senate.

straight-lined rent In compliance with GAAP, REITs "straight line" the rental income they receive by reporting the average annual rent to be received over the life of a lease instead of the actual cash received. The straight-lined rent adjustment REITs report is the amount to be added to or subtracted from GAAP rents to arrive at cash rents received. Please refer to Chapter 8.

taxable REIT subsidiary (TRS) Taxable REIT subsidiaries are stand-alone corporations for tax purposes that are owned directly or indirectly by a REIT. Created as part of the REIT Modernization Act of 1999, TRSs allow REITs to compete more effectively with other landlords by enabling REITs to provide nontraditional services to tenants or provide traditional real estate management services to third parties. TRSs also allow REITs the (limited) ability to invest in and derive income from nonrental real estate assets.

Tax Reform Act of 1986 The federal law that substantially altered the real estate investment landscape by permitting REITs not only to own but also to operate and manage most types of income-producing commercial properties. It also eliminated real estate tax shelters that had attracted capital from investors based on the amount of losses that could be created.

total market capitalization The sum of a REIT's equity market capitalization, plus the liquidation value of any preferred stock outstanding, and the principal amounts of debt outstanding.

total return A stock's dividend income plus capital appreciation, before taxes and commissions.

Transparency Corporate transparency describes the extent to which a corporation's actions are observable by outsiders.

Treasury inflation-protected securities (TIPS) First issued by the U.S. government in 1997, TIPS are a Treasury security that is indexed to inflation. According to Vanguard Investment Counseling & Research, TIPS are like most other bonds in that they are issued with a fixed coupon interest rate and a fixed maturity date. Unlike traditional bonds, TIPS have a principal value that the Treasury raises (or lowers) each month to keep pace with inflation. As a result, the semiannual coupon payments to investors also change, because they are derived by applying the fixed coupon rate to an inflation-adjusted principal amount.

triple-net lease See **net, double-net, and triple-net lease**, as well as Chapter 4.

UPREIT Umbrella partnership real estate investment trust. Please refer to Chapter 6 for information.

Index

Note: Page references followed by "f" and "t" indicate an illustrated figure and table, respectively.